THE LYRICS

VOLUME 2

Paul McCartney

THE LYRICS

1956 TO THE PRESENT

Edited with an Introduction by Paul Muldoon

LIVERIGHT PUBLISHING CORPORATION
A Division of W. W. Norton & Company
Independent Publishers Since 1923

Volume 2

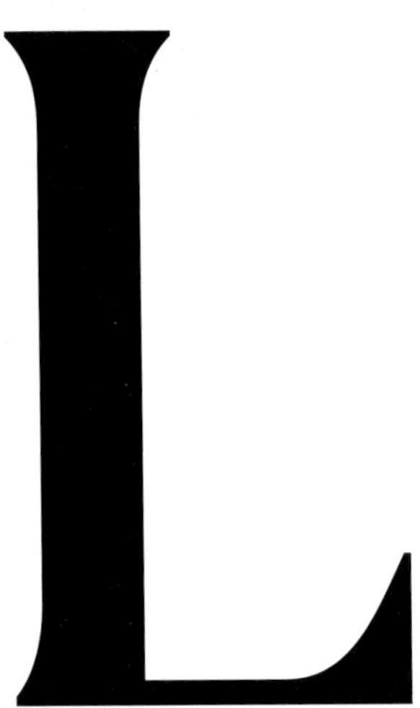

Kellogg's
ALL-BRAN
Vaseline

Lady Madonna

WRITERS	Paul McCartney and John Lennon
ARTIST	The Beatles
RECORDED	Abbey Road Studios, London
RELEASED	Single, 1968

Lady Madonna, children at your feet
Wonder how you manage to make ends meet
Who finds the money when you pay the rent?
Did you think that money was heaven sent?

Friday night arrives without a suitcase
Sunday morning creeping like a nun
Monday's child has learned to tie his bootlace
See how they run

Lady Madonna, baby at your breast
Wonders how you manage to feed the rest

See how they run

Lady Madonna, lying on the bed
Listen to the music playing in your head

Tuesday afternoon is never-ending
Wednesday morning papers didn't come
Thursday night your stockings needed mending
See how they run

Lady Madonna, children at your feet
Wonder how you manage to make ends meet

THE FACT THAT MY MOTHER MARY DIED WHEN I WAS FOURTEEN is something I never got over. A song that portrays a very present, nurturing mother has got to be influenced by that terrible sense of loss. The question about how Lady Madonna manages 'to feed the rest' is particularly poignant to me, since you don't have to be a psychoanalyst to figure out that I myself was one of 'the rest'. I must have felt left out. It's really a tribute to the mother figure, a tribute to women.

My single favourite aspect of the song is the recurring phrase 'See how they run'. It comes from the nursery rhyme 'Three Blind Mice', with that rather less-than-nurturing farmer's wife who cuts off their tails with a carving knife. That reference lends a slightly dark aspect to the song. In any case, the word 'run' also refers to stockings. One of my abiding memories of growing up was that, in addition to the other rather more important problems women faced, they were always laddering their stockings - 'Thursday night, your stockings needed mending'.

This repetition in 'See how they run' is one of the most powerful components in songwriting. The technical term for that repeated phrase is 'refrain'. We're having a little fun with that idea in another song from this same period, 'Hey Jude', with its exhortation 'And anytime you feel the pain / Hey Jude, refrain'.

With The Beatles, we were always operating on the cusp between being conscious of how a 'refrain' contributed to a song and basically having no idea what we were doing. One of the things I always thought was the secret of The Beatles was that our music was self-taught. We were never consciously thinking of what we were doing. Anything we did came naturally. A breathtaking chord change wouldn't happen because we knew how that chord related to another chord. We weren't able to read music or write it down, so we just made it up. My dad was exactly the same. And there's a certain joy that comes into your stuff if you didn't mean it, if you didn't try to make it happen and it happens of its own accord. There's a certain magic about that. So much of what we did came from a deep sense of wonder rather than study. We didn't really study music at all.

Right and below: Family portraits with mum Mary and brother Mike.

Let 'Em In

WRITERS	Paul McCartney and Linda McCartney
ARTIST	Wings
RECORDED	Abbey Road Studios, London
RELEASED	*At the Speed of Sound*, 1976 Single, 1976

Someone's knocking at the door
Somebody's ringing the bell
Someone's knocking at the door
Somebody's ringing the bell
Do me a favour
Open the door and let 'em in
Let 'em in

Sister Suzy, Brother John
Martin Luther, Phil and Don
Brother Michael, Auntie Jin
Open the door and let 'em in
Oh yeah

Sister Suzy, Brother John
Martin Luther, Phil and Don
Uncle Ernie, Auntie Jin
Open the door and let 'em in
Oh yeah, yeah

Someone knocking at the door
Somebody ringing the bell
Someone's knocking at the door
Somebody's ringing the bell
Do me a favour
Open the door and let 'em in
Oh yeah, yeah, let 'em in now

Sister Suzy, Brother John
Martin Luther, Phil and Don
Uncle Ernie, Uncle Ian
Open the door and let 'em in
Yeah, yeah

Someone's knocking at the door
Somebody's ringing the bell
Someone's knocking at the door
Somebody's ringing the bell
Do me a favour
Open the door and let 'em in
Yeah, yeah, yeah, yeah, yeah

Above: With Mary and Linda. Jamaica, 1972

A STOCKING FILLER. THAT'S HOW I THINK OF SOME SONGS. It's a fun little item, but it's not your main Christmas present. I can get a bit perfectionist about things and think, 'This is just not one of my grand pieces,' and often I'll get a bit down on them. I remember being very down on a song called 'Bip Bop' and thinking, 'Oh God, how banal can you get?' But I once said that to a producer named Trevor Horn, who produced Frankie Goes to Hollywood, Grace Jones and a lot of cool recording artists, and he said, 'That's one of my favourites of yours!' And then I could see what he saw in it, which is what I saw in it when I wrote it and wanted to record it, so he made me feel better about that.

'Someone's knocking at the door / Somebody's ringing the bell' – I'm imagining this is in Liverpool. A party of some sort. When we were in Jamaica, all the Jamaican guys would say to Linda, being blonde, 'Hey Suzy, Suzy!' To them a blonde, white woman was 'Suzy'. So, Linda got a group and called herself Suzy and the Red Stripes, after the beer brand. So, 'Sister Suzy' – that's Linda. 'Brother John' is either her brother, John Eastman, or John Lennon, 'Martin Luther' is Martin Luther King Jr, 'Phil and Don' are The Everly Brothers, and then you get 'Brother Michael', so that's my brother, or it might have been Michael Jackson – the timing's right for that, as we'd invited The Jackson 5 to the *Venus and Mars* album party on the *Queen Mary* the year before. And then 'Auntie Jin', which is spelt with a *J* rather than a *G* because her name was Jane. But in Liverpool that sounded too formal, so she would say, 'Just call me Jinny.' Then 'Uncle Ernie' – my cousin's name was actually Ian, but they called him Ern. And by this point, I'm not really fussed. I'm just playing with words. 'Uncle Ian'? Oh, come on guys, you're just not pay-

ing attention. Never mind. There is no Uncle Ian . . . and he certainly was not married to Auntie Jin.

Then the strangest of strange happenings: fast-forward a million years and I marry Nancy Shevell, whose sister is named Susie and whose brother is named Jon. So, suddenly I'm singing about Nancy's family: 'Sister Suzy, Brother John'. It's quite a coincidence.

It's been suggested that 'Martin Luther' is here because he's associated with banging on a door, nailing the articles of faith to a door. That's not something I was aware of when I wrote the song, but out in the collective unconsciousness, maybe it's possible. It definitely does happen that songs can come from some mysterious place. Much of the time, if you're lucky, the words and music come together. You just sit down and start. You're blocking stuff out with various sounds, and eventually, you hear a little phrase that's starting to work. Then you follow that trail. As artists, we seem to instinctively know that if we're open to it and if we play around enough with this bunch of words or notes, something will come of it. Something will come in. You don't even have to let it in.

Above: With Susie Shevell, Nancy and Merissa Simon, 2011

Right: Photo shoot for Suzy and the Red Stripes, for the release of the 'Seaside Woman' single, 1977

SUZY
and
The
RED
STRIPES

Left: With Trevor Horn. Music Mill, London, 1987

Below: With cousin Ian Harris. Liverpool, 1982

Right: Sheet music artwork for 'Let 'Em In'

It definitely does happen that songs can come from some mysterious place. Much of the time, if you're lucky, the words and music come together. You just sit down and start. You're blocking stuff out with various sounds, and eventually, you hear a little phrase that's starting to work.

1976-141-MPL COMMUNICATIONS
LET 'EM IN
LET 'EM IN

Let It Be

WRITERS	Paul McCartney and John Lennon
ARTIST	The Beatles
RECORDED	Apple Studio, London
RELEASED	Single, 1970
	Let It Be, 1970

When I find myself in times of trouble
Mother Mary comes to me
Speaking words of wisdom
Let it be
And in my hour of darkness
She is standing right in front of me
Speaking words of wisdom
Let it be

Let it be, let it be
Let it be, let it be
Whisper words of wisdom
Let it be

And when the broken-hearted people
Living in the world agree
There will be an answer
Let it be
For though they may be parted
There is still a chance that they will see
There will be an answer
Let it be

Let it be, let it be
Let it be, let it be
There will be an answer
Let it be
Let it be, let it be
Let it be, let it be
Whisper words of wisdom
Let it be

Let it be, let it be
Let it be, let it be
Whisper words of wisdom
Let it be

And when the night is cloudy
There is still a light that shines on me
Shine until tomorrow
Let it be
I wake up to the sound of music
Mother Mary comes to me
Speaking words of wisdom
Let it be

Let it be, let it be
Let it be, let it be
There will be an answer
Let it be
Let it be, let it be
Let it be, let it be
There will be an answer
Let it be
Let it be, let it be
Let it be, let it be
Whisper words of wisdom
Let it be

STING ONCE SAID TO ME THAT 'LET IT BE' WASN'T A GOOD CHOICE for me to sing at Live Aid. He thought it was implicit that action was required, and that leaving well enough alone wasn't an appropriate message on the occasion of the huge call to action that Live Aid represented. But 'Let It Be' isn't about being complacent, or complicit. It's about having a sense of the complete picture, about being resigned to the global view.

The context in which the song was written was one of stress. It was a difficult time because we were heading towards the breakup of The Beatles. It was a period of change partly because John and Yoko had got together, and that had an effect on the dynamics of the group. Yoko was literally in the middle of the recording session, and that was challenging. But it was also something we had to deal with. Unless there was a really serious problem - unless one of us said, 'I can't sing with her there' - we just had to let it be. We weren't very confrontational, so we just bottled it up and got on with it. We were northern lads, and that was part of our culture. Grin and bear it.

One interesting thing about 'Let It Be' that I was reminded of only recently is that, while I was studying English literature at the Liverpool Institute High School for Boys with my favourite teacher, Alan Durband, I read *Hamlet*. In those days you had to learn speeches by heart because you had to be able to carry them into the exam and quote them. There are a couple of lines from late in the play:

O, I could tell you -
But let it be. - Horatio, I am dead

I suspect those lines had subconsciously planted themselves in my memory. When I was writing 'Let It Be', I'd been doing too much of everything, was run ragged, and this was all taking its toll. The band, me - we were all going through times of trouble, as the song goes, and there didn't seem to be any way out of the mess. I fell asleep exhausted one day and had a dream in which my mum (who had died just over ten years previously) did, in fact, come to me. When you dream about seeing someone you've lost, even though it's sometimes for just a few seconds, it really does feel like they're right there with you, and it's as if they've always been there. I think anyone who's lost someone close to them understands that, especially in the period of time just after they've passed away. Still to this day I have dreams about John and George and talk to them. But in this dream, seeing my mum's beautiful, kind face and being with her in a peaceful place was very comforting. I immediately felt at ease, and loved and protected. My mum was very reassuring and, like so many women often are, she was also the one who kept our family going. She kept our spirits up. She seemed to realise I was worried about what was going on in my life and what would happen, and she said to me, 'Everything will be all right. Let it be.'

I woke up thinking this would be a great subject for a song. I just started with the circumstances surrounding me - the 'trouble at t'mill'.

Around the time we recorded 'Let It Be', I'd been pushing the band to go back out and play some club dates - to get back to basics and just bond again as a band, end the decade like we'd begun it, just playing for the love of it.

We didn't get to do that as The Beatles, but that idea did inform the direction of the *Let It Be* album. We didn't want any studio trickery. It was supposed to be an honest, no-overdubbing album. It didn't exactly end up that way, but that had been the plan.

The sad thing is that The Beatles didn't ever get to play the song at a show. So the performance at Live Aid was, for many people, probably the first time they saw it sung onstage.

'Let It Be' has now been in the live show for a while, though. It's always been a communal song, about acceptance, and I think those moments work really well with a crowd. You see a lot of people holding their partners or friends or family in their arms and singing along. In the beginning, thousands of cigarette lighters would be held up in the air during the song too. Then you couldn't smoke at shows anymore, and the lights came from people's phones. You can always tell which songs aren't so popular, because the phones get put away. But they come out for this one.

Then, a few years ago, we were in Japan and played the Budokan in Tokyo. We had just done three nights at the Tokyo Dome, a huge fifty-five-thousand-seat baseball stadium. To balance it out, we finished the tour with a night at the Budokan, which is very intimate by comparison. It wasn't quite fifty years since The Beatles had played there, but it was a special show and a venue with a lot of memories. My tour crew likes to surprise me, and in this instance they gave out wristbands to everyone in the venue. I didn't know this was going to happen, but during 'Let It Be' the whole room just lit up with these swaying arms. It's sometimes difficult to continue singing at moments like that.

Some people have said that 'Let It Be' has slight religious connotations, and it does sound a little like a gospel song, especially the piano and organ. The term 'Mother Mary' is probably primarily interpreted as a reference to Mary the Virgin Mother of God. As you may recall, my mother Mary was a Catholic, though my father was a Protestant, and my brother and I were christened. So, as far as religion goes, I'm obviously influenced by Christianity, but there are many great teachings in all the religions. I'm not particularly religious in any conventional sense, but I do believe in the idea that there is some sort of higher force that can help us.

So, this song becomes a prayer, or mini-prayer. There's a yearning somewhere at its heart. And the word 'amen' itself means 'so be it' - or 'let it be'.

Right: Notes and sketch from school copy of *Hamlet*

It's always been a communal song, about acceptance, and I think those moments work really well with a crowd. You see a lot of people holding their partners or friends or family in their arms and singing along.

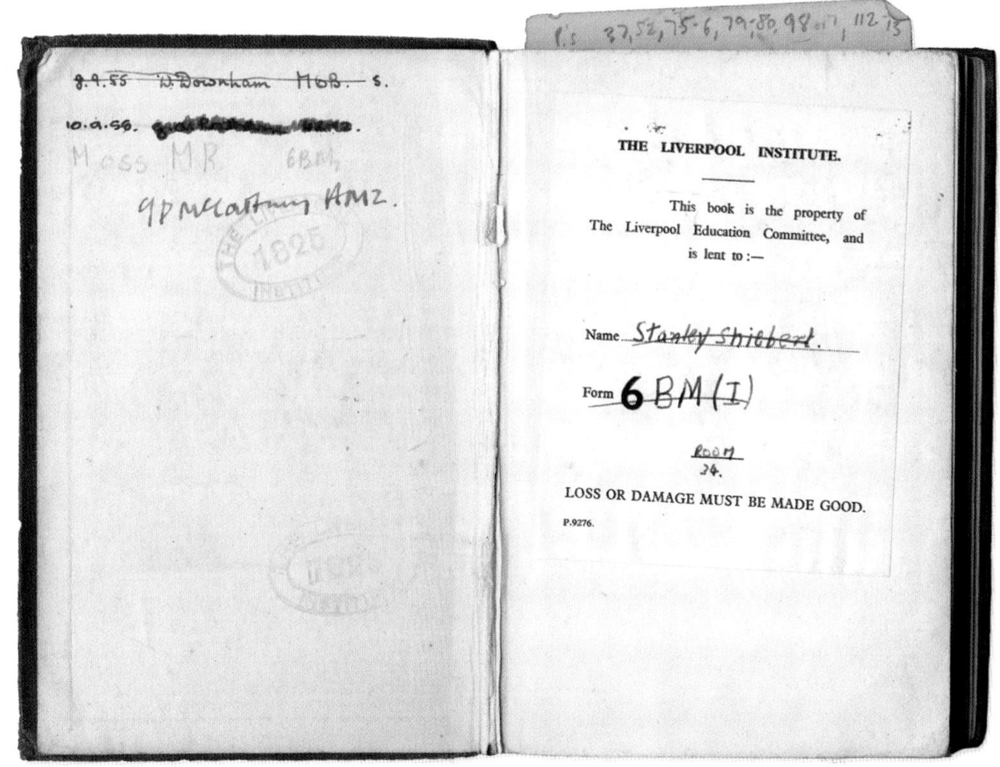
THE LIVERPOOL INSTITUTE.
This book is the property of The Liverpool Education Committee, and is lent to :—
Name Stanley Shibbert.
Form 6 BM (I)
ROOM 34.
LOSS OR DAMAGE MUST BE MADE GOOD.
P.9276.
Moss MR 6BM
1825

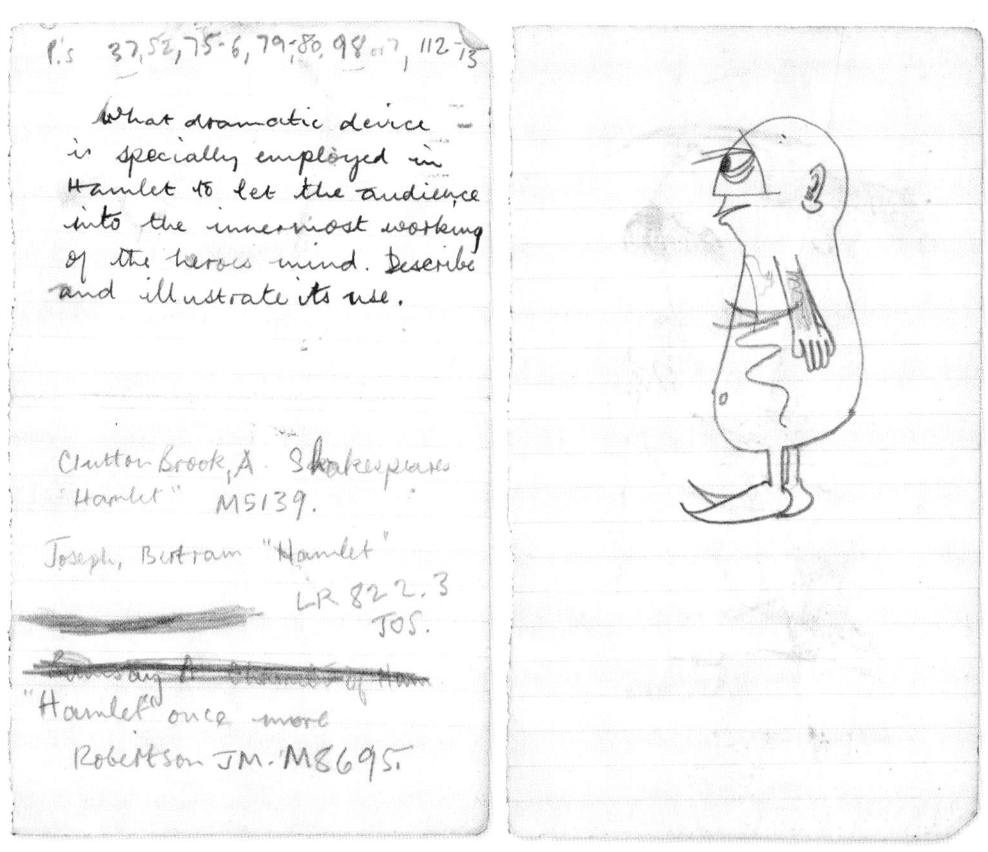
P.'s 37, 52, 75-6, 79-80, 98 or 7, 112-13
What dramatic device is specially employed in Hamlet to let the audience into the innermost working of the heroes mind. Describe and illustrate its use.
Clutton Brook, A. Shakespeares "Hamlet" M5139.
Joseph, Bertram "Hamlet" LR 822.3 JOS.
"Hamlet" once more
Robertson JM. M8695.

Left: Mum, Mary McCartney

Right: Recording sessions. Apple Studio, London, 1969

Pages 418–419: Performing 'Let It Be'. *Out There* tour, Budokan, Tokyo, 28 April 2015

My mum was very reassuring and, like so many women often are, she was also the one who kept our family going. She kept our spirits up. She seemed to realise I was worried about what was going on in my life and what would happen, and she said to me, 'Everything will be all right. Let it be.'

YAMAHA

Let Me Roll It

WRITERS	Paul McCartney and Linda McCartney
ARTIST	Paul McCartney and Wings
RECORDED	EMI Studios, Lagos; and AIR Studios, London
RELEASED	*Band on the Run*, 1973
	B-side of 'Jet' single, 1974

You gave me something
I understand
You gave me loving in the palm of my hand

I can't tell you how I feel
My heart is like a wheel
Let me roll it
Let me roll it to you
Let me roll it
Let me roll it to you

I want to tell you
And now's the time
I want to tell you that
You're going to be mine

I can't tell you how I feel
My heart is like a wheel
Let me roll it
Let me roll it to you
Let me roll it
Let me roll it to you

BOG ECHO. WE ALWAYS CALLED IT BOG ECHO BECAUSE IT'S LIKE the echo in a toilet, known to us as a 'bog'. We'd shout up to the control room, 'Can we have the bog echo, please?' And they would ask, 'Do you want it at 7.5 inches per second or 15 inches per second?' We would say, 'We don't know. Play them both.' The echo was on tape in those days. Short bog echo, long bog echo. It was very Gene Vincent. Very Elvis.

John loved this tape echo and used it more than any of us, so it became a signature sound on his solo records. I'm acknowledging that by using it here. I remember first singing 'Let Me Roll It' and thinking, 'Yeah, this is very like a John song.' It's in John's area of vocalisation, needless to say, but the most Lennon-esque thing is the echo.

The single most significant element in this song is not the echo, though. It's not the vocalisation. It's not the lyrics. It's the guitar riff. The word that comes to mind is 'searing'. It's a searing little thing. We can talk about lyrics till the cows come home, but a good riff is a rare beauty. This one is so dramatic that people in the audience gasp when they hear it. Because it stops so abruptly, it feels like everything freezes. Time freezes.

When we do talk about the lyrics, I think it's fair to say that to 'roll it' has to do with rolling a joint. I don't think that's going to come as a surprise to anyone. There was a lot of pot-smoking in an audience, back in the day when smoking was still allowed in venues. When I play live now, I sometimes wonder whether the audience isn't a bit prudish. Then I smell marijuana and I think, 'Well, that's alright. That smells good.' That probably happens more at festivals, though. It's probably easier not to get caught by security.

'Let Me Roll It' is a love song at its heart. The other, erotic, sense of rolling that is part and parcel of rock and *roll* is very much part of it. The image of 'My heart is like a wheel' so 'Let me roll it to you' is one that anyone can connect with. Anyone can understand how exposed you feel when you offer your heart to, or reveal your affections for, another person. It's very difficult.

The hesitation we feel in that situation - of wanting to reach out but being reluctant to be completely open - is made physical in the abrupt starting and stopping of the riff. The constant cutting short of the momentum of the song mimes the subject matter. We all relate to that situation. A year or two back, I saw a musical called *Be More Chill* by Joe Iconis and Joe Tracz, about a nerdy boy who can't say he loves someone. He has a speech impediment, a nervous stammer. 'Let Me Roll It' is a sort of long, drawn-out stammer.

Roll It

(1) You gave me something
I understand
You gave me loving
in the palm of my hand

(2) I want to tell you
And now's the time
I want to tell you
That you're going to be mine

Chorus
I can't tell you how I feel
My heart is like a wheel
Let me roll it to you

LET ME ROLL IT.

(1) You gave me something.
I understand.
You gave me loving in the palm of hand

Refrain
I can't tell you how I feel
my heart is like a wheel
LET ME ROLL IT
let me roll it to you
let me roll it
let me roll it to you.

(2) I want to tell you
And now's the time.
I want to tell you that
you're going to be mine

Refrain.

LET ME ROLL IT

Words & Music by Paul & Linda McCartney

As Recorded by
PAUL McCARTNEY
and
WINGS

MUSIC PUBLISHING COMPANY OF AFRICA (PTY.) LTD
McCARTNEY MUSIC LTD.

60¢ PA 4245

Sole Selling Agents for the Republic of South Africa and Rhodesia.
GALLO (AFRICA) LIMITED
P.O. Box 6216, JOHANNESBURG CAPE TOWN: 43 Somerset Road DURBAN: 593 Smith Street.

With Fender Jazz bass guitar during *Band on the Run* recording sessions. Lagos, Nigeria, 1973

Bog echo. We always called it bog echo because it's like the echo in a toilet, known to us as a 'bog'. We'd shout up to the control room, 'Can we have the bog echo, please?' And they would ask, 'Do you want it at 7.5 inches per second or 15 inches per second?' We would say, 'We don't know. Play them both.' The echo was on tape in those days. Short bog echo, long bog echo.

Live and Let Die

WRITERS	Paul McCartney and Linda McCartney
ARTIST	Paul McCartney and Wings
RECORDED	AIR Studios, London
RELEASED	Single, 1973

When you were young
And your heart was an open book
You used to say live and let live
You know you did
You know you did
You know you did
But if this ever-changing world in
which we're living
Makes you give in and cry

Say live and let die
Live and let die
Live and let die
Live and let die

What does it matter to ya?
When you got a job to do
You got to do it well
You gotta give the other fellow hell

You used to say live and let live
You know you did
You know you did
You know you did
But if this ever-changing world in
which we're living
Makes you give in and cry

Say live and let die
Live and let die
Live and let die
Live and let die

MOST SONGS ARE SELF-COMMISSIONED: YOU WRITE THEM FOR your own pleasure or to get yourself out of trouble, but in some cases somebody else commissions a song, and that's a nice thing; that's where the craft comes in. In some ways I liked to see myself as a jobbing writer. I'm the kind of guy that, if we needed a table I'd say, 'Well, I'll build one,' and that would give me weeks, months of pleasure - just drawing it, figuring out how I would make it.

In the case of 'Live and Let Die', the guy who had been the head of Apple Records for a while was Ron Kass, whom I liked a lot and got on with very well. He knew somebody connected with the Bond franchise, and one day in October 1972 he phoned me, and we were just chatting and he said, 'You don't have any interest in doing a Bond film, do you?' I said, 'Yeah, I'd probably be interested' - you know, trying not to seem too enthusiastic.

Writing a Bond song is a bit of an accolade, and I always had a sneaking ambition to do it. Ron told me the film was called *Live and Let Die*. The screenplay wasn't finished at that point, so I got the Ian Fleming book, and it's a real page-turner. I just spent that afternoon immersing myself in the book, so when I sat down to write the song, I knew how to approach it. I didn't want the song to be, 'You've got a gun. Now go kill people. Live and let die'. That's just not me. I wanted it to be, 'Let it go. Don't worry about it. When you've got problems, just live and let die'. Once I had that thought in my head, the song almost wrote itself. I think I read the book on a Saturday, and I sat down at my piano in the living room and spent that Sunday putting it together, with Linda helping on the reggae bit. It came together really quickly.

Then I took it round to George Martin, who was doing the music for the film. I showed him the chords and how the song was structured, and the central riff. I knew it had to have explosions in it, but I left the Bondian arrangements completely to him. This was one of the first times we had worked together since The Beatles, and it was a joy. His score was pure George - that perfectly stated balance of grandiose, without being over the top. I was very happy with that.

In those days you'd have an acetate, a little pressing of the record, and George went out to the Caribbean where they were already filming. He brought a little record player with him to play it to Cubby Broccoli, one of the movie's producers, who listened to it and said, 'That's nice, George. That's a nice demo. When are you going to make the finished record?' George replied, 'This is it.' They'd thought I was going to write it for someone else to sing.

I didn't rate it too much alongside some of the Bond themes that had gone before, like those for *From Russia with Love* or *Goldfinger*, which are *very* Bondian. I wasn't sure whether mine was, whether it would hold up with such classics, but a lot of people have put it on their list of top Bond songs. Then, when it was released, it became the most successful Bond theme so far and was nominated for an Oscar for Best Original Song - 'When you got a job to do / You got to do it well.'

In the early nineties, Guns N' Roses did a version of it, and the interest-

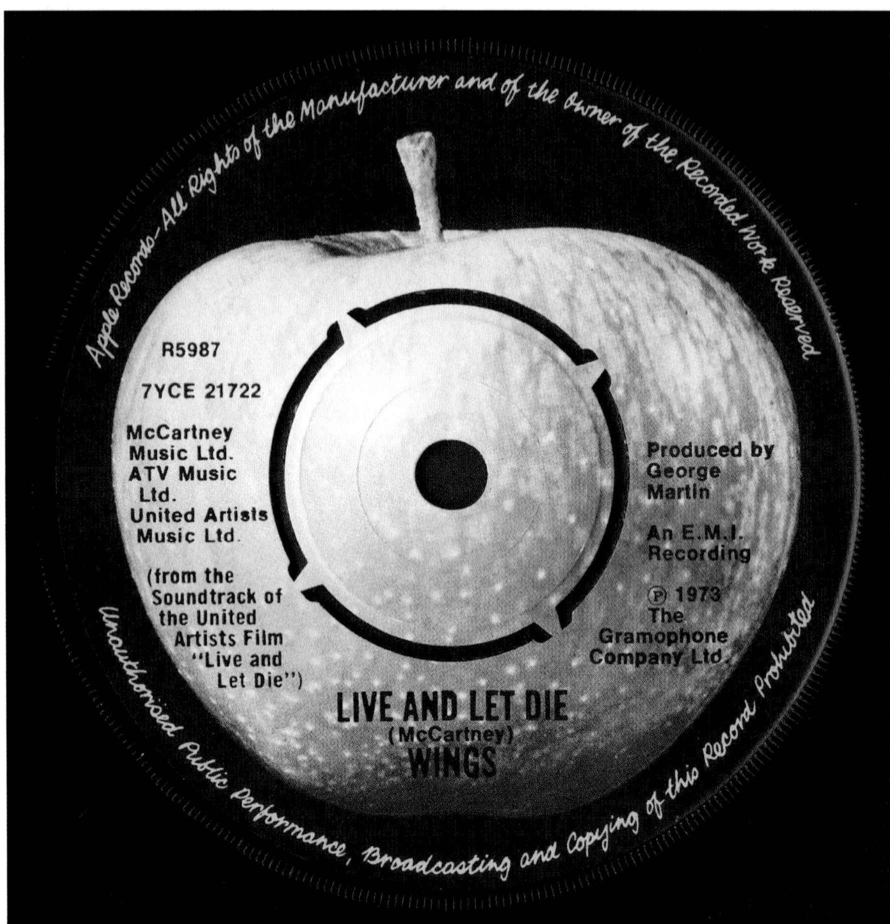

Left: 'Live and Let Die' single, 1973

Right: George Martin's handwritten score for 'Live and Let Die', 1972

Pages 430–431: Performing 'Live and Let Die' 2016–19

ing thing was that my kids went to school and said, 'My dad wrote that,' and their friends said, 'No, he didn't. It's Guns N' Roses.' Nobody would believe them. But I was very happy that they'd done it. I thought it was a pretty good version actually. I was amazed that they would do it – a young American group. I always like people doing my songs. It's a great compliment.

It's still a big show tune for us to this day. We have pyrotechnics, and the thing I think I like most about it is that we know the explosion's about to happen, that big first explosion. Often I look at the people, particularly in the front row, who are blithely going along, 'Live and let . . .' BOOM! It's great to watch them; they're shocked.

One night I noticed a very old woman in the front row, and I thought, 'Oh shit, we're going to kill her.' But there was no stopping, I couldn't stop the song and say, 'Cover your ears, love!' So when it came to that line, I looked away. 'Live and let . . .' BOOM! And I looked back at her, and she hadn't died after all. She was grinning from ear to ear and loving it.

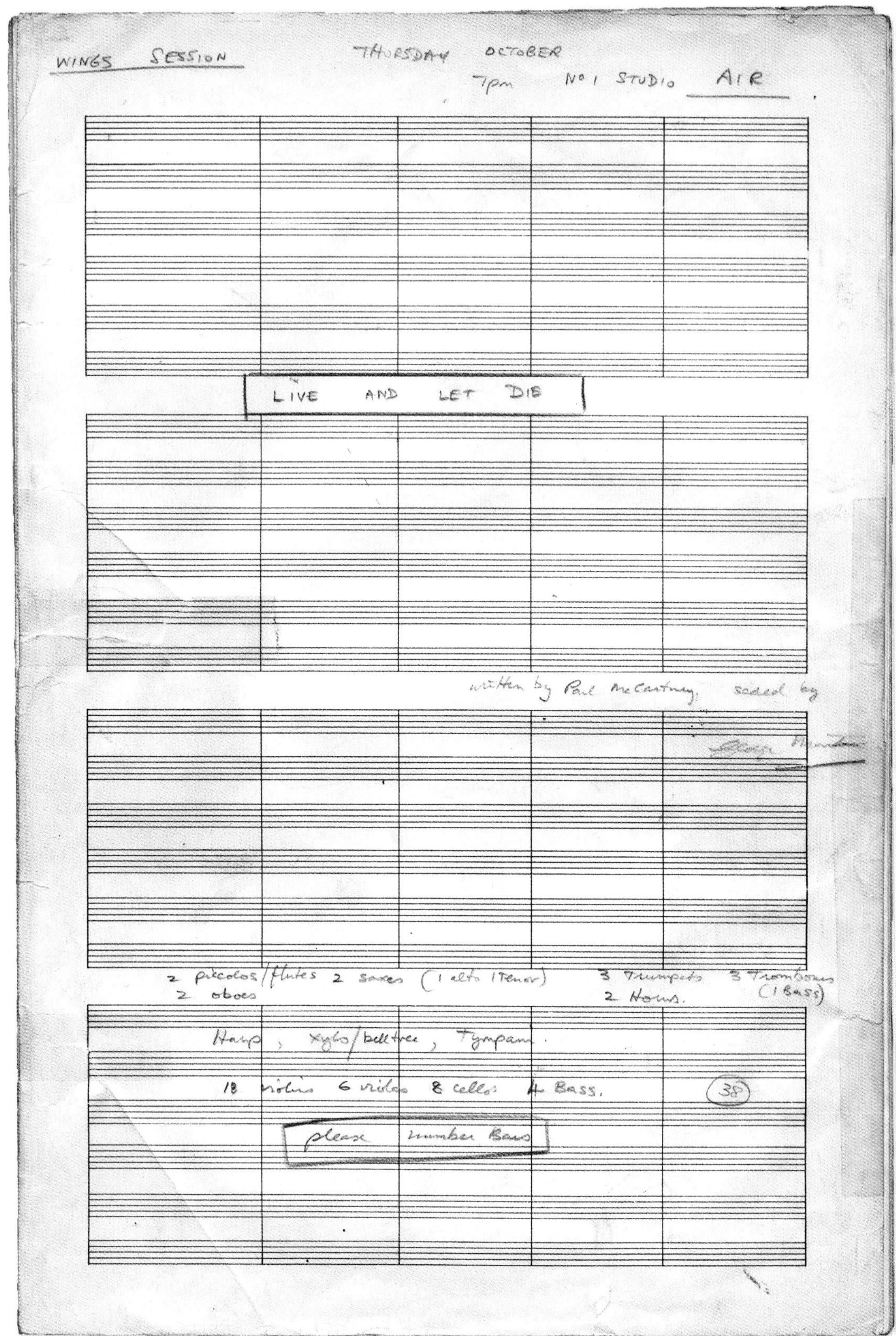
WINGS SESSION
THURSDAY OCTOBER
7pm No 1 STUDIO AIR
LIVE AND LET DIE
written by Paul McCartney scored by
2 piccolos/flutes 2 saxes (1 alto 1 Tenor) 3 Trumpets 3 Trombones (1 Bass)
2 oboes 2 Horns.
Harp, xylo/belltree, Tympani.
18 violins 6 violas 8 cellos 4 Bass.
38
please number Bars

YAMAHA

London Town

WRITERS	Paul McCartney and Denny Laine
ARTIST	Wings
RECORDED	Abbey Road Studios, London
RELEASED	*London Town*, 1978 Single, 1978

Walking down the sidewalk on a purple afternoon
I was accosted by a barker playing a simple tune
Upon his flute
Toot toot toot toot

Silver rain was falling down
Upon the dirty ground of
London Town

People pass me by on my imaginary street
Ordinary people it's impossible to meet
Holding conversations that are always incomplete
Well I don't know

Oh where are there places to go?
Someone somewhere has to know
I don't know

Out of work again the actor entertains his wife
With the same old stories of his ordinary life
Maybe he exaggerates the trouble and the strife
Well I don't know

Oh where are there places to go?
Someone somewhere has to know

Crawling down the pavement on a
Sunday afternoon
I was arrested by a rozzer wearing a pink balloon
About his foot
Toot toot toot toot

Silver rain was falling down
Upon the dirty ground of
London Town

Someone somewhere has to know
Silver rain was falling down
Upon the dirty ground of
London Town

As is so often the case in my songs, I'm a watercolourist. I'm just painting a scene: here's me walking down the sidewalk on a purple afternoon, I'm accosted by a barker and he's playing a simple tune on his flute – 'Toot toot toot toot'. I'm just dredging my imagination, saying, 'Okay, what shall we do now?'

'Sidewalk' is an American usage, I know. When I look at it now I think, 'Why wasn't it "pavement"?' But I like the word 'sidewalk'. The US features large in all my thoughts, musically; I was married to an American woman then, and I'm married to an American woman now. And I'm in New York a lot. Obviously, I know I've got a choice of 'pavement' or 'sidewalk', but 'sidewalk' just happened to pop out and I thought, 'Yeah, that'll do.'

'Ordinary people it's impossible to meet' has a double meaning. It's almost impossible to meet anyone. It's impossible to meet new people. You could also say it's impossible to meet people you know. 'The dirty ground of London Town' – that's a bluesy thing, as well as folky. So now we've got people passing me by, and then it gets quasi-philosophical, with me realising that we're just passing each other in life, ships in the night. 'Oh where are there places to go? / Someone somewhere has to know' – that's coming off the back of that little philosophical thing about the people, and then, with 'Out of work again', we're getting a bit more story line. The actor is telling stories to his wife of their ordinary life, and it's almost like a dig at him: he's out of work; he entertains his wife instead of people.

There are parallel lines that run through a song. You set up a pattern and you don't have to stick to it, but it's kind of nice to. In 'Here, There and Everywhere', for example, the pattern is informed by the title. Those three words come in order at certain points of the song and move the story along. So, with 'London Town', whereas before I was walking down the sidewalk, I'm

Above: London, 1978

Walking Down the sidewalk
on a purple afternoon
I was accosted by
a barker playing a certain simple
tune upon his flute - toot toot
Silver rain was falling
down upon the dirty
ground of London town.

now doing a variation on that: I'm 'crawling down the pavement', this time 'on a Sunday afternoon'. It's the same rhyming pattern, but now the story's kind of advanced. It sounds like I got drunk, and then I was arrested by a rozzer with a pink balloon tied to his foot, and it's just daft, but you can also read into it that pink could signify something like a certain gayness. 'Rozzer' is just another word for a policeman, or copper, but 'Toot toot toot toot' refers to cocaine. And this was the freedom of Wings: I could just throw in surreal lines because I like surrealism in painting, people like Magritte, who had been a big influence on me since I came across his work in the 1960s. I like the freedom of being able to throw it in a song for no reason whatsoever.

Whenever you make reference to drugs, you're connecting with a group of people; you're just sort of saying that you kind of know what they're doing, and it doesn't mean that you're doing it too, or that you advocate it, but you're hooking into a secret little group, a secret little crowd. When John and I wrote, 'I'd love to turn you on', we knew it was a perfectly harmless phrase, but we also knew it would hook into the Timothy Leary crowd. There's an impishness about it, a schoolboy thing. There are some old songs that mention it – Cole Porter's 'I Get a Kick Out of You', or the song 'Cocaine Blues' (covered by Johnny Cash and Bob Dylan) – and it's a nod, a wink and a nod, because you're using a perfectly ordinary word when you're talking about a guy on a flute going 'toot toot toot toot' – that's what flutes do – but you're also playing a little bit of naughtiness.

Above left: Linda's handwritten lyrics for 'London Town', alongside poster for the single

Right: Nancy. New York, 2019

The Long and Winding Road

WRITERS	Paul McCartney and John Lennon
ARTIST	The Beatles
RECORDED	Apple Studio, London; and Abbey Road Studios, London
RELEASED	*Let It Be*, 1970
	US single, 1970

The long and winding road that leads to your door
Will never disappear, I've seen that road before
It always leads me here, lead me to your door

The wild and windy night that the rain washed away
Has left a pool of tears crying for the day
Why leave me standing here?
Let me know the way

Many times I've been alone and many times I've cried
Anyway you'll never know the many ways I've tried
But still they lead me back to the long winding road
You left me standing here a long, long time ago
Don't keep me waiting here, lead me to your door

FROM THE BEDROOM WINDOW OF MY FARMHOUSE ON THE MULL of Kintyre, in Argyllshire, I could see a road that twisted away into the distance towards the main road. That's how you got into town. Campbeltown, to be precise.

I'd bought High Park Farm back in 1966. It was a very remote retreat, and the farmhouse was virtually derelict and probably would've stayed that way if Linda hadn't said we should do the place up. It wasn't until two years later that the image of this distant, winding road would become fully developed as a song. It was released in 1970, becoming The Beatles' twentieth American number one. It was also our last number one.

One of the fascinating aspects of this song is that it seems to resonate in very powerful ways. For those who were there at the time, there seems to be a double association of terrific sadness and also a sense of hope, particularly in the assertion that the road that 'leads to your door / Will never disappear'.

Often when I write a song, I do a bit of a disappearing trick myself. For example, I imagine it having been recorded by somebody else - in this case Ray Charles. As usual, the last thing I'd want to be writing is a Paul McCartney song. This is a strategy for keeping things fresh.

I had a similar experience when I painted. For years and years, I simply couldn't bring myself to paint, though I liked drawing and had a bit of talent. I even got a little art prize at school. But the thought of this blank canvas was so daunting that I could never do it. Then I just happened to meet Willem de Kooning at his studio. He'd given us a little picture, and I took all my courage in my hand and said, 'Bill, what is it?' I don't suppose that's what you ask an abstract expressionist! But he was a very patient fellow, and he said, 'Oh, I don't know. It looks like a couch.' And I realised that all these worries about the significance of what a painting might be about weren't the issue at all.

So, I went out and bought a load of canvases, paints, brushes, and everything and proceeded to paint about five hundred pictures. I imagined that a friend who owned a restaurant had asked me to paint a picture for his alcove. So, I could think of a picture I was working on as being for Luigi's alcove - less pressure. Or, when I was blending colours, I was transformed into a certain 'Mr Blendini'. It was all tricks.

In songwriting I've got similar tricks. In the earliest days we were pretending to be Buddy Holly. Then we were writing like Motown. Then we were writing like Bob Dylan.

There's always someone else you can invoke. You can put on a mask and a cloak as you're writing something, and it takes away a lot of the anxiety. It frees you up. You discover as you get through it that it wasn't a Ray Charles song anyway; it was yours. The song takes on its own character. The road leads not to Campbeltown, but to somewhere you never expected.

Scotland, 1968

Right: With Willem de Kooning. East Hampton, 1983

Often when I write a song, I do a bit of a disappearing trick myself. For example, I imagine it having been recorded by somebody else – in this case Ray Charles. As usual, the last thing I'd want to be writing is a Paul McCartney song. This is a strategy for keeping things fresh.

Love Me Do

WRITERS	Paul McCartney and John Lennon
ARTIST	The Beatles
RECORDED	Abbey Road Studios, London
RELEASED	UK single, 1962
	Please Please Me, 1963
	Introducing... The Beatles, 1964
	US single, 1964

Love, love me do
You know I love you
I'll always be true
So please
Love me do
Whoa love me do

Love, love me do
You know I love you
I'll always be true
So please
Love me do
Whoa love me do

Someone to love
Somebody new
Someone to love
Someone like you

Love, love me do
You know I love you
I'll always be true
So please
Love me do
Oh love me do

Love, love me do
You know I love you
I'll always be true
So please
Love me do
Whoa love me do
Yeah love me do
Whoa love me do

THE BIGGEST INFLUENCE ON JOHN AND ME WAS THE EVERLY BROTHers. To this day, I just think they're the greatest. And they were different. You'd heard barbershop quartets, you'd heard The Beverley Sisters - three girls - you'd heard all that. But just two guys, two good-looking guys? So we idolised them. We wanted to be like them.

Then, Buddy Holly came along when we were fifteen or sixteen. Buddy's look fitted with the fact that John wore glasses. John had a perfect reason to pull his glasses back out of his pocket and put them on. Buddy Holly was also a writer, a lead guitarist and a singer. Elvis wasn't a writer or a lead guitarist; he was just a singer. Duane Eddy was a guitar player but not a singer. So, Buddy had it all. And the name, The Crickets. We also wanted something with a dual meaning.

The actual origin of the name 'The Beatles' is clouded in mystery, but my memory is that we were striving to find something with a dual meaning because of The Crickets: you have cricket the game, and crickets the little grasshoppers. What if we could find an insect that also had some double meaning? When you take 'Beatles' out of context and imagine it as just the insect, it's not immediately attractive. But now that it's been around awhile, you totally accept it and you don't even think of the creepy-crawlies.

'Love Me Do' was written in one of our sessions at 20 Forthlin Road, up a little garden path, past my dad's lavender hedge, up by the front door where he had planted a mountain ash, which was his favourite tree. You would come to the front door and then into a small parlour to the left of the door, and then you could go through the parlour to the dining room behind that,

Above: The Beatles. Liverpool, 1962

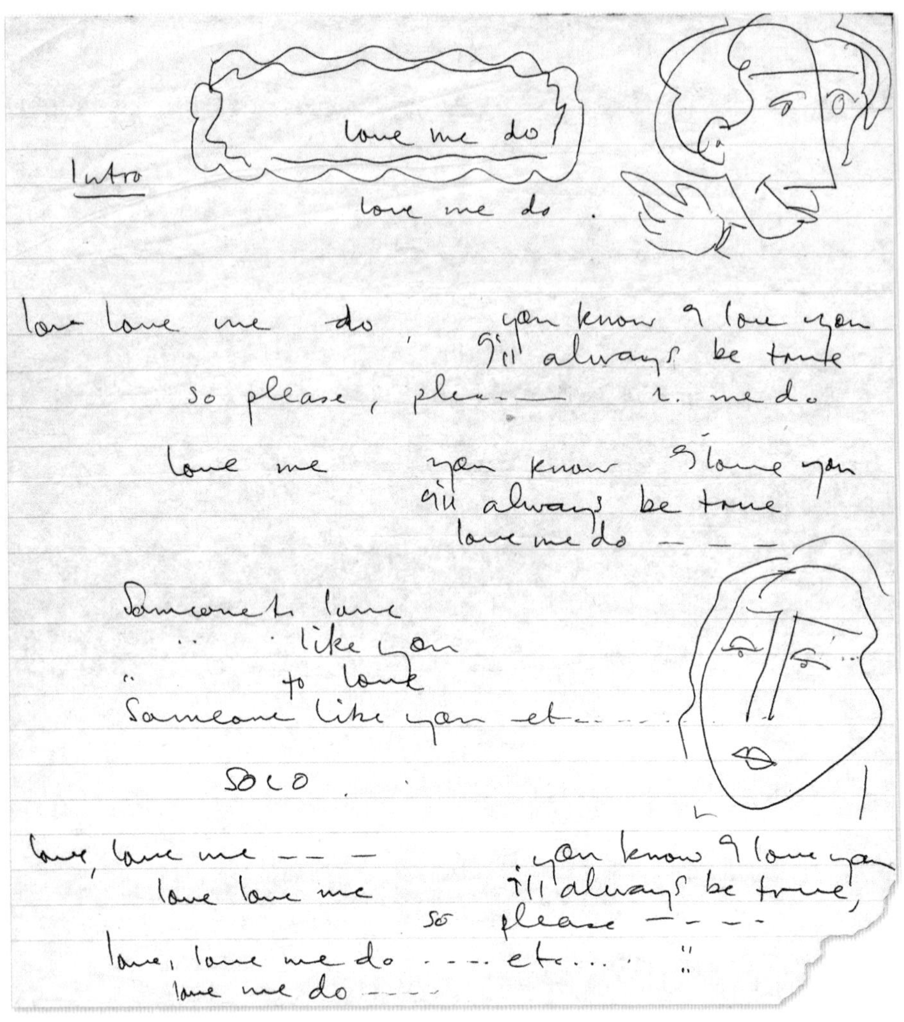
Intro

love me do

love me do .

love love me do, you know I love you
I'll always be true
so please, plea— l. me do

love me you know I love you
I'll always be true
love me do — — —

Someone to love
" " like you
" to love
Someone like you etc....

SOLO .

love, love me — — — you know I love you
love love me I'll always be true,
so please — — —
love, love me do ... etc....
love me do ----

which is where we did most of our composing when we were teenagers. I visualise it again and again. John came up with this riff, the little harmonica riff. It's so simple. There's nothing to it; it's a will-o'-the-wisp song. But there's a terrific sense of longing in the bridge which, combined with that harmonica, touches the soul in some way.

I think our image and our energy as the four Beatles were what was potent. 'Love Me Do' wasn't a major hit; it just sort of crept into the charts. We'd been touring the country since summer 1960, so we had a lot of fans around Britain. We had a very fresh sound; that's the sort of thing people notice. And we had a very fresh image.

Nobody looked like us. Before not too long, of course, *everybody* looked like us.

"BUDDY AT 60"
by Jeff Cummins
Commissioned by Paul McCartney

Lovely Rita

WRITERS	Paul McCartney and John Lennon
ARTIST	The Beatles
RECORDED	Abbey Road Studios, London
RELEASED	*Sgt. Pepper's Lonely Hearts Club Band*, 1967

Lovely Rita, meter maid
Lovely Rita, meter maid

Lovely Rita, meter maid
Nothing can come between us
When it gets dark I tow your heart away

Standing by a parking meter
When I caught a glimpse of Rita
Filling in a ticket in her little white book
In a cap she looked much older
And the bag across her shoulder
Made her look a little like a military man

Lovely Rita, meter maid
May I enquire discreetly
When are you free to take some tea with me, Rita?

Took her out and tried to win her
Had a laugh and over dinner
Told her I would really like to see her again
Got the bill and Rita paid it
Took her home I nearly made it
Sitting on the sofa with a sister or two

Lovely Rita, meter maid
Where would I be without you?
Give us a wink and make me think of you

Lovely Rita, meter maid
Lovely Rita, meter maid

NOBODY LIKED PARKING ATTENDANTS, OR METER MAIDS, as they were known in that benighted era. So, to write a song about being in love with a meter maid - someone nobody else liked - was amusing in itself. There was one particular meter maid in Portland Place on whom I based Rita. She was slightly military-looking. I know it's a terrible thing to say, but those meter maids were never good-looking. You never heard anybody say, 'God, that's one stunning parking attendant.'

In any case, I caught a glimpse of Rita opposite the Chinese embassy in Portland Place. She was filling in a ticket in her little white book. The cap, the bag across her shoulder. It's sheer observation, like painting *en plein air*. I've said it before and I'll say it again: the secret to successful songwriting is the ability to paint a picture.

One of the complicating factors in this picture is just how taken the speaker is with Rita. You might recall that her suitor got the bill, but 'Rita paid it'. It would have been considered ungentlemanly in that era to allow her to do that. Set against that is the idea that the speaker seems slightly miffed by the fact that he and Rita end up on the sofa 'with a sister or two'. The line suggests that he might quite like to have been alone with her rather than to have the sister or two as third and fourth wheels. Of course, another implication is the possibility of 'making it' not only with Rita but with the sister or two in tow. I've already had fun with that idea in the line 'When it gets dark I *tow* your heart away'.

At the end I can't quite suppress my weakness for naughtiness. In the phrase 'Give us a wink', for example, a wink may conjure up an idea like 'a nod and a wink', but it's also a euphemism, I admit. We always liked to put in things like 'finger pie', which you'll find in 'Penny Lane'. We knew people would get it. And the BBC wouldn't ban a song like this because they couldn't say for sure what you meant when you said, 'Give us a wink and make me think of you'. And it amuses me to think that the BBC, that bastion of respectability, was also in Portland Place, not too far from the Chinese embassy where I first saw Rita in the flesh.

Above: At Abbey Road Studios, London

Right: 'Lovely Rita' handwritten lyrics by John Lennon, with additional notes by Paul. Written on the reverse of an invitation to the Million Volt Light and Sound Rave held at the Roundhouse, London, 1967

B I N D E R   E D W A R D S   V A U G H A N

invite you to share a new experience.

London's first Light and Sound Show, at the Round House.

The first showing is on the 28th January from 8:30 pm. Please come in something white or wear a sheet.

This admits two.

D Ed[illegible]

HARANHURST LTD. 13 WIGMORE ST. LONDON W1 LAN 2824 N. SHULMAN, Secy.

I'm real, in a world that is tur[ning]
And sunlight is filtered away,
of our misfortune.

I'm grey, in a ~~night~~ day that is chang[ing]
And memory means living right,
of our misfortune

ing to grey
ith the veils

g + ~~day~~ night
ling tales

(2)

Standing by a parking meter
when I caught a glimps of Rita
filling in a ticket in her
little white book.

(1)
Lovely Rita, meter maid
Nothing can come between us
when it get's ~~night~~ dark I'll
~~tow~~ your heart away.

(3)
in a cap she looked ~~so stunning~~ much older
~~with~~ a bag across her shoulder
made her look a little like a military man.

(4) Lovely Rita meter maid

May I inquire discreetly
when ~~you~~ are you free to take some tea with me.

what would I do without you

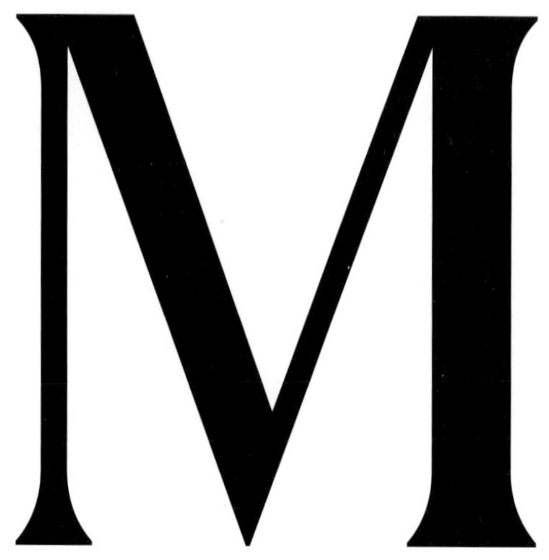

Magneto and Titanium Man

WRITERS	Paul McCartney and Linda McCartney
ARTIST	Wings
RECORDED	Sea-Saint Recording Studio, New Orleans
RELEASED	*Venus and Mars*, 1975
	B-side of 'Venus and Mars'/'Rock Show' single, 1975

Well I was talking last night
Magneto and Titanium Man
We were talking about you, babe
They said

You was involved in a robbery
That was due to happen
At a quarter to three
In the main street

I didn't believe them
Magneto and Titanium Man
But when the Crimson Dynamo
Finally assured me, well I knew

You was involved in a robbery
That was due to happen
At a quarter to three
In the main street

So we went out
Magneto and Titanium Man
And the Crimson Dynamo
Came along for the ride

We went to town with the library
And we swung all over that
Long tall bank
In the main street

Well there she were
And to my despair
She's a five-star criminal
Breaking the code

Magneto said, now the time has come
To gather our forces and run
Oh no
This can't be so

And then it occurred to me
You couldn't be bad
Magneto was mad
Titanium too
And the Crimson Dynamo
Just couldn't cut it no more
You were the law

IN 1975, AROUND THE TIME I WROTE 'MAGNETO AND TITANIUM Man', I was reading and looking at a lot of comic books, and as far as I was concerned, that was real art. It took some skill - not to mention perspective and imagination - to pull off these illustrations. So, I decided it would be nice to bring these two comic book characters into a song. Magneto is the archrival of the X-Men. Michael Fassbender has been playing him in the recent Marvel films. Titanium Man is one of Iron Man's enemies. And the Crimson Dynamo turns up as well; he's a bad guy too. So we have three baddies, and I made up a story that could have been in one of these comic books.

The mid-seventies also marked the rise of glam rock - people like David Bowie and T. Rex. Instead of a band just standing on the stage and simply playing their instruments, we were moving into a period when shows were using theatrical lighting and various stage effects. Bands like Pink Floyd were putting on big, spectacular shows. So when we did this onstage, we had big illustrations of the comic book characters Magneto and Titanium Man on the screens behind us.

To me, these comic book characters are drawn really well. And I've always thought that pop art and comic book art are near to madness. I studied John Dryden in school, since it was a time when school kids still read poets like Dryden, and have always been struck by these lines of his:

Great wits are sure to madness near allied,
And thin partitions do their bounds divide.

The sixties was the time when pop art really reached its peak. Roy Lichtenstein was literally doing comic book characters, Peter Blake was painting his wrestlers and The Beatles had contributed *Sgt. Pepper*. There was a lot of that about - which is really a part of that same conversation, where people are taking what you would call working-class pleasures, working-class themes, soup cans, and making a place for them in the art gallery and the museum.

It was a fascinating period for me, getting to meet some of these artists and see their work, even working with some of them. I'd won a little essay prize when I was in school in Liverpool, I think when I was about ten or eleven. The

Above: With Peter and Chrissy Blake. London, 1985

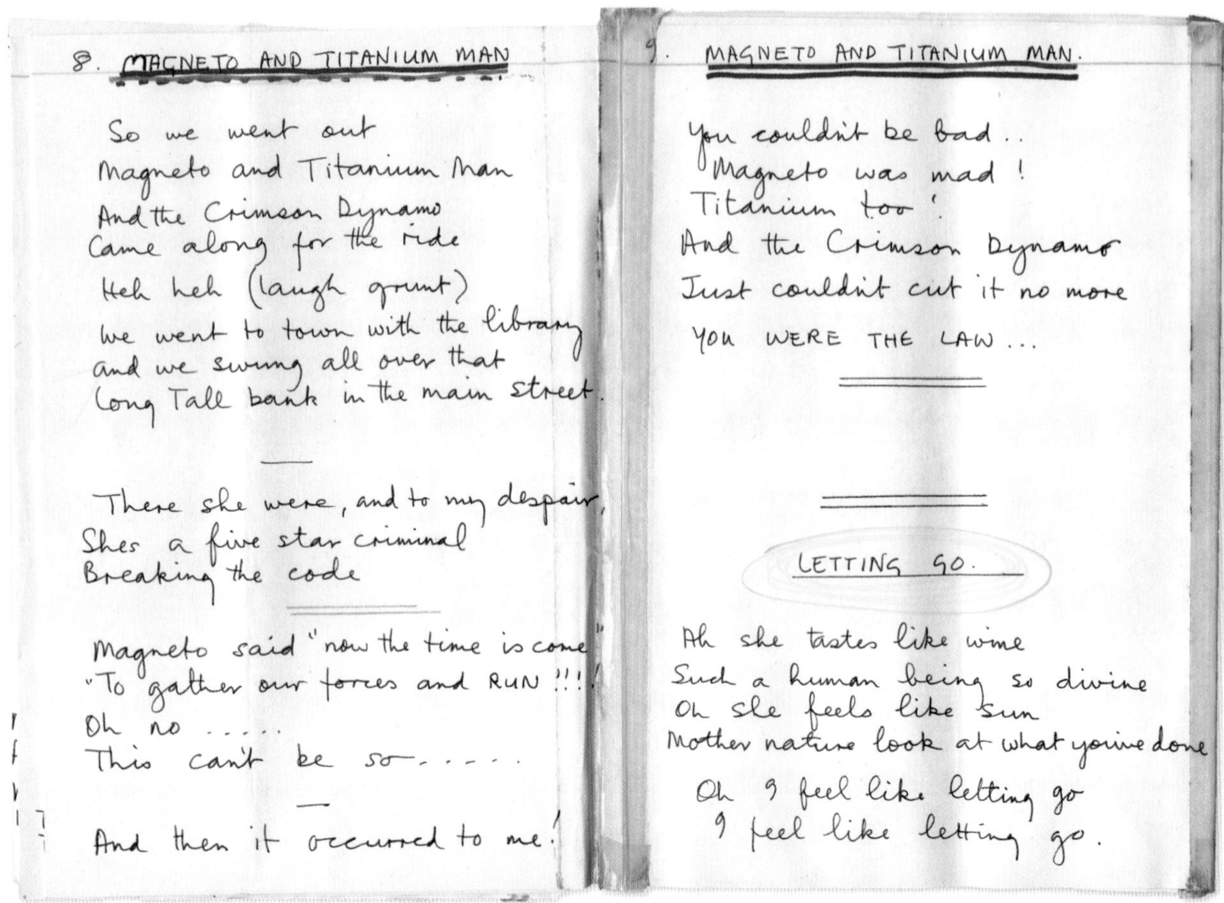

8. MAGNETO AND TITANIUM MAN

So we went out
Magneto and Titanium Man
And the Crimson Dynamo
Came along for the ride
Heh heh (laugh grunt)
We went to town with the library
and we swung all over that
Long Tall bank in the main street.

—

There she were, and to my despair,
Shes a five star criminal
Breaking the code

Magneto said "now the time is come"
"To gather our forces and RUN!!!"
Oh no .....
This can't be so.....

—

And then it occurred to me!

9. MAGNETO AND TITANIUM MAN.

You couldn't be bad..
Magneto was mad!
Titanium too!
And the Crimson Dynamo
Just couldn't cut it no more
YOU WERE THE LAW...

LETTING GO.

Ah she tastes like wine
Such a human being so divine
Oh she feels like sun
Mother nature look at what you've done
Oh I feel like letting go
I feel like letting go.

prize was a book, a modern art book, and it was lovely. It just fascinated me, so when I got a bit of money and was living in London, I would go into art galleries and buy little bits of art. I met Robert Fraser, a gallery owner, in 1966, and he became quite a formative art influence for me. We ended up becoming quite collaborative. A little later, he helped us out on *Sgt. Pepper* very much, put me in touch with quite a few people, like Peter Blake and Richard Hamilton, and we'd just hang out with them or go to a club.

I met Andy Warhol through Robert around the same time too, and he used to come over to London and we would go for a meal occasionally at this place called the Baghdad House, which had good curries, and one evening we went back to my house in North London. We set up for Andy to show a film of his, called *Empire*, which he'd made a few years before. It was a single shot of the Empire State Building, for eight hours. We all watched it. We kind of came and went a bit, but I watched it with Andy. He didn't talk much, so it wasn't easy to get to know him, and because there wasn't much to talk about in the film, it wasn't exactly the liveliest of evenings.

So, this song is my nod to comic books being high art.

With Robert Fraser.
London, 1981

I met Robert Fraser, a gallery owner, in 1966, and he became quite a formative art influence for me. We ended up becoming quite collaborative. A little later, he helped us out on *Sgt. Pepper* very much, put me in touch with quite a few people, like Peter Blake and Richard Hamilton, and we'd just hang out with them or go to a club.

Above: 'Magneto and Titanium Man' was released as the B-side to the 'Venus and Mars'/'Rock Show' single in 1975. The Crimson Dynamo character also appears on the sleeve as well as in the lyrics

Right: *Wings Over the World* tour. Detroit, 1976

Martha My Dear

WRITERS	Paul McCartney and John Lennon
ARTIST	The Beatles
RECORDED	Trident Studios, London
RELEASED	*The Beatles*, 1968

Martha my dear
Though I spend my days in conversation
Please remember me
Martha my love
Don't forget me
Martha my dear

Hold your head up, you silly girl
Look what you've done
When you find yourself in the thick of it
Help yourself to a bit of what is all around you, silly girl

Take a good look around you
Take a good look, you're bound to see
That you and me were meant to be
For each other, silly girl

Hold your hand out, you silly girl
See what you've done
When you find yourself in the thick of it
Help yourself to a bit of what is all around you, silly girl

Martha my dear
You have always been my inspiration
Please be good to me
Martha my love
Don't forget me
Martha my dear

BECAUSE MY MUM AND DAD BOTH WORKED AND WERE OUT ALL day, and my brother Mike and I were at school, there was no one to look after a dog. I remember one time we heard tell of puppies being given away in the next street, so we legged it round the corner, where, sure enough, there was a litter of puppies. We took a very cute little puppy home, but my mother told us we couldn't keep it. We were crestfallen. Totally crushed.

When I grew up and was in The Beatles, I had a house of my own in London. More than that, I actually had a housekeeper looking after the house. The time was ripe to get a dog. I had always liked the look of Old English sheepdogs, so I went along to a place in Milton Keynes, about an hour north of London, and selected this little dog. I named her Martha.

I'm pretty sure I was taken by Old English sheepdogs because of those television ads for Dulux paint. Dulux had started using an Old English sheepdog as a brand mascot back in 1961. It's a terrible thing to admit, but I'm a sucker for ads. The Dulux dog looked so loveable. It's not the only choice I've made because of what you might call product placement. For instance, I got myself the Aston Martin I mentioned earlier because I'd seen the first James Bond films and was quite impressed by the car.

Anyhow, I got Martha and she was a lovely little dog. I just adored her. One of the unlikely side effects was that John became very sympathetic towards me. When he came round and saw me playing with Martha, I could tell that he liked her. John was a very guarded person, which was partly where all his wit came from. He'd had a very difficult upbringing, what with his father leaving home, his uncle dying, and his mother getting killed in a traffic accident. By the time I knew him, he could be very sarcastic. Not that I couldn't be too. It was my own way of dealing with my mother's death, I expect. We were both quite into the witty put-down. But seeing me with Martha, with my guard down, all of a sudden he started warming to me. And so he let his guard down too.

The funny thing is, at the time almost no one listening to the song knew that Martha was a dog. And actually, as the song proceeds, Martha morphs into a person. As it happens, I had a relative who was having an affair and came down to London to tell me about it. Maybe for some hand-holding. If you think about it, by 1968 I represented a breath of freedom. I was now slightly outside the circle. This relative could confide in me in a way that maybe wouldn't have been possible with other members of a gossipy Liverpool family. I'm the only person who knew the song was about someone having an affair, and that gives a line like 'When you find yourself in the thick of it' an added layer of poignancy.

Left: With Martha and Eddie. London, 1968

Above: With Martha. London, 1969

Below: Recording 'Martha My Dear'. Trident Studios, London, 1968

Maxwell's Silver Hammer

WRITERS	Paul McCartney and John Lennon
ARTIST	The Beatles
RECORDED	Abbey Road Studios, London
RELEASED	*Abbey Road*, 1969

Joan was quizzical, studied pataphysical
Science in the home
Late nights all alone with a test tube
Oh oh oh oh
Maxwell Edison majoring in medicine
Calls her on the phone
Can I take you out to the pictures, Joan?
But as she's getting ready to go
A knock comes on the door

Bang bang Maxwell's silver hammer
Came down upon her head
Clang clang Maxwell's silver hammer
Made sure that she was dead

Back in school again, Maxwell plays the fool again
Teacher gets annoyed
Wishing to avoid an unpleasant scene
She tells Max to stay when the class has gone away
So he waits behind
Writing fifty times I must not be so
Oh oh oh
But when she turns her back on the boy
He creeps up from behind

Bang bang Maxwell's silver hammer
Came down upon her head
Clang clang Maxwell's silver hammer
Made sure that she was dead

PC Thirty-One said, we've caught a dirty one
Maxwell stands alone
Painting testimonial pictures
Oh oh oh oh
Rose and Valerie screaming from the gallery
Say he must go free
The judge does not agree and he tells them so
Oh oh oh
But as the words are leaving his lips
A noise comes from behind

Bang bang Maxwell's silver hammer
Came down upon his head
Clang clang Maxwell's silver hammer
Made sure that he was dead

Silver hammer man

ZOOMING UP THE MOTORWAY FROM LONDON TO LIVERPOOL IN the aforementioned Aston Martin, I fiddled around on the radio for something and happened on a BBC Radio 3 production of *Ubu Cocu*. It was first broadcast on 21 December 1965, with a repeat on 10 January 1966. It's one of three plays, including the better-known *Ubu Roi*, by the French dramatist Alfred Jarry and is subtitled 'a pataphysical extravaganza'. 'Pataphysical' is a nonsense word Jarry made up to poke fun at toffee-nosed academics. I was then thrilled when I was able to rhyme 'quizzical' with 'pataphysical' in this song. How often do you get that chance? I liked that people wouldn't necessarily know what 'pataphysical' was, so I was being a little bit obscure on purpose.

Maxwell is possibly a descendant of James Clerk Maxwell, who was a pioneer of electromagnetism. Edison is obviously related to Thomas Edison. They're two inventor types. Part of the fun here is that Edison is connected to the lightbulb and the phonograph, and here we were making a gramophone record. Speaking of lightbulbs, they're going off all the time, particularly when those little chimes happen. 'Edison' and 'medicine'. 'Valerie' and 'gallery'.

The thing about Maxwell is that he's a serial killer, and his hammer isn't an ordinary household hammer but, as I envision it, one that doctors use to hit your knee. Not made of rubber, though. Silver.

Also invoked is the world of the children's nursery rhyme, where people are always getting their heads chopped off – and of course, there's also the Queen of Hearts from *Alice's Adventures in Wonderland*, who's always saying, 'Off with their heads!' Ian Brady and Myra Hindley, the Moors murderers, had been jailed for life in 1966 for committing serial murders. That case was quite likely in my mind, as it was front page news in the UK.

I was very keen on this song, but it took a bit long to record, and the rest of the guys were getting pissed with me. This recording period coincided with the visit to Abbey Road of Robert Moog, the inventor of the Moog synthesizer, and I was fascinated with what could be done with these new sounds. That's one reason why it took a little longer than our normal songs. Not crazy compared to today's standards – it was something like three days – but a long time by the standards of the day. This song is also an analogy for when something goes wrong out of the blue, as I was beginning to find happening around this time in our business dealings. Recording sessions were always good because no matter what our personal troubles were, no matter what was happening on the business front, the minute we sat down to make a song we were in good shape. Right until the end there was always a great joy in working together in the studio.

So there we were, recording a song like 'Maxwell's Silver Hammer' and knowing we would never have the opportunity to perform it. That possibility was over. It had been knocked on the head like one of Maxwell's victims. Bang bang.

Back in school again Maxwell plays the fool again
Teacher gets annoyed.
wishing to avoid an unpleasant scene
She tells Max to stay when the class has
gone away so he waits behind, no no no
writing 50 times I must not be so,
~~And as she turns her back to the board,~~
But when she turns her back on the boy,
he creeps up from behind . . .
Bang Bang — Maxwells . . . .

P.C. thirty one
says "we caught a dirty one"
Maxwell stands alone
Painting testimonial pictures — o oh oh oh
Rose + Valerie, screaming from the gallery
say he must go free,
The judge cannot agree and he tells them so,
But as the words are leaving his lips
a noise comes from behind.

Maxwell's Silver Hammer

(1) Joan was quizzical
Studied pataphysical
Science in the home
Late nights all alone with a test tube
Oh ho ho ho

Maxwell Edison, majoring in medicine
Calls her on the phone
Can I take you out to the pictures
Joa — oa — an

But as she's getting ready to go,
a knock comes on the door....
Bang bang Maxwell's Silver Hammer

(2) Back in school again
maxwell plays the fool again
teacher gets annoyed
~~How can she avoid him a third time~~
~~wishing to avoid~~ an unpleasant scene
How can she avoid

Left: Playing the Minimoog synthesizer. Lagos, 1973

Diary entry including the time of the *Abbey Road* album cover shoot, August 1969

So there we were, recording a song like 'Maxwell's Silver Hammer' and knowing we would never have the opportunity to perform it. That possibility was over. It had been knocked on the head like one of Maxwell's victims. Bang bang.

Maybe I'm Amazed

WRITER	Paul McCartney
ARTIST	Paul McCartney
RECORDED	Abbey Road Studios, London
RELEASED	*McCartney*, 1970

Baby, I'm amazed at the way you love me all the time
And maybe I'm afraid of the way I love you
Maybe I'm amazed at the way you pulled me out of time
You hung me on a line
Maybe I'm amazed at the way I really need you

Baby, I'm a man
Maybe I'm a lonely man who's in the middle of something
That he doesn't really understand
Baby, I'm a man
And maybe you're the only woman who could ever help me
Baby, won't you help me to understand

Maybe I'm amazed at the way you're with me all the time
Maybe I'm afraid of the way I leave you
Maybe I'm amazed at the way you help me sing my song
You right me when I'm wrong
And maybe I'm amazed at the way I really need you

THIS IS SUPPOSEDLY LIZA MINELLI'S FAVOURITE OF MY SONGS. I expected her to go for something a bit more ballady. But she really likes this one. It dates from the time, the end of the 1960s, when Linda and I were first living together. In much the way that Linda wanted to flee from New York society - the constrictions of Park Avenue and Scarsdale - I wanted to flee from what The Beatles had become. I was hoping to escape, she was hoping to escape. So we had this feeling that we had each pulled the other 'out of time'.

Though the song was written immediately after The Beatles' breakup, it was somehow included under the Lennon-McCartney rubric, where it doesn't belong. It was one of my first solo songs, but because of the deal, it got caught in the publishing net. That was very annoying.

Actually, Linda and I were probably already married, because I can now visualise sitting at the lovely black Steinway piano that we got after our wedding. I was playing on it one day, and this song came to me - the central idea being that there's so often a split between the inner and outer. For example, I was in the gym this morning, looking at the girls on the TV, and I was thinking, 'Oh God, I really shouldn't be doing this, because I'm married. If people knew what was in my head, I'd be so busted.' You can think anything, so you do think anything, and then your conscience has to check it and control it.

I use this as an extreme example of the kind of intense, interior conversation that's going on in the song. The elements of fear and loneliness are very much to the fore. 'Maybe I'm afraid of the way I love you' is itself a troubling idea.

While it's true that Linda is the person I'm addressing, it's also true that I'm dealing in fiction. Starting with myself, the characters who appear in my songs are imagined. I can't state that often enough. I know that in some quarters it's felt you can't write about gay people unless you're gay, or about Asian Americans unless you're an Asian American.

I think that's silly. That's like saying that because James Joyce wasn't Jewish, he shouldn't have written about Leopold Bloom. The whole point about being a writer is that you should be free to write about anything. In fact, it's part of your job to go to the places where others might not feel comfortable.

In any event, this song isn't the conventional way of presenting a relationship, or of some of the contradictions that can arise from being in love. That's maybe why Liza Minnelli likes it so much. It shows the fragility of love.

(13) Maybe I'm Amazed

Baby I'm Amazed at the way you
love me all the time.
and maybe I'm afraid of the way I love you
Maybe I'm amazed at the way you pulled
me out of time, hung me on a line,
and maybe I'm amazed at the way I really
need you.

MIDDLE
Baby I'm a man, maybe I'm a lonely man
whose in the middle of something
That he doesn't really understand
Baby I'm a man ~~lg~~ maybe you're the
~~of~~ only woman who could ever help me,
Baby won't you help me to understand,

Maybe I'm amazed at the way you're
with me all the time,
+ maybe I'm afraid of the way I leave you.
maybe I'm amazed at the way you

(13) ~~maybe I'm as~~ amazed (cont....)

help me sing my song,
right me when I'm wrong,
and maybe I'm amazed at the way I
really need you.

MIDDLE
Baby I'm a man, (REPEAT,) . . . . .

(14) Kreen-Akrore
— instrumental.

MAYBE I'm amazed

Maybe I'm amazed at the way you
love me all the time
maybe I'm afraid of the way I love you
~~maybe~~ Baby I'm amazed at the way you pulled me
out of time
hung me on a line
~~maybe~~ I'm ~~af~~ amazed at the way
I really need you.

MIDDLE
Baby I'm a man
maybe I'm a lonely man
who's in the middle of something
That he doesn't really understand.
Baby I'm a man
maybe you're the only woman
who could ever help me
Baby won't you help me understand . . .

Maybe I'm amazed at the way you're
with me all the time,
maybe I'm afraid of the way I leave you
maybe I'm amazed at the way you

help me sing my song
right me when I'm wrong
maybe I'm amazed at the way I really
need you.

middle. Baby I'm a man . . .

TAKING THINGS EASY,

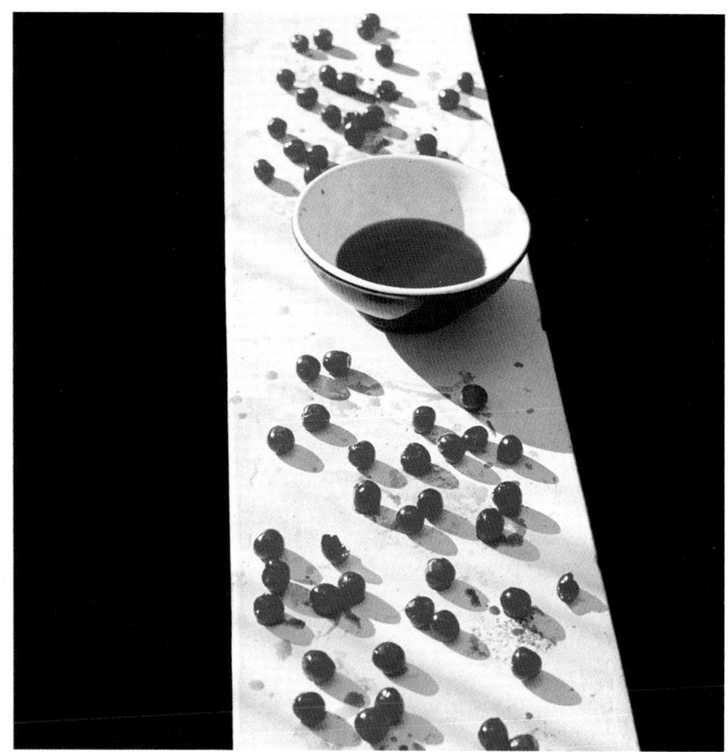

Left: Linda. Antigua, 1969. Her photograph of the cherries to her right is later used for the cover of *McCartney*, 1970

Left: Linda. London, 1969

Right: Linda on the farm. Scotland, 1970

The elements of fear and loneliness are very much to the fore. 'Maybe I'm afraid of the way I love you' is itself a troubling idea.

Michelle

WRITERS	Paul McCartney and John Lennon
ARTIST	The Beatles
RECORDED	Abbey Road Studios, London
RELEASED	*Rubber Soul*, 1965

Michelle, ma belle
These are words that go together well
My Michelle

Michelle, ma belle
Sont les mots qui vont très bien ensemble
Très bien ensemble

I love you, I love you, I love you
That's all I want to say
Until I find a way
I will say the only words I know that
you'll understand

Michelle, ma belle
Sont les mots qui vont très bien ensemble
Très bien ensemble

I need to, I need to, I need to
I need to make you see
Oh what you mean to me
Until I do I'm hoping you will know what I mean
I love you

I want you, I want you, I want you
I think you know by now
I'll get to you somehow
Until I do I'm telling you so you'll understand

Michelle, ma belle
Sont les mots qui vont très bien ensemble
Très bien ensemble

And I will say the only words I know that
you'll understand
My Michelle

JOHN, BEING OLDER AND AT ART SCHOOL, WOULD TAKE ME TO art school parties. I remember going to one and sitting in the corner with my black polo-neck sweater on, trying to look interesting to this older crowd. I had the acoustic guitar with me, and I was playing a French-sounding song and making guttural noises. I was half hoping that someone would think I was French, possibly even a French intellectual.

So that's where it all started, with my memory of having this faux French song that must have been influenced by Édith Piaf's 'Milord', a big hit in 1959. 'Milord' was interesting because it was out of left field, whereas with other songs you knew what genre they were. In 'Milord', Piaf does the old trick of slowing down in the course of the song. I must have had a memory of that in the hopper.

Another element was the fact that George Harrison and I liked learning new chords and finding ways to put them into songs. We knew a guy called Jim Gretty, who worked in Hessy's guitar shop in Liverpool. We used to love going into this shop, even though it meant we had to pay our dues with our little books because, of course, we'd bought our guitars on an instalment plan. Jim Gretty would often stand behind the counter in Hessy's, playing a bit of guitar, as guys in music shops so often do. We really admired his skills. He was far more advanced than us. One chord we heard him play was particularly lush, and he took the trouble to demonstrate it to us. It was what we knew as an F chord, a simple F shape, down at the first position, down at the nut. But Jim used two more of his fingers to cover the first two strings up on the fourth fret, which would be A-flat and E-flat, so there was an extra component to the F chord. The good thing was that if he showed something to both of us, we were bound to remember it because if George forgot it I'd remember it, and vice versa. We called Gretty's lush F chord 'F demented'.

In the Beatles period we were looking for new songs, and John once said to me, 'Remember that daft French thing you used to do at parties?' I happened to meet up with Ivan Vaughan, who was probably my best friend in school. By then he'd been to University College London to study the classics. He and his wife Jan lived in Islington, and I used to visit them. Jan taught French, so I asked if she could think of a rhyme for 'Michelle', two syllables. She said '*Ma belle*'. So, how could I say 'these words go together' in French? So, Jan also gave me '*sont les mots qui vont très bien ensemble*'. You must sound the *b* in '*ensemble*'. I'd always said '*ensemble*' with a silent *b*.

In addition to the 'F demented', which would have had an official name like an F augmented ninth or something, I put in a second naughty chord. Again, I don't know its name - maybe D diminished? I got it off the Coasters record *Along Came Jones*. I used these two chords and this melody, and grunted along like a cod Frenchman, and there was 'Michelle'.

Left: With Ivan Vaughan and his son. London, 1968

Above left and right: At home in Liverpool, photographed by brother Mike, late 1950s

I love you I love you I love you
that's all I want to say
until I find a way
I will use the only words I know that you
understand.

Michelle.

I ~~need~~ want you
I think you know by now
I'll get to you somehow
until I find – – –

Mother Nature's Son

WRITERS	Paul McCartney and John Lennon
ARTIST	The Beatles
RECORDED	Abbey Road Studios, London
RELEASED	*The Beatles*, 1968

Born a poor young country boy
Mother Nature's son
All day long I'm sitting singing songs
For everyone

Sit beside a mountain stream
See her waters rise
Listen to the pretty sound of music
As she flies

Find me in my field of grass
Mother Nature's son
Swaying daisies
Sing a lazy song beneath the sun

Mother Nature's son

PEOPLE USE THE EXPRESSION 'LIVING ON THE EDGE'. WE lived literally on the edge of the city of Liverpool because my mother was a midwife, and anytime a new housing estate was built, the council would provide a midwife's house. The city kept spreading like a stain. In this case, the midwife's house was in Western Avenue, and I have memories of my mum cycling off on her bike in the snow.

After that we were moved to a new house at 12 Ardwick Road in the area called Speke, just ten minutes by bike down the road, five minutes by bus. Lots of houses were going up. There were building sites everywhere, and the road wasn't quite built yet, so it was muddy in the winter. We played on the building sites, and they were really quite dangerous. I once pulled my brother out of a lime pit because he couldn't get up the steep, slippery side. It was scary, but we were kids and we knew no better than to be there. That was our playground.

If you went about a mile from where we lived, you would suddenly be in rural Lancashire, and it was as if you'd fallen off the end of the Earth. It was all woods and streams and fields of golden corn waving – everything you love about the countryside. There was a lot of bird life there because, in those days, things were more or less organic. They just hadn't quite got round to buying expensive pesticides and fertilisers; nature was much more in balance.

Top and above: With brother Mike and mum Mary, late 1940s

So that was something I would often do – just go walking, either into the woods or to dam up a stream or to climb a tree or to wander into the fields and get chased by farmers. Even now, as I walk through my own fields, or ride through them on my horse, I often think of those farmers: 'Get out of here! You're ruining my field!'

There was that strong sense of the countryside, and I was very lucky to access it so easily. I had the privilege - the joy, really - of watching a skylark rising. In the middle of a field there's a bird that just rises, vertically, singing as if its life depends on it, and it goes up this column of air till it gets to the top, and then it stops singing and just glides down. That's how it leads you away from its nest, fluttering like the solo violin in *The Lark Ascending*, that lovely piece of music by Ralph Vaughan Williams. It's now a golden memory. Most people I meet these days haven't seen this behaviour of the skylark, but it was very powerful for me, the sheer glory of nature. I was living in London and imagining it, trying to think like a country boy. Mother Nature's son.

'Sit beside a mountain stream' - which it wouldn't have been; it would have been a field stream or a woodland stream. 'See her waters rise / Listen to the pretty / Sound of music as she flies'. I was very fascinated by streams, and still am. I just like to see them burrowing their way to the sea, or wherever it is they go. 'My field of grass' was a definite nod to marijuana, because at that time we were all smoking pot and, as you may recall, I always enjoyed sticking in any little reference to that. I just incorporated the phrases because I liked having a little in-joke.

The song was partly inspired by being in Rishikesh with the Maharishi, as well as by Nat King Cole's 'Nature Boy', but I seem to remember writing it at my dad's house in Liverpool. I was in my folk-singing 'California' mindset, but the actual terrain was Speke or, later on, Scotland. Swaying daisies, buttercups - it was memories of summer in the beautiful fields. This is a love song - a love song to the natural world.

Left: Ireland, 1971

Right: On horseback, late 1940s

(3)

MOTHER NATURES SON.

1. Born a poor young country boy
Mother Natures son,
All day long I'm sitting singing songs
For everyone.

2. Sit beside a mountain stream
See her waters run,
Listen to the pretty sound of music
As she flies ...
Mother Natures son

Riding in Sussex, photographed by daughter Mary, 2020

Mrs. Vandebilt

WRITERS	Paul McCartney and Linda McCartney
ARTIST	Paul McCartney and Wings
RECORDED	EMI Studios, Lagos; and AIR Studios, London
RELEASED	*Band on the Run*, 1973

Down in the jungle, living in a tent
You don't use money, you don't pay rent
You don't even know the time
But you don't mind

Ho hey ho

When your light is on the blink
You never think of worrying
What's the use of worrying?
When your bus has left the stop
You'd better drop your hurrying
What's the use of hurrying?
Leave me alone Mrs. Vandebilt
I've got plenty of time of my own

What's the use of worrying?
What's the use of hurrying?
What's the use of anything?

Ho hey ho

When your pile is on the wane
You don't complain of robbery
Run away, don't bother me
What's the use of worrying?
What's the use of anything?
Leave me alone Mrs. Washington
I've done plenty of time on my own

What's the use of worrying?
What's the use of hurrying?
What's the use of anything?

Ho hey ho

When we were first in the Beatles, we used to get asked whether we were worried that we might have joined the Establishment. We thought The Establishment was a club in London - which indeed it was. We didn't really know precisely what it meant, except that we were now part of the status quo. Of course, we insisted we weren't part of anything posh. We knew a few posh people, but that was it.

If you were on a quiz show and had to come up with a list of names that embodied vast wealth, you'd have Rockefeller, Getty, Vanderbilt. There are certain names you know because they're in the newspapers all the time - the super-rich.

The problem with being rich is that what comes with it is often quite bothersome. For example, I've got a little sailboat which I can sail by myself. I can get it in and out of the water by myself. Just the other day someone reminded me it was really a kid's boat. I went, 'Okay, I'm a kid.' I'm not sure if they would understand that I just don't want a bigger boat, the kind 'adults' might have. If I have a bigger boat I'll need a crew, and I don't want a crew.

The problem with getting involved with Mrs Vandebilt is that it comes with a lot of society's rules. I've got to invite for cocktails all these people whom I don't like. I'm the kind of person who'll go to Mrs Vandebilt's cocktail party - once.

That's the way I've led my life. I like this idea of the alternative being the norm and then dipping into, or playing with, this other world that I don't really want and to which I'll never quite belong. 'Down in the jungle, living in a tent / You don't use money, you don't pay rent' is a riff on a song by the British comedian Charlie Chester, who was a mainstay of radio when I was a kid. It's also a worldview that I find very attractive. Hippiedom. Dropping out.

I don't want Mrs Vandebilt or her ilk to intrude on my tranquil time. She's going to spoil it for me. She's going to make me obey rules that I don't want to obey. She's going to pull me up into her cloud of money and influence and authority, and I would rather be spending my time with the Eleanor Rigbys of the world.

Just as Mrs Vandebilt morphs into Mrs Washington, who represents the political capital of America, so the phrase 'I've got plenty of time of my own' turns into 'I've done plenty of time on my own'. Even though this song was written long before my 1980 arrest in Japan, when I spent nine nights in jail for possession of marijuana, I'd been incarcerated a couple of times before in Hamburg too. Only for a day, not overnight. So this feeling was familiar to me.

In short, Mrs Vandebilt is a figure of authority and wealth and rules and money that the protagonist of the song doesn't want to know about. He wants to be left alone. And that's me, very much who I am. I'm never happier than when I'm in the middle of the woods, on a horse, making a trail. Any chance I have, I like to be out on my own in the woods.

MRS. VANDEBILT

Down in the jungle living in a tent
You dont use money you dont pay rent
" " even know the time
But you dont mind

CHORUS HO HEY HO
" " "
" " "
" " "

When you light is on the blink
You never think of worrying
What's the use of worrying?
When your bus has left the stop
You'd better drop your hurrying
What's the use of " ?
Leave me alone Mrs. Vandebilt
I've got plenty of time of my own
What's the use of worrying?
" " " " hurrying?
" " " ..anything?

CHORUS HO HEY HO

What's the use of worrying?
hurrying?
anything?

HO HEY HO

When your pile is on the wane
You don't complain of robbery
Run away don't bother me
What's the use of worrying?
anything?
Leave me alone Mrs. Washington,
I've done plenty of time on my own

What's the use of worrying?
hurrying? (no use!)
anything?

CHORUS HO HEY HO

Above: On horseback. Sussex, 1992

Left: Sunfish sailboat. 1990

Right: Menorca, 1986

FUSION

Mull of Kintyre

WRITERS	Paul McCartney and Denny Laine
ARTIST	Wings
RECORDED	Spirit of Ranachan Studio, Scotland
RELEASED	'Mull of Kintyre'/'Girls' School' double A-side single, 1977

Mull of Kintyre
Oh mist rolling in from the sea
My desire is always to be here
Oh Mull of Kintyre

Far have I travelled and much have I seen
Dark distant mountains with valleys of green
Past painted deserts, the sunset's on fire
As he carries me home to the Mull of Kintyre

Mull of Kintyre
Oh mist rolling in from the sea
My desire is always to be here
Oh Mull of Kintyre

Sweep through the heather like deer in the glen
Carry me back to the days I knew then
Nights when we sang like a heavenly choir
Of the life and the times of the Mull of Kintyre

Mull of Kintyre
Oh mist rolling in from the sea
My desire is always to be here
Oh Mull of Kintyre

Smiles in the sunshine and tears in the rain
Still take me back where my memories remain
Flickering embers grow higher and higher
As they carry me back to the Mull of Kintyre

Mull of Kintyre
Oh mist rolling in from the sea
My desire is always to be here
Oh Mull of Kintyre

THE SONG WAS RECORDED IN SCOTLAND IN A LITTLE STUDIO ON the farm, a mobile unit that we had set up. Unfortunately, it was too small a space to get a whole pipe band in. If you are in an orchestral session, the musicians will count 'One two three four, two two three four, . . .', but a Scottish pipe band won't. It counts, 'One two three four five six seven eight nine ten eleven twelve . . .', which was great. The English can only get to four!

We'd already been spending a lot of time on our farm in Scotland by the mid-seventies. It's in Kintyre, as it happens, not actually on the Mull of Kintyre. I think a lot of English people, or non-Gaelic people, have a Gaelic dream, a romantic idea of Scottish history, or Irish history, and if your ancestors were from Ireland, as mine were, it's even more important to you because you have a right to play into the dream. Very early on, John had Scottish relatives, and he would go up there and stay in a croft somewhere, and I thought, 'Wow, that's wildly romantic,' so this song was a way of plugging into that feeling and being proud of this area where I was living. One day it occurred to me that there were no new Scottish songs; there were lots of great old songs that the bagpipe bands played, but nobody had written anything new. So, that was an opportunity to see whether I could. A new Scottish song written by a Sassenach? That would be fun.

One of the things you do as an artist is try to make sense of, and maybe even honour, the place in which you find yourself. You do that for your homeplace, and I always tried to do that for Liverpool because I'm proud of it. I really like remembering where I've come from; not only does it honour the place, but it reminds me of how far I've come. It relates to the class system in the UK – that it's a great achievement to have come from a place that's thought of as being quite lowly compared to other places that are not. There's considerable satisfaction in that.

When Linda and I first met and were getting to know each other, she said, 'Have you got a place up in Scotland? I heard you do.' I did, though to tell you the truth, I wasn't that keen on it then, but when we went up there, she said, 'Oh, this is fantastic. I love it!' I also found it very lovely, and so I was very happy to romanticise it. I thought my way into the minds of travellers, soldiers returning home, and that dream of coming back to the beautiful country, the beautiful village. The point of view of the homecoming person is deep in people's souls. Sometimes we do this song in concert when we're in expat places like Canada and New Zealand. We've got some security guys who are Scottish, and you see them welling up.

When the time came to record, I had the local pipe major come up to the house with his pipes, a gentleman named Tony Wilson. It was a very little house, and when he played it was so loud that I said, 'Let's go out into the garden,' which again was a very little garden, and we just sort of played and I got some ideas. I figured out which chords would work with what he was playing – what key he was in, because you can't change key on the bagpipes; what you hear is what you've got. I made the song, and we recorded the basic tracks. Then, a few days later, we had a recording session up there in the

evening with lots of McEwan's beer for all the boys in the band, although they weren't allowed to drink it until afterwards because some of them were quite young and it could have gone horribly wrong. And there they were all dressed up in their pipers' outfits. It was pretty emotional, hearing the band play; it was so loud, and they did it in a few takes. It was a very fun evening, and they loved it. 'Oh, aye, it's a number one hit!'

The big thought from me, and from everyone, was that it was 1977; we couldn't release the song in those days of punk. I mean, it was madness, but I just thought, 'Well, sod it.' But even though I was a Sassenach, it became a big Scottish song. It ended up spending nine weeks at number one, and I think it's still something like the fourth best-selling single in the UK ever. And the strange thing was, even punks liked it. One day, Linda and I were in traffic in London in the West End somewhere, and there was a big gang of punks who looked very aggressive, and we were kind of crouching a little bit, trying not to get noticed, and thinking, 'Jesus, what are they gonna do?' And then they noticed us, and one of them comes to the car, so I wound down the window a little bit, and he goes, 'Oy, Paul, that "Mull of Kintyre" is fucking great!'

Above: With pipe major Tony Wilson. Scotland, 1977

Right: Campbeltown Pipe Band. Scotland, 1977

Above, left and top right: With Wings and Campbeltown Pipe Band. Spirit of Ranachan Studio, Scotland, 1977

Bottom right: Mary and Stella preparing post-recording refreshments for the Pipe Band, 1977

Mull OF KINTYRE.

Chorus.

Mull of Kintyre

Oh mist rolling in from the sea
my desire is always to be here
Oh mull of Kintyre.

(1) Far have I travelled + much have I seen
Dark distant mountains with vallies of green
Past painted deserts the sun sets on fire
as he carries me home to the mull of Kintyre.

— CHORUS mull of Kintyre.

✳ 4 Bars PIPE BAND — drone starting.

KEY CHANGE TO D — PIPE SOLO (chorus.)

(2) Sweep through the heather, like deer in the glen
Carry me back ~~where my memories remain~~ to the days I knew then.
Nights when we sang like a heavenly choir
of the life and the times of the mull of Kintyre.

CHORUS — PIPE RIFF D — to A
Repeat. once.

(3) (BACK IN A.)
Smiles in the sunshine - tears in the rain
Carry me back where my memories remain
Flickering embers grow higher + higher
as they carry me back to the mull of Kintyre.

CHORUS Mull of Kintyre. (TWICE) CHORUS in D ..
PIPE RIFF — D to A ~~fade out~~ END.

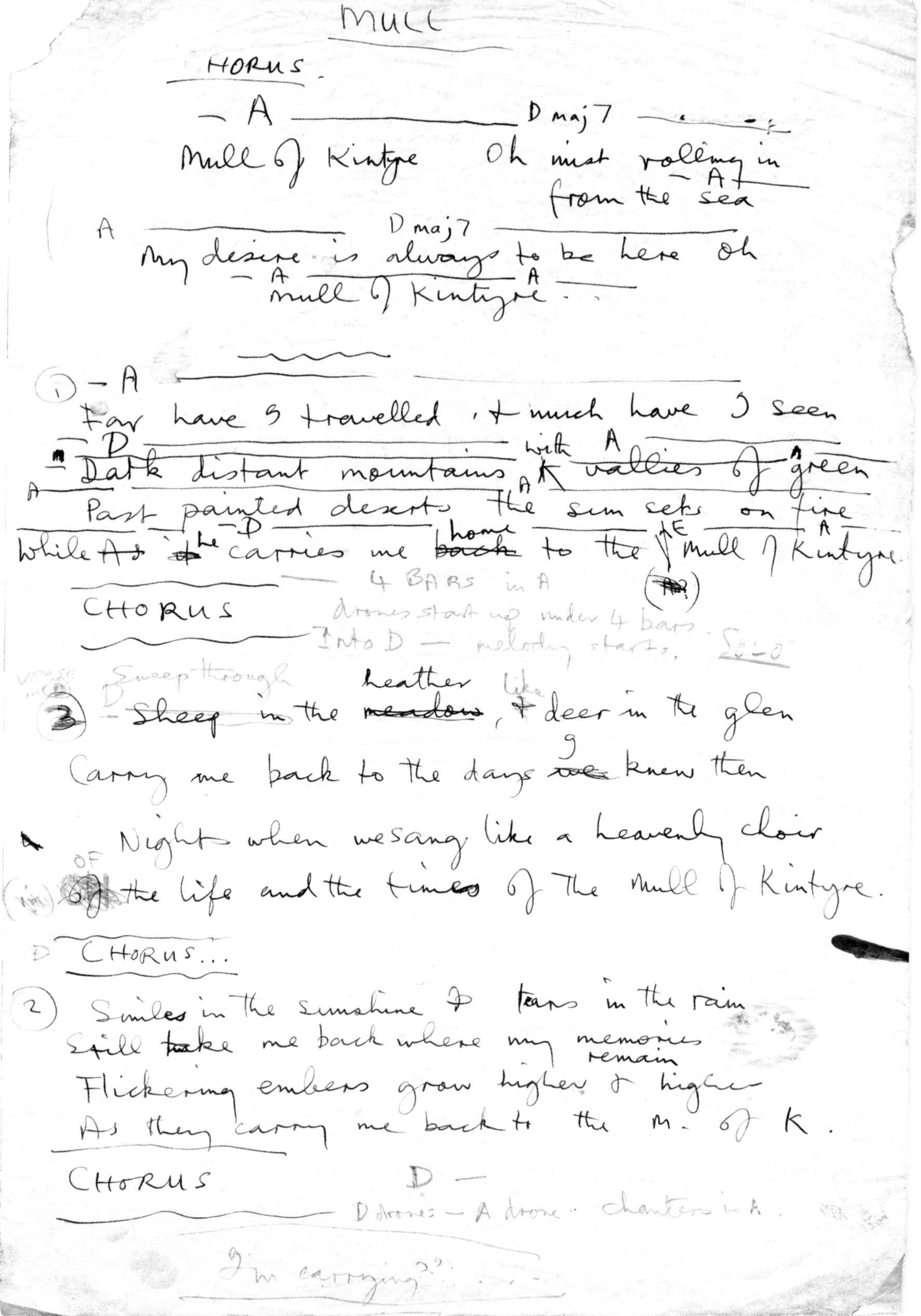

MULL

CHORUS.

A D maj 7

Mull of Kintyre Oh mist rolling in
A
from the sea

A D maj 7

My desire is always to be here Oh
A A
Mull of Kintyre...

(1) A

Far have I travelled, & much have I seen
D A
Dark distant mountains with valleys of green
A A
Past painted deserts the sun sets on fire
D E A
While he carries me home to the Mull of Kintyre.

4 BARS in A

CHORUS

drones start up under 4 bars
INTO D — melody starts, SOLO

Sweep through
D heather like
(3) Sheep in the heather, & deer in the glen

Carry me back to the days I knew then

Nights when we sang like a heavenly choir

Of the life and the times of the Mull of Kintyre.

D CHORUS...

(2) Smiles in the sunshine & tears in the rain
Still take me back where my memories remain
Flickering embers grow higher & higher
As they carry me back to the M. of K.

CHORUS D —

D drones — A drone · chanters in A.

I'm carrying?" ...

My Love

WRITERS	Paul McCartney and Linda McCartney
ARTIST	Paul McCartney and Wings
RECORDED	Abbey Road Studios, London
RELEASED	Single, 1973
	Red Rose Speedway, 1973

And when I go away
I know my heart can stay with my love
It's understood
It's in the hands of my love
And my love does it good
My love does it good

And when the cupboard's bare
I'll still find something there with my love
It's understood
It's everywhere with my love
And my love does it good
My love does it good

I love
My love
Only my love holds the other key to me
My Love
My love
Only my love does it good to me
My love does it good

Don't ever ask me why
I never say goodbye to my love
It's understood
It's everywhere with my love
And my love does it good
My love does it good

I love
My love
Only my love does it good to me

STEPHEN SONDHEIM AND I ONCE SPENT A VERY PLEASANT COUPLE of hours chatting about this and that, and eventually got round to songwriting methods. When he asked what my process was, I told him I started out by finding the chords. What chords work well next to each other, what progression suggests a new melody. He seemed a little surprised that what I did was all chord based. For him, it's all about melody and counterpoint, how various melodies can work together and complement each other. It had never occurred to me that his music and classical music mightn't be chord based, so that was an interesting insight into how classical music is written.

The Abbey Road recording session for 'My Love' was really cool because our guitarist, Henry McCullough, a Northern Ireland boy, played such a role in it. We'd worked out a solo in rehearsal because it was going to be live in the studio with an orchestra. And I remember Henry walking around the studio before one of the takes and whispering to me that he had an idea for a solo. Would I mind if he tried it out? I could have said no. I could have said I'd prefer him to stick to the script, but I said, 'Yeah, sure.'

So, the solo came pretty much out of the blue. None of us had heard it before. It's an absolutely beautiful solo, and I think it was lovely for me to give Henry his freedom when he'd been in the band only about a year. It was great for him to be bold enough not only to want it but to take it.

It's a comparative freedom, mind you. Henry's solo and the notes he chose still had to be operating within the framework of those basic chords for it to work within the song. In that sense the music is informing – perhaps even instructing – him.

There's a lot of musical history lying behind even a phrase like 'My love does it good'. A phrase like that is a classic case of the nongrammatical

Above: 'My Love' recording sessions with Denny Seiwell and Henry McCullough. Abbey Road Studios, London, 1972

Left: Linda photograph titled *My Love*. London, 1978

Right: Linda. Spain, 1972

somehow being the perfect choice. It started off in blues music, but I often think of Elvis Presley's double negative in 'You ain't nothing but a hound dog'. That double negative is so effective because it sounds just like people speaking in their day-to-day lives. In 'Getting Better' from *Sgt. Pepper*, for example, we use the phrase 'it can't get no worse'. We were proud of ourselves for that one, particularly because the song was set partly in a classroom. It's always satisfying to subvert the rules of grammar. Instead of writing 'my love does it well' or 'my love does it marvellously' or 'my love does it with panache' or even 'my love's a good shag', we have her do it 'good'. It leaves a lot to the imagination.

I love the idea of finding some interesting chords, then finding a melody that goes over those chords and then finding some lyrics that work with them both, maybe are even inspirational. Then I hope it will widen out and inspire not only me but others.

In this case, it's a pure love song to Linda, a reaffirmation of my love for her. But, as always, it doesn't just refer to 'My Linda'. It refers to 'My Love', so that other people will be able to relate to it. One of the things I found particularly gratifying about this song was that it had great success in the American R & B charts, which for me was special because I didn't normally do that. I'm normally in the white charts, but the Black charts, given their influence, have always been so important to me. In this case, it was a thrill for me to imagine Black couples thinking, 'Yeah, I identify with that.'

My Love

1. And when I go away, I know my heart can stay with my love

it's understood, it's in the hands of my love, + my love does it good

Woh! ... my love does it good.

2. And when the cupboards bare, I'll still find something there with my love, it's understood it's everywhere with my love, my love does it good. Woh!

MIDDLE. Oh ~~my~~ I love, oh my love
only my love holds the other key
TO ME —
Oh my love oh my love
only my love does it good to me.
Solo

Don't ever ask me why
I never say goodbye to my love
it's understood it everywhere with my love
and my love does it good,
only my love does it good to... me!

On the set of the 'My Love' music video. London, 1973

I love the idea of finding some interesting chords, then finding a melody that goes over those chords and then finding some lyrics that work with them both, maybe are even inspirational. Then I hope it will widen out and inspire not only me but others.

My Valentine

WRITER	Paul McCartney
ARTIST	Paul McCartney
RECORDED	Avatar Studios, New York
RELEASED	*Kisses on the Bottom*, 2012

What if it rained
We didn't care
She said that someday soon the sun was gonna shine
And she was right, this love of mine
My valentine

As days and nights
Would pass me by
I'd tell myself that I was waiting for a sign
Then she appeared, a love so fine
My valentine

And I will love her for life
And I will never let a day go by
Without remembering the reasons why
She makes me certain that I can fly

And so I do
Without a care
I know that someday soon the sun is gonna shine
And she'll be there, this love of mine
My valentine

HERE'S WHAT HAPPENED. I HAD FALLEN IN LOVE WITH MY LADY, Nancy, but we weren't an item yet. We went on holiday to Morocco, to a quiet little hotel I knew, but because we weren't an item, we didn't stay together in the same room.

Nancy got a room and I had a room, and my brother Mike and his wife, who were on holiday with us, also had a room. But it rained the whole bloody time, and we had paid all this money to come away to this paradise, and we might as well have stayed in Manchester!

The rain was relentless, but we had a great time, and the lovely thing was that I was getting to know Nancy, as you do in that kind of situation. I kept apologising to her for the rain, like it was my fault. I said, 'I'm really sorry, darling, about all this rain.' And she said, 'It doesn't matter.' And that attitude was so sweet that it really resonated with me. I thought, 'That's great.'

There was a pianist in the foyer of the hotel where we were staying, and every evening we would go down there and have drinks and listen to a guy playing a few tunes. He was an old Irish military man who had hung out in Morocco for one reason or another – we don't even dare dream about why – but he was a great guy. He was particularly good on the piano, and he played just like my dad, all the old songs, so they were songs that took me back. We really enjoyed that, and he'd do requests and then we'd go and have dinner.

The piano was sitting in the foyer all day long, till the pianist came for cocktail hour in the evening, and because the rain would not stop, I sometimes went and just noodled on the keys. Some of the waiters would be clearing up, but there wouldn't be many people around, so it was nice. It was just like the cupboard I always like to write in. I was just noodling, and although I didn't know it at the time, I think I was influenced by him, the restaurant pianist, and perhaps even by my dad too, as I was going in a sort of old-fashioned direction with my chords. And it was Valentine's Day.

I thought, as I often do when I've come up with something good, 'How the hell am I going to remember this?' So I raced to my room and got my Handycam – this was before iPhones, but I did have a little camera – and I just set it up on the piano and sang the song, so at least I'd have the soundtrack to remind me.

It was all very romantic. I was thinking all sorts of loving thoughts towards Nancy, and while I was at the piano, I could see that the waiters who were clearing up were listening. You can tell when someone's got half an ear on you, even when they're pretending just to do their work. But it was nice and romantic, it was a perfect moment, and I thought to myself, we're not going to stay in separate rooms tonight.

I've always really liked that attitude: *Don't worry; it's gonna be alright*. 'As days and nights / Would pass me by / I'd tell myself that I was waiting for a sign'. This is my life's philosophy, and this is what happened before I met Nancy; I would always be thinking, 'I'm gonna see something that's gonna say, "Oh, this is the woman for you."' I had just been in Paris for my daughter Stella's fashion show, and I'd bought a pink outfit in a shop window, thinking, 'This'll be for my next woman,' and I ended up giving it to Nancy.

I knew from very early on that my relationship with Nancy was going to last, but we had to keep it under cover, at least for a while. I'm always having to look over my shoulder for paparazzi, so we'd go to things and Nancy would have to keep out of the way.

We just wanted to announce ourselves as an item in our own way at our own pace, but they always catch you out. They always end up outing you. You'll be on a Mediterranean beach, holding hands on one of those innocently beautiful spring days and thinking, 'This is so good, nobody around for miles.' And the next day you'll look online and see yourselves caught on the beach in the most unflattering pose.

If you had to say one word about Nancy, it's that she's *real*. I have a beautiful picture of when we went to the White House. It's of Nancy and me talking to Barack and Michelle Obama, and we're laughing at something the president said, and Nancy is paying such attention. She's a great person. She's multifaceted. She ran a trucking company, so there's that side to her, which is very blue collar-esque. Nancy's got that superpractical administrative side; she's very interesting to talk to about things. She's a sweetie - really, as the song says, 'My valentine'.

The phrase 'for life' in this song is something Nancy picked up on. We know the painter Ed Ruscha, who often uses lettering in his pictures, so she asked him whether he would do a picture for my birthday. It's one of Ed's most beautiful pictures, and it just says, 'For life'.

Above: Nancy, 2008

MY VALENTINE.

FEB 10 · 11

(1) What if it rained
we didn't care
She said that someday soon
The sun was going to shine
And she was right
This love of mine
my valentine.

(2) As days and nights
would pass me by
I'd tell myself that I
was waiting for a sign
Then she appeared.
A love so fine.
My valentine

[MIDDLE] And I will love her
for life,
I know I'll never
let a day go by
without remembering the reasons why
she makes me certain that I can fly

(3) And so I do
without a care
I know that someday soon
The sun is going to shine
And she'll be there
This love of mine
My valentine

SOLO
(MIDDLE)

VERSE
(1)

Left: With Nancy to receive the Library of Congress Gershwin Prize for Popular Song. The White House, Washington, DC, 2010

Right: Nancy, 2007

It was all very romantic. I was thinking all sorts of loving thoughts towards Nancy, and while I was at the piano, I could see that the waiters who were clearing up were listening. You can tell when someone's got half an ear on you, even when they're pretending just to do their work. But it was nice and romantic, it was a perfect moment.

Nineteen Hundred and Eighty Five

WRITERS	Paul McCartney and Linda McCartney
ARTIST	Paul McCartney and Wings
RECORDED	EMI Studios, Lagos; and AIR Studios, London
RELEASED	*Band on the Run*, 1973
	B-side of 'Band on the Run' US single, 1974

Oh no one ever left alive
In nineteen hundred and eighty five
Will ever do
She may be right
She may be fine
She may get love but she won't get mine
'Cause I got you

Oh I oh I
Well I just can't get enough of that sweet stuff
My little lady gets behind

Oh my mama said the time
Would come when I would find myself
In love with you
I didn't think
I never dreamed
That I would be around to see it
All come true

Woh I oh I
Well I just can't get enough of that sweet stuff
My little lady gets behind

Above: Filming live documentary film *One Hand Clapping*. Abbey Road Studios, London, 1974

WHEN I READ GEORGE ORWELL'S *1984* I WAS JUST A KID, AND I thought it was so far into the future I mightn't live to see it. Like the movie *2001: A Space Odyssey* – impossibly distant. Now they're well behind us.

The idea behind the song is that this is a relationship that was always meant to be. No one in the distant future is ever going to get my attention, because I've got you. But when this was written, 1985 was only twelve years away; it wasn't the very distant future – only the future in this song. So, this is basically a love song about the future.

Sometimes you try to avoid using the word 'love' in a song, but I also wrote a song asking what's wrong with silly love songs. It's something I think about. 'Love' is a staggeringly important word, and a staggeringly important feeling, because it's going on everywhere, in the whole of existence, right now. I think about this whole planet and the whole human race. I think about how in China right now there are two people who love each other and they're getting married and committing their whole lives to each other, or in South America right now there's a mother having a baby and loving this baby and the father is loving the baby too. The point I'm making is obvious – that this 'love thing' is global, really universal. And it's true not only for humans but also for animals, which we too often forget about, and that commonality outweighs the fact that it might be soppy. But you're always trying to say it in a way that's not soppy. That's why I write about it.

Band on the Run recording sessions. EMI Studios, Lagos, 1973

Sometimes you try to avoid using the word 'love' in a song, but I also wrote a song asking what's wrong with silly love songs. It's something I think about. 'Love' is a staggeringly important word, and a staggeringly important feeling, because it's going on everywhere, in the whole of existence, right now. I think about this whole planet and the whole human race.

NINETEEN HUNDRED AND
EIGHTY FIVE.

(1) Oh No one ever left alive in 1985, will ever
She may be right do
" " " fine
She may get love but she won't get mine
Cos I got you
Oh I — Oh I
Well I just cant get enough of that sweet
Stuff my little lady gets behind

INTERLUDE

Oh my mama said the time would come when I would
(2) → In love with you find myself
I didnt think
I never dreamed ~~that I would be around~~
That I would be around to see it all come
woh I - Oh I true
Well I just cant get enough of that sweet stuff
My little lady gets behind.

INTERLUDE

Repeat (1)

FINALE

No More Lonely Nights

WRITER	Paul McCartney
ARTIST	Paul McCartney
RECORDED	AIR Studios, London
RELEASED	Single, 1984
	Give My Regards to Broad Street, 1984

I can wait another day
Until I call you
You've only got my heart on a string
And everything aflutter

But another lonely night
Might take forever
We've only got each other to blame
It's all the same to me, love
'Cause I know what I feel to be right

No more lonely nights
No more lonely nights
You're my guiding light
Day or night I'm always there

May I never miss the thrill
Of being near you
And if it takes a couple of years
To turn your tears to laughter
I will do what I feel to be right

No more lonely nights
Never be another
No more lonely nights
You're my guiding light
Day or night I'm always there

And I won't go away until you tell me so
No I'll never go away

Yes I know what I feel to be right

No more lonely nights
Never be another
No more lonely nights
You're my guiding light
Day or night I'm always there

And I won't go away until you tell me so
No I'll never go away
I won't go away until you tell me so
No I'll never go away

No more lonely nights

'WORD DANCING' I CALL IT. YOU BEGIN WITH A THOUGHT, and then you start word dancing and then it's step, step, step. This was a straightforward love song, really, about a lonely person saying, 'Can't wait till we're together.' There are a few more lines to reinforce that idea: ''Cause I know what I feel to be right' and 'You're my guiding light'. It's about the heartache of being apart from your loved one and, when you're back together, not wishing to be apart from them again – 'May I never miss the thrill / Of being near you'.

David Gilmour plays the solo on the record. I've known him since the early days of Pink Floyd. Dave is a genius of sorts, so I was pulling out all the stops. I admired his playing so much, and I'd seen him around; I think he'd just done his solo *About Face* album. So I rang him up and said, 'Would you play on this?' It sounded like his kind of thing.

I wrote this song specifically for a film that I also wrote: *Give My Regards to Broad Street*. The song did better than the film. Originally, the opening of the film was me walking around Broad Street station with some sound effects played over the top. But I wanted to do a film tune, so I wrote this song to go with the music. I then later rearranged it as an up-tempo version so that when it played out at the end there was a dance version.

Above: On the set of *Give My Regards to Broad Street*. London, 1983

Below: With Sir Ralph Richardson, 1983

The film's title was a play on the old show tune 'Give My Regards to Broadway'. We made it around the same time as my solo album *Pipes of Peace* and, I think, I wrote some of the screenplay on the train between Sussex and London. The plot's a bit of a caper. It's a dreary, wet day, and I fall asleep on the way to a meeting and have a dream about losing the master tape for a new album. We think Harry, a reformed criminal, is back to his old ways and he's going to bootleg it. We have to find the tapes before midnight; otherwise Mr Rath, the film's baddie, is going to take over the record label.

It was a lot of fun to make, and people like Ringo and his wife Barbara got involved. Linda was there too, plus George Martin and Tracey Ullman. Wrestler Giant Haystacks was also in it, and Bryan Brown. We had some nice set pieces, re-creating the old Liverpool dances of the fifties for the song 'Ball-

Left and top right:
Ringo Starr, Barbara Bach and Paul on the set of *Give My Regards to Broad Street*. Buckinghamshire, 1983

Bottom right and left:
With Dave Gilmour. Hog Hill Mill, Sussex, 1984

room Dancing', and it was fun to do 'Eleanor Rigby' onstage at the Royal Albert Hall.

In the film, just as things are getting really bad and we can't find Harry or the missing tape, I pop into the pub to see Ralph Richardson, who plays Jim, a bit of a Polonius-type father figure. Sir Ralph was an incredible Shakespearian actor, so it was great to act in a scene with him, and I think this was the last film he released. Ralph's character, Jim, tells me off for running around too much, but then he gives me some words of wisdom, paraphrasing W. H. Davies's poem 'Leisure':

> *What is this life if, full of care,*
> *We have no time to stand and stare.*

I think I would have read that at school in English class. Anyway, I can't slow down, because I have to get to Broad Street train station, as the station plays an important role in the plot. And that's where the film's title comes from.

This was getting into the days of the big music video, and we did two for this song. One was shot in the train station at night, and the other was a bit of a clip reel with highlights from the film. The single did really well but just missed being number one, which I think was Wham!'s 'Freedom'.

But Gilmour really goes to town on that solo, especially on the album version, which is longer and gives him more space to play. It's a really nice solo, with that signature Fender Stratocaster sound of his. He played guitar at a show I did at The Cavern Club in December 1999, which they'd reopened along the street from where it had been when The Beatles originally played there. So, that was a pretty good way to see out the twentieth century.

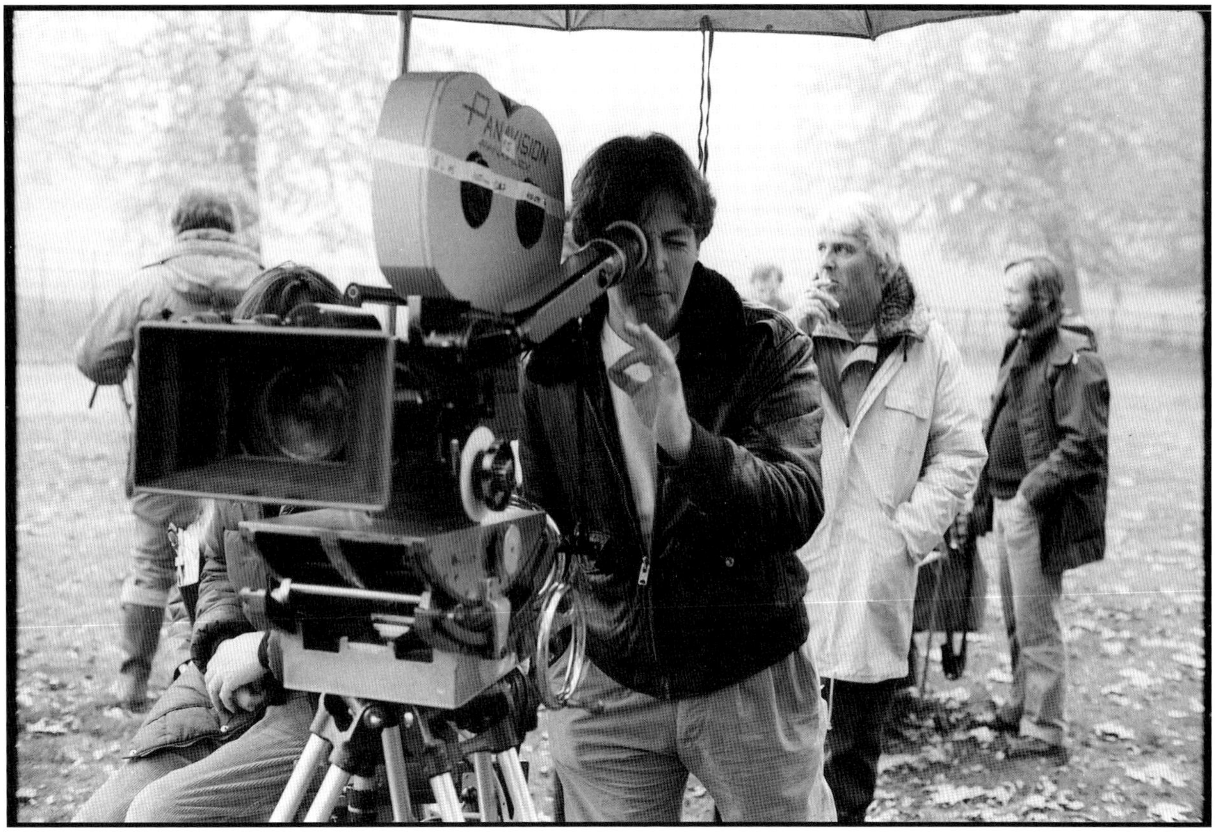

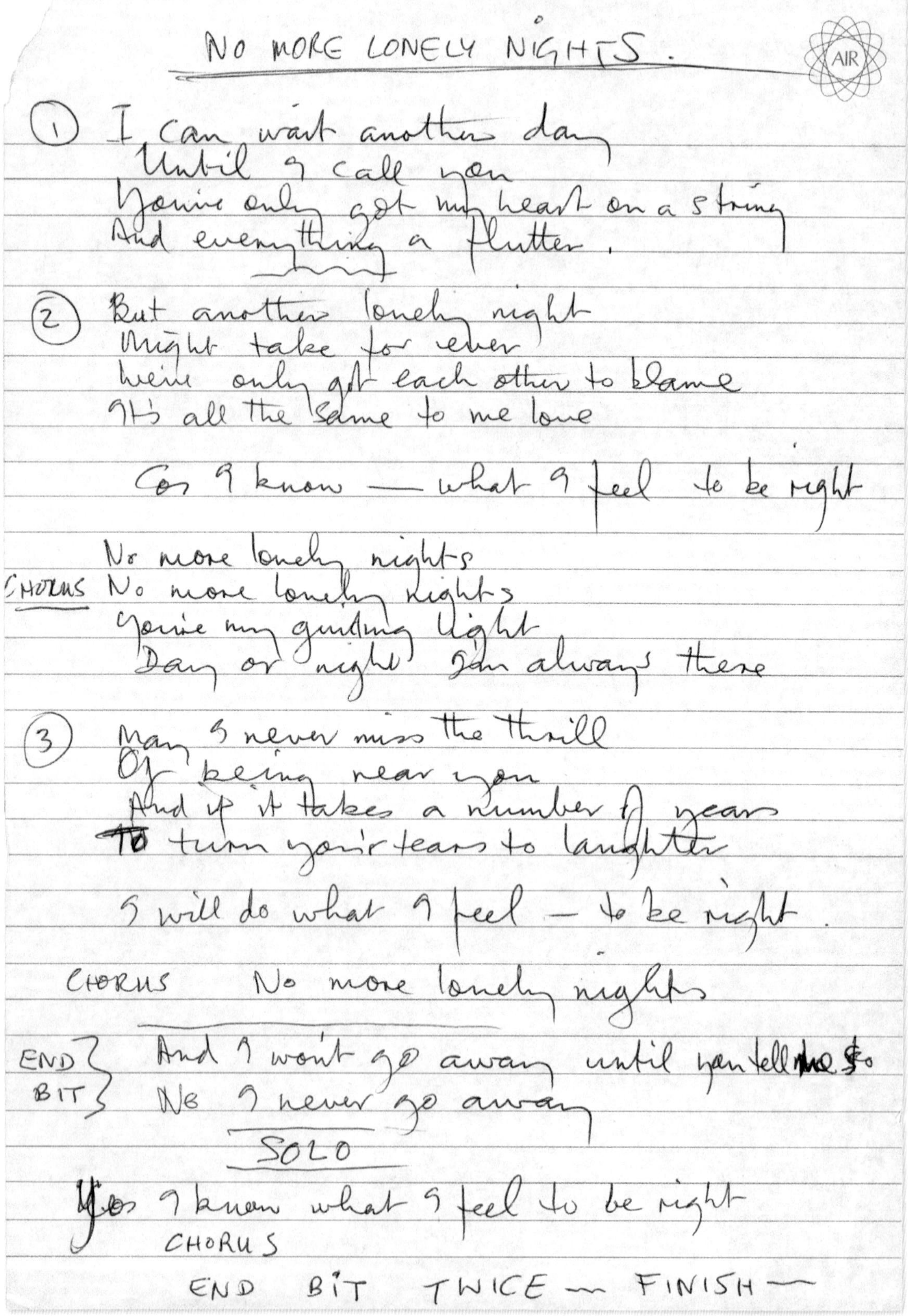

NO MORE LONELY NIGHTS.

AIR

(1) I can wait another day
Until I call you
You've only got my heart on a string
And everything a flutter.

(2) But another lonely night
Might take for ever
We've only got each other to blame
It's all the same to me love

Cos I know — what I feel to be right

No more lonely nights
CHORUS No more lonely nights
You're my guiding light
Day or night I'm always there

(3) May I never miss the thrill
Of being near you
And if it takes a number of years
To turn your tears to laughter

I will do what I feel — to be right.

CHORUS No more lonely nights

END BIT } And I won't go away until you tell ~~me~~ so
No I never go away

SOLO

~~If~~ Cos I know what I feel to be right
CHORUS

END BIT TWICE — FINISH —

(1) I can wait another day
Until I ~~see~~ call you
You've only got my heart on a string
And everything's a flutter........

(2) But another lonely night
~~Could~~ Could be take for ever (could break the camel)
We'd only have each other to blame
~~It's all the same to me love~~ IT SEEMS A SHAME TO ME LOVE........,
~~But~~ I know
What I feel
To be right........

CHORUS.
You're my guiding light
(Let the world know)

You're my guiding light
You're my guiding light
Day or night you're always there.

(3) May I never miss the thrill
Of being NEAR you

But I know
What I feel
To be right

CHORUS
You're my guiding light
" " " " (never need another)
" " " "
day or night you're always there.

(N.B. goes through...)

The Note You Never Wrote

WRITERS	Paul McCartney and Linda McCartney
ARTIST	Wings
RECORDED	Abbey Road Studios, London
RELEASED	*At the Speed of Sound*, 1976

Later on the story goes
A bottle floated out to sea
After days when it had found the perfect spot
It opened up

And I read the note
That you never wrote to me

After all I'm sure you know
The Mayor of Baltimore is here
After days now he can finally appear
Now at last he's here

But he never is gonna get my vote
'Cause he never is gonna get a quote
From the little note
That you never wrote to me

Further on along the line
I was arrested on the shore
Holding papers of governments galore
I was taken in

But I read the note that you never wrote
Yes I read the note that you never wrote
Oh I read the note that you never wrote to me
To me

THE LEAD GUITARIST IS JIMMY McCULLOCH – NOT TO BE CONFUSED with Henry McCullough – and his solo is quite amazing. A little reminiscent of Dave Gilmour. The arrangement as a whole is kind of dreamy and Floydian. It's what we call a 'Floydian slip'.

Pink Floyd made some great records in the 1970s. *Dark Side of the Moon* had come out in 1973, and it would have been natural for Wings to do something in their style. A lot of people did. A few years back, Beck's record *Morning Phase* was very like a Floyd record. It won Album of the Year at the Grammys. I listened to it and I thought, 'That owes a lot to Pink Floyd.' Pink Floyd's world was almost an extraterrestrial world, so it was a nice place to go. Of course, I had to make up the Mayor of Baltimore character. Why? Because it sounded good. I wasn't too worried about the meaning. Maybe the song would develop a meaning at some point. Or maybe someone would find a meaning.

With nursery rhymes, we don't necessarily know what they mean. We don't even really know the theories about what they mean; they're just handed down from generation to generation. They mean this or that, or they mean nothing at all in some cases, but it actually doesn't matter. We get hooked on this idea that everything must mean something, and there must be some logic behind everything, and that's simply not true. You have to give yourself over to the power of what used to be known as inspiration.

Normally, for me, a song takes a few hours. Sometimes they fall out more quickly, but normally it's about three or four hours of sitting there and thinking about it, and the first verse comes in and then the second verse. In the early days, when John and I first started writing songs, that's about how long it would take. I'd go round to his house, we'd sit opposite each other, and by twelve o'clock, one o'clock, we'd start writing and I'd leave about three or four o'clock. You'd think there'd be a few days when we'd just go, 'Can't get it. Sorry, man; I'm feeling a bit, you know, unproductive.' No. Every single time we sat down, a song came out. That's pretty amazing. And I find that's still roughly true. The danger now is having devices like the iPhone that think a sketch is a song; it comes too easily in some ways. Or you put it down and you think, 'I'll finish that later,' whereas John and I couldn't have done that. It wouldn't have made sense for us to meet and write, 'Let me take you down / 'Cause I'm going to . . .' and then say, 'Okay, see you tomorrow' or 'We'll finish this later.' It just wouldn't make any sense.

So we'd say, 'Strawberry Fields. Yeah, that's right,' and we'd just grab a pad and that was our manuscript; that was the music. We knew that this line came next and whoever wrote it would fill it in. After three or four hours you were getting a bit bored and losing stamina, so you'd finish it up. The *Liverpool Oratorio*'s Carl Davis, whom I collaborated with on the project, used to say that your brain gets addled after about three hours, and you're just not doing as well as you were. I've always found that to be true.

With Wings I was lucky. There wasn't any pressure from the record company, which for Wings was mostly Parlophone in the UK and Capitol in the US. And Columbia for a short while too. I would just get my managers or

Sheet music artwork for 'The Note You Never Wrote'

business people to do a deal for three or four records or something. So, I knew that was five years or so, and I'd pretty much do a record every one or two years. I was lucky to have that freedom, so I would write whenever I felt like writing, which was nearly always when I just had some time off, and I'd fit it in around the family's plans. Instead of sitting around, I'd write something. Always with a guitar or a piano, never with anything else, and a pad and a pencil with a rubber on the end (even then, I was old school). When you've written enough, it's time to put those songs in a bottle, so you can write some more. I like to get them out, get them away and clear the deck, let them 'float out to sea'.

And I read the note
That you never wrote
To me.
Harmony
NEVER
TO ME
(or)
I AM A NO MAD
by NO MAD
NO MAD
NEVER TO ME
I AM A
NO MAD

With Jimmy McCulloch.
Abbey Road Studios,
London, 1977

Nothing Too Much Just Out of Sight

WRITER	Paul McCartney
ARTIST	The Fireman
RECORDED	Hog Hill Mill, Sussex
RELEASED	*Electric Arguments*, 2008

Yeah na
Oh na na na na na
Yeah road too all bright

Now nothing too much just outta sight
You say you love me this is true
The best thing to do is to lie down beside me
I said I love you
Now nothing too much just outta sight

Yeah na na na na na
Oh don't you want to be fair
In the beautiful air in the twilight
Of the half-night
It was all bright all bright

I said I love you
I thought you knew
The last thing to do was to try to betray me
The new morning light, I'll never forget it
That's just outta sight

Yeah na na na na na
Twilight of the half-night
Southwest
I was barely obsessed
Nothing too much all bright

All I can remember the beautiful air
I can't remember why did you take me there
Don't you try to betray me
You don't wanna betray me
I was barely obsessed
I was barely obsessed
With the way she undressed

Bright nothing too half-night
It was all right all bright
Now nothing too much just outta sight

Now nothing too much just outta sight
In the beautiful air

Oh don't you wanna be frightened of the half-night
Beautiful air
On the road to the west
I was barely obsessed
By the way she undressed in the moonlight
In the twilight of the half-night
It was all right all bright

All bright
Well nothing too much
It was all right
Just outta sight

The last thing to do was to try to betray me

'NOTHING TOO MUCH, JUST OUT OF SIGHT' WAS AN EXPRESSION that a Nigerian friend of mine called Jimmy Scott taught me. We used to meet in the London clubs in the 1960s, and he had some great expressions. Jimmy was the guy who taught me 'Ob-La-Di', so you can kind of say that he had a legendary status. This - 'Nothing too much, just out of sight' - was another expression he had. In those days, expressions were like fashion. I guess it's the same for every generation, but I think it was during the sixties when language started to become a little less formal, especially in song lyrics. We had expressions like 'far out', and another one was 'too much'. I remember saying, 'Oof, too much.' And Jimmy would say, 'Nothing too much, just out of sight.' I thought, 'I like that; it's very good.'

This song is from a side project called The Fireman. I have a producer friend who goes by the name 'Youth' - real name Martin Glover - and he was in a group called Killing Joke. He did a remix for me years ago. I used to take a song and give it to someone, so they'd have a fresh view of it. I became friendly with Youth, so I said, 'Come down to my studio. We'll do something.'

We did very improvisational stuff, and it was a thrill. I really love to work that way. You can't do it if you're trying to write 'Lady Madonna' or 'Eleanor Rigby'. You can't just make up songs like those on the spot in the studio; you've got to be a bit more disciplined. But he came down, and we started on this project. We decided we would call ourselves The Fireman, and we released our first record, *Strawberries Oceans Ships Forest*, in 1993, which was in the vein of ambient trance music. It was as if he'd stayed up till dawn to do the mix. We released it, and it did hardly anything, which was kind of what we wanted; people like to think that I'm always aiming for a number one hit, but the truth is that I really like an underground project, where people have to sniff around. 'Who is The Fireman?' We'd say, 'We've no idea.' That anonymity was quite freeing and fun.

Above: With Keith Smith, Eddie Klein, Hugo Nicholson, John Hammel, Youth (Martin Glover) and Paul Taylor during the *Rushes* recording sessions. Hog Hill Mill, Sussex, 1995

Eventually we did a second album, *Rushes*, and now we've done three. The first two were instrumental, but eventually we did one where Youth said, 'Go out on the microphone. Imagine you're a morning DJ in Arizona, and just give me a bit of rap. Just keep going.' He would select the best bit, loop it, cut it up, and just play with it. So I would get on the mic and go, 'Well, hello there, it's a beautiful morning and that sun shine, shine, shining!' and he'd cut it all up and put it together. Until then we hadn't done any songs with lyrics.

On the most recent album - in 2008, where this song is from - Youth said to me, 'Well, Paul, why don't you sing some words?' I said, 'Well, I've got no words,' and he gave me a knowing look, meaning, 'Come on! You can do it.' And I thought, 'Oh, damn you, alright,' so I went out on the mic, and I said to everyone in the room - just the engineer and the roadies and the guys - 'Okay, disclaimer: I have no idea what's gonna come out here, so this could be like a real embarrassment. Probably the most embarrassing moment in my recording career.'

I had the idea of using 'nothing too much, just outta sight' - my friend Jimmy Scott's expression - and we agreed that was a good starting point. Then I would just go out on the microphone, and we'd have some kind of backing before I did the vocal - the pretty insistent drums and the distorted slide guitar on this one - and then I knew I was going to scream a bit.

Normally, I've got some idea what I'm going to sing, but I didn't on these things. Maybe I'd scribble something down on a piece of paper and then just sing that and see whether something came off the back of it. In my usual way of songwriting, I've got to conform to a rhythm and the metres that I set myself, but the stream of consciousness is obviously less constricted, so you get something like this, which reads like a sort of beat poem. I think I just went through it a few times and screamed at it, just freewheeling and trying to grab rhymes. When you're sitting down writing, you can think, 'Well, I can do better than that,' but here it has everything to do with free association, so there's no time for any preparation. You're just grabbing the first rhymes.

The title of the album - *Electric Arguments* - comes from an Allen Ginsberg line in his poem 'Kansas City to St. Louis'. Allen, whom I knew a little, always used to say, 'First thought, best thought,' but then I would notice him correcting his poems!

Right: Working with Youth on the *Electric Arguments* album artwork. London, 2008

In my usual way of songwriting, I've got to conform to a rhythm and the metres that I set myself, but the stream of consciousness is obviously less constricted, so you get something like this, which reads like a sort of beat poem.

Above and left: *Electric Arguments* artwork

Right: With Youth. London, 2008

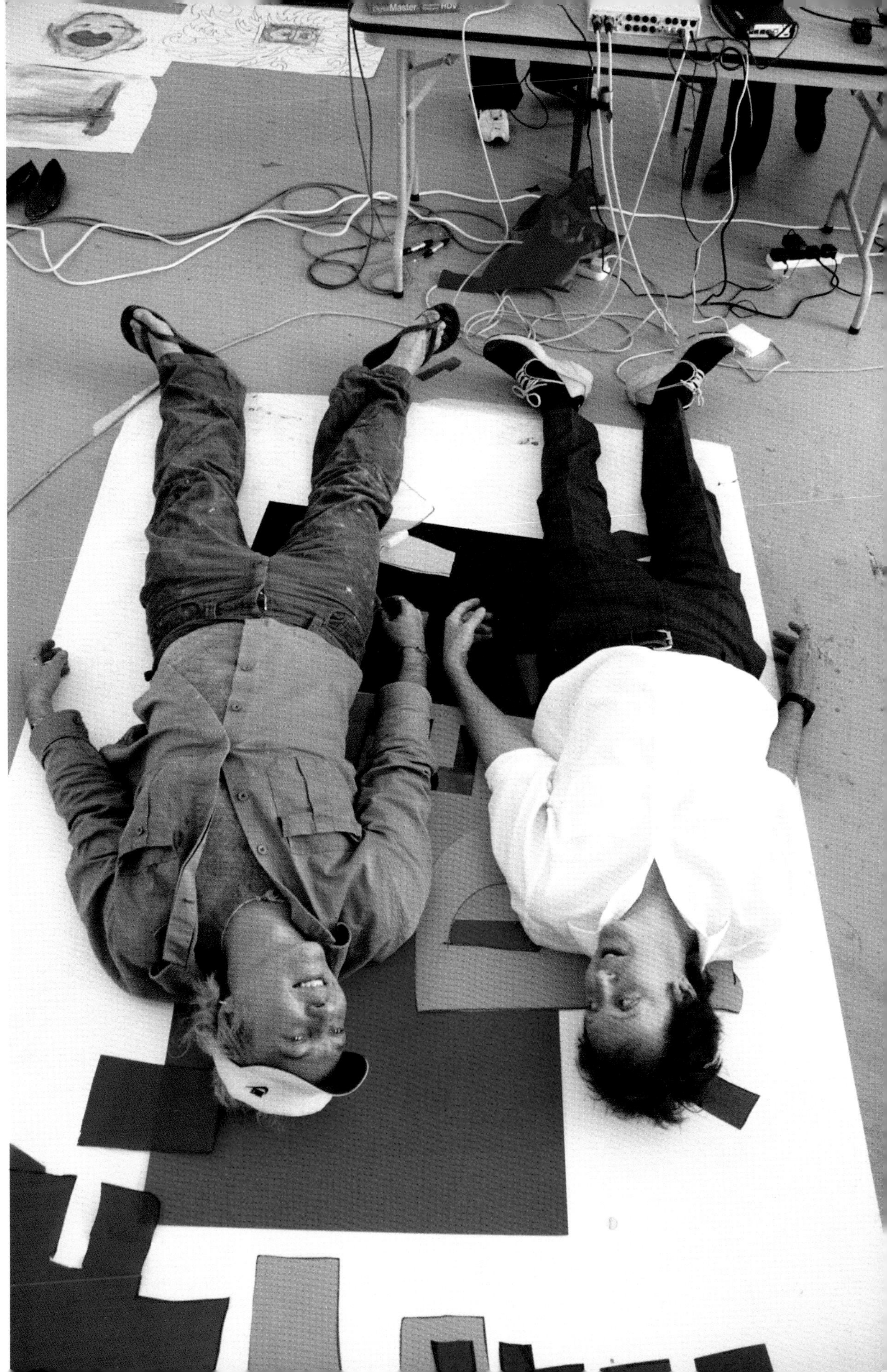

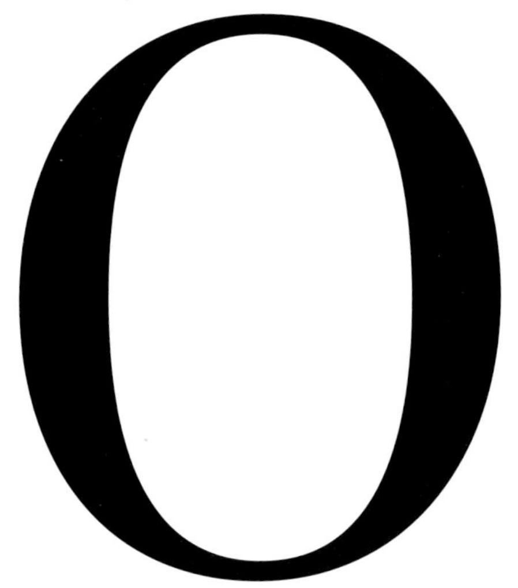

Ob-La-Di, Ob-La-Da

WRITERS	Paul McCartney and John Lennon
ARTIST	The Beatles
RECORDED	Abbey Road Studios, London
RELEASED	*The Beatles*, 1968

Desmond has a barrow in the market place
Molly is the singer in a band
Desmond says to Molly, Girl, I like your face
And Molly says this as she takes him by the hand

Ob-la-di, Ob-la-da, life goes on
Bra, la-la how the life goes on
Ob-la-di, Ob-la-da, life goes on
Bra, la-la how the life goes on

Desmond takes a trolley to the jeweller's store
Buys a twenty carat golden ring
Takes it back to Molly waiting at the door
And as he gives it to her she begins to sing

Ob-la-di, Ob-la-da, life goes on
Bra, la-la how the life goes on
Ob-la-di, Ob-la-da, life goes on
Bra, la-la how the life goes on

In a couple of years
They have built a home sweet home
With a couple of kids running in the yard
Of Desmond and Molly Jones

Happy ever after in the market place
Desmond lets the children lend a hand
Molly stays at home and does her pretty face
And in the evening she still sings it with the band

Ob-la-di, Ob-la-da, life goes on
Bra, la-la how the life goes on
Ob-la-di, Ob-la-da, life goes on
Bra, la-la how the life goes on

In a couple of years
They have built a home sweet home
With a couple of kids running in the yard
Of Desmond and Molly Jones

Happy ever after in the market place
Molly lets the children lend a hand
Desmond stays at home and does his pretty face
And in the evening she's a singer with the band

Ob-la-di, Ob-la-da, life goes on
Bra, la-la how the life goes on
Ob-la-di, Ob-la-da, life goes on
Bra, la-la how the life goes on
And if you want some fun
Take Ob-la-di-bla-da

THE PROBLEM WAS, OUR GIGS FINISHED SO LATE THAT RESTAURANTS and pubs had closed by the time we got back to London, so the only way we could get a drink and something to eat was to 'go down a club', as they used to say. That became a way of life. We would drive home from a gig and immediately go to a club. The Bag O'Nails was one of my favourites. The Speakeasy. The Revolution. The Scotch of St James. The Cromwellian. Later when the other guys were married and living in the suburbs, I would often go by myself.

It was in one of these clubs that I met Jimmy Scott, the Nigerian conga player whom I liked a lot. Jimmy had a couple of catchphrases he used all the time, one of which was 'Ob-La-Di, Ob-La-Da, life goes on, bra'. Some people think 'Ob-La-Di, Ob-La-Da' is a Yoruba phrase that means something like *comme ci, comme ça*. Some people think it's a phrase Jimmy Scott made up. And there are others who think 'bra' refers to a brassiere, rather than an African version of 'bro'.

I liked the *comme ci, comme ça, que sera sera* sentiment. So I set out to write a humorous little 'character song' about Desmond and Molly and their kids. It's a combination of African and Jamaican elements. I'm pretty sure Desmond is named after Desmond Dekker, the Jamaican ska and reggae artist whose 'Israelites' was a hit later in 1969. He'd already had a big hit in the UK in 1967 with '007'.

When Desmond takes a 'trolley', I may be thinking of the San Francisco tram system. San Francisco is where The Beatles had done our last concert. There's a world of difference between 'Desmond takes a tram' and 'Desmond takes a trolley'. Some things either fit rhythmically or they don't, and 'tram' is awkward in a song, whereas 'trolley' allows for more possibilities rhythmically. John and I used to have conversations about trying to write songs that had a very conversational tone. 'Desmond takes a trolley to the jeweller's store' isn't too flowery. It's something you could actually hear people saying. That could be a secret of why the Beatles stuff is still very accessible to people. It's because we're just talking straight.

No matter how straight you're talking, though, there's still room for interpretation. Going back to the word 'trolley', I can see there's actually a lot to be said for the 'shopping cart' reading. The idea of going to a jeweller's store with a shopping cart to load up on stuff is pretty funny, particularly when Desmond comes back with a 'twenty carat' engagement ring. One way or another, it's pretty everyday stuff.

That's something I'm still looking out for. I'm very much switched on to the power of the ordinary. My camera is looking around and sweeping life for clues, for stories. When I'm on a bus or a plane or a train, my imagination starts going. I love simple truths. I love that the vast majority of people, whether they're Mongolian or Indian or American, relate immediately to the idea of family and family life, to the image of a couple of kids running in the yard. If I plug into that, I'm going to relate to people.

SONG TITLES.

I'M SO TIRED, John in bed.

DON'T PASS ME BY, Ringo as fiddler (C+W handout.)

BLACKBIRD, Blackbird from bird book.

EVERYBODYS GOT SOMETHING TO HIDE EXCEPT FOR ME AND MY MONKEY, Black space.

GOODNIGHT, Ringo saying goodnight to his kids.

YER BLUES, Blues.

OB LA DI, OB LA DA, Jimmy Scott and wife in market

ROCKY RACCOON, Mal as Rocky being shot by Dan while

~~WILD~~ HONEY PIE, — (Hollywood handout) Lil sits on 4 poster.

MOTHER NATURES SON, Paul by stream.

BACK IN THE U.S.S.R. Paul throwing flowers to fat Russian (BOAC.)

SEXY SADIE, Black vinyl special.

WHILE MY GUITAR GENTLY WEEPS, Guitar rain splashed window

NOT GUILTY, George smiling behind bars.

HELTER SKELTER, Beatles on helter skelter

CRY BABY CRY, Alice fancy dress party on lawn.

REVOLUTION NO. 9, White space

WHAT'S NEW MARY JANE, Alexis machine.

CHILD OF NATURE, John standing in hot sun.

HAPPINESS IS A WARM GUN, Johns hand on steel gun.

THE CONTINUING STORY OF BUNGALOW BILL, Ringo as tiger. John as heavily armed Bill.

JULIA, Picture of Julia – or of cloud.

POLYTHENE PAM, In person.

MAXWELLS SILVER HAMMER,

Desmond has a barrow in the market place
Molly is the singer in a band
Desi says to Molly girl I like your face,
And Molly says this as she takes him by the hand

CHORUS Obla dee Obla da, life goes on, bra,
la-la how the life goes on. -

Desmond takes a trolley to the jewellers store
Buys a twenty-carat golden ring,
Takes it back to Molly waiting at the door
And as he gives it to her, she begins to sing

CHORUS. ----

In a couple of years they have built a home sweet home
with a couple of kids running in the yard of
Desmond & Molly Jones ----
~~Desmond~~ Happy ever after in the market place
Desmond lets the children lend a hand
Molly stays at home + does her pretty face
And in the evening she still sings this with the band

CHORUS ---------

Left: Album notes by Paul and John, 1968

Oh Woman, Oh Why

WRITER	Paul McCartney
ARTIST	Paul McCartney
RECORDED	CBS Studios, New York
RELEASED	B-side of 'Another Day' single, 1971

Woman, oh why why why why why
What have I done?
Oh woman, oh where where where where where
Did you get that gun?
Oh what have I done?
What have I done?

Well I met her at the bottom of a well
Well I told her I was tryin' to break a spell
But I can't get by, my hands are tied
Don't know why I ever bother to try myself
'Cause I can't get by, my hands are tied

Oh woman, oh why why why why why
What have I done?
Oh woman, oh where where where where where
Did you get that gun?
Oh what have you done?
Woman, what have you done?

Well I'm fed up with your lying cheating ways
But I get up every morning and every day
But I can't get by, my hands are tied
Don't know why I ever bother to try myself
'Cause I can't get by, my hands are tied

Oh woman, oh why why why why why
What have I done?
Oh woman, oh where where where where where
Did you get that gun
Woman, what have I done?
What have you done?
Woman, what have I done?
Oh woman, oh why

A SUBGENRE OF THE BLUES I REALLY LIKE IS THE 'WOMAN, YOU done me wrong' song. I don't know whether all these bad things could really have happened to all these blues players. It does seem that there are an awful lot of wrongdoing women out there. I suspect there might be a few wrongdoing men too!

This is a song that's somewhat in the vein of 'Frankie and Johnny', a tale of dirty doings that has innumerable manifestations, sung by innumerable artists, including Lead Belly's version of 1935:

It was not murder in the first degree
It was not murder in the third
A woman simply dropped her man
Like a hunter drops a bird
He was her man, but she shot him down

I was plugging into that system of imagery when I wrote, 'I met her at the bottom of a well'. I thought that was a more interesting image than, say, 'I met her on Bourbon Street' or 'I met her in a brothel in Paris'. I like to be direct but not necessarily literal.

The well itself is more associated with the folk tradition. There's an erotic subtext to the image of the well. I think of William Bell's 'You Don't Miss Your Water'. The other reason I gravitate towards these songs is that I'm looking for a vehicle for my voice. I want to get dirty with my voice, and I want to make a nice dirty backdrop. I try to let my voice have a go at singing something more bluesy rather than trying to hold a melody. It's nice to cut loose on the vocals.

When you get right down to it, in everything I've ever done - in The Beatles, Wings, solo - there's an undercurrent of Black music. You could say it's blues, but it could be soul. So many of the white groups looked to the Black players and singers for inspiration. If you think of The Beatles' early stuff, it was mostly covers of Black guys: 'You Really Got a Hold on Me', 'Twist and Shout'. We loved Chuck Berry, Fats Domino, Little Richard. Then there were the white guys - Elvis, Gene Vincent, Buddy Holly, Carl Perkins, Jerry Lee Lewis - who were already influenced by the Black guys. So, even though we were admiring these white guys, we were admiring white guys who admired Black guys. That's definitely the underpinning of almost everything I've done.

— Guitar
Drums
Guitar

Chorus Oh woman oh why why ...

Verse I met her, at the bottom of the well

— — — — — —

— — —

Chorus - Oh woman

I don't ~~feel~~ sick I don't feel so bad
any more
I got over it — — — —

(rode all night till I finally
hit the daybreak — — —)

Right: Song list, late 1950s

1. That's Alright Mama.
2. I'm a gonna love you too.
3. Blue moon of Kentucky.
4. Mean Woman Blues.
5. Bad Boy.
6. Honey Don't
7. Clarabella
8. Whole lotta Shaking.
9. My Baby Left Me.
10. Baby lets play house
11. One side love affair.
12. ~~Good Rockin' Tonight.~~
13. I don't care if the sun don't shine.
14. A Fool such as I.
15. ~~Fools~~ Everyday
16. Honky Tonk Blues.
17. Ain't that a shame.

Fool's Paradise

Donny.

} ?

I sign & seal this document.

Oedipus

16 TRACK IDENTIFICATION CHART
CBS RECORDS Paul McCartney

SESSION	JOB NO.	PRODUCER	ENGINEER	DATE
Studio B	216827	PM	TB	10/30/70

5782

NO.	CC. NO. / TITLE							
1	Sunshines Sometimes							
	1 Bass Drum	2 Drums Cowbell + Cymbal	3	4 Bass	5 Paul / Dave Ending O.D. Guitar	6 Amp Dave Guitar	7 Acoustic Paul Guitar	8 Rough Vocal
	9	10 Chorus Linda/Paul	11 Solo Vocal	12 Hi Lindas Chorus + Solo Double	13	14	15	16 Triangle
2	Oh Woman Oh Why Why Why							
	1 Bass Drum	2 Snare	3 Hi Hat Small Tom	4 Large Tom Cymbal	5 Bass	6 Hugh Guitar	7 Paul Guitar	8 Rough Vocal
	9 O.D. Hugh Guitar	10 O.D. Paul Guitar	11 1/26/71 Paul + Linda Background voc. Bounce 13, 14, 15, + maracas	12 1/26/71 Paul lead voc.	13 1/26/71 Background P&L + maracas TBE	14 1/26/71 Background P&L TBE	15 1/26/71 BG Voc P&L TBE	16 1/27/71 Gun
3	Monkberry Moon Delight							
	1 Bass Drums	2 Snare Hi Hat Small Tom	3 Large Tom Cymbal	4 Vocal Background Linda	5 Vocal Background Linda	6 Hugh Guitar Hold	7 Piano	8 Rough Vocal
	9 Paul #1 Leslie Guitar	10 Paul #2 Leslie Guitar	11 Bass	12 Solo OK	13 Hugh O.D. #1 + 2 Comb.	14 Solo OK Erace	15 Solo Comp. Main	16 Tamb.

CR 1721

I was plugging into that system of imagery when I wrote, 'I met her at the bottom of a well'. I thought that was a more interesting image than, say, 'I met her on Bourbon Street' or 'I met her in a brothel in Paris'. I like to be direct but not necessarily literal.

Above: Track sheet from *RAM* recording sessions, 1970

Right: Recording gunshot overdub for 'Oh Woman, Oh Why'. A&R Studios, New York, 1970

The Beatles with Fats Domino. New Orleans, 1964

Old Siam, Sir

WRITER	Paul McCartney
ARTIST	Wings
RECORDED	Spirit of Ranachan Studio, Scotland
RELEASED	Single, 1979
	Back to the Egg, 1979

In a village in old Siam, sir
Lived a lady who lost her way
In an effort to find a man, sir
She found herself in the old UK

She waited round in Walthamstow
She scouted round in Scarborough
She waited round in Walthamstow
She scouted round in Scarborough

In a village in old East Ham, sir
She met a fellow who made her reel
Took her rushes to show his mam, sir
Met his dad at the wedding meal

In a letter from old Siam, sir
Came a terrible tale of woe
She decided the only answer
Was to get up a pile of dough

She waited round in Walthamstow
She scouted round in Scarborough
She waited round in Walthamstow
She scouted round in Scarborough

When a relative told her man, sir
He directed her not to stay
In a village in old Siam, sir
Lives a lady who lost her way

In a village in old Siam, sir
Lived a lady who lost her way
In an effort to find her man, sir
She found herself in the old UK

She waited round in Walthamstow
She scouted round in Scarborough
She waited round in Walthamstow
She scouted round in Scarborough

THE RATHER FANCY-SOUNDING SPIRIT OF RANACHAN STUDIO was basically a barn with a control room window at one end of it. Wackiness was the order of the day during this period - garish outfits and the punk and disco era - and they don't come much wackier than 'Old Siam, Sir'. If I had to rate the elements of it, I think the lyric would come third to the feel of the song and then the attack of the vocal. I'm doing a bit of alliteration here, playing around with the words - 'waited' and 'Walthamstow', 'scouted' and 'Scarborough'. I think the reason I'm ever so slightly embarrassed by it is that it doesn't really make much sense.

Maybe I should just relax, though, because it doesn't necessarily have to make sense. There's a nonsensical aspect to it, but when you've read things like Lewis Carroll's 'Jabberwocky', it gives you licence to do pretty much anything. Another consideration is that the song is a representation of an Asian immigrant in the UK, and the song gives a sense of her culture shock.

Ninety-eight per cent of my songs come from a musical idea, not a lyrical idea, and it's likely this song began with the riff. Sometimes words just come out when I'm writing a song, particularly if it's around a riff, and they'll fit with the song and work for the singing. Even in this enlightened era, they're called 'dummy' lyrics, placeholder lyrics while you map out the structure of the song. I think these could actually still be the dummy lyrics.

There's only one song I can think of where I wrote the words first, and that was 'All My Loving', because I was on a tour bus. Mainly I sit down with an instrument, and it begins that way. Even 'Eleanor Rigby' started with an E minor chord. Then I start getting ideas off that chord, and I'm either going to do something gentle and melodic or I'm going to get up and scream - whichever seems the most appropriate thing. And sometimes the words just slip out, and next thing you know you've got 'Old Siam, Sir'.

All the way back at the very beginning, when John and I were listening to records, we didn't really care a lot of the time about the words - just the sound. People would say, 'Well, what about those lyrics?' and we'd realise we hadn't even noticed some of the nuances people were picking up on. We'd say, 'Oh yeah, suppose so.' There is a song called 'Just Walk On By' by Jim Reeves that was a hit in the early 60s, and I remember a vicar complaining about it, saying it was about a divorce or about a man having an affair. We said, 'What? He's crazy!' We'd never thought about the lyrics. We'd had absolutely no idea what that song was about. We just liked the sound of it.

Left: 'Old Siam, Sir' single and artwork layout, 1979

Right: Lympne Castle, Kent, 1979

OLD SIAM, SIR.

In a village in Old Siam, Sir
Lived a lady who lost her way
In an effort to find a man, Sir
Found herself in the Old U.K.

She waited round in Walthamstow
She scouted round in Scarborough

Repeat.

In the village Old East 'am, Sir
MET a fella that made, a reel
Took her rushes to show his mam, sir
Met his dad at the wedding meal

In a letter from Old Siam, Sir
Came a terrible tale of woe
She decided the only answer
Was to get up a pile of dough
She waited round in Walthamstow
She scouted " " Scarborough.

Repeat.

When a relative told her man, Sir,
He directed her not to stay
In a village in Old Siam, Sir
Lives a lady who lost her way

She waited round in Walthamstow

Spirit of Ranachan Studio.
Scotland, 1979

There's a nonsensical aspect to it, but when you've read things like Lewis Carroll's 'Jabberwocky', it gives you licence to do pretty much anything.

On My Way to Work

WRITER	Paul McCartney
ARTIST	Paul McCartney
RECORDED	Hog Hill Mill, Sussex; Abbey Road Studios, London; Henson Studios, Los Angeles; and AIR Studios, London
RELEASED	*NEW*, 2013

On my way to work
I rode a big green bus
I could see everything
From the upper deck
People came and went
Smoking cigarettes
I picked the packets up
When the people left

But all the time I thought of you
How far away the future seemed
How could I have so many dreams
And one of them not come true?

On my way to work
I bought a magazine
Inside a pretty girl
Liked to waterski
She came from Chichester
To study history
She had removed her clothes
For the likes of me

But all the time I thought of you
How would you know that I was there?
How could a soul search everywhere
Without knowing what to do?

On my way to work
As I was clocking in
I could see everything
How it came to be
People come and go
Smoking cigarettes
I pick the packets up
When the people leave

But all the time I think of you
How far away the future seems
How could I have so many dreams
And one of them not come true?

On my way to work

But all the time I thought of you
How would you know that I was there?
How could a soul search everywhere
Without knowing what to do?

On my way to work
On my way to work

Above: View of Liverpool from the Royal Liver Building, 1955

MY DAD WAS FROM THE CLASS THAT BELIEVED YOU shouldn't hang about doing nothing when you're in your teenage years. It's not a good idea to sit at home not paying any rent. At that point, after our mum died, it was just him and my brother and me, so there wasn't an awful lot of money coming into the house.

My first job was at this place called SPD, Speedy Prompt Deliveries, which was down on the old Liverpool docks. I was what you call a 'second man' on a lorry, which could have been a very important position. But in my case it really wasn't, so I asked the driver, who was obviously 'first man' on the lorry, 'What's my job - second man on the lorry?' And he said, 'Well, when we get to the place where we're delivering' - normally shops and factories - 'you'll help me with the stuff.' So, that's what I would do.

He was very cool, I recall - the driver I was buddied up with - and he knew I was a teenage slob, so he would let me sleep while he drove to the place, and he'd only wake me up when we got there. We'd get out, he'd roll up the back of the truck and pull out the parcels, and I'd carry them in or we'd carry them in together.

This is a thing I always thought when I was young: 'How on earth am I going to meet the right person with these billions of people teeming about the planet? How could a soul search everywhere, without knowing what to do? How am I going to run into the right one?' It was very much a teenage worry for me. The other was, 'What job am I going to have?' I could see no future on the delivery truck or working as a coil winder in a factory (another job of mine), or going into the cotton trade like my dad had done.

Above: John Lennon performing with The Quarry Men at St. Peter's Church Fête, 6 July 1957

Left: Still from 'Penny Lane' promotional film featuring Liverpool's distinctive green bus

I see kids nowadays with those same worries, and they're very real worries, very much like the ones I described when I wrote this song. 'On my way to work / I bought a magazine / Inside a pretty girl / Liked to waterski / She came from Chichester'. I was very happy to get that detail in. I would sometimes do that on my way to Speedy Prompt Deliveries. I could get nudie magazines, now that I was a working man and I was actually allowed to buy them! And besides them, a few years later *The Sun* newspaper started doing this sort of thing on page 3: 'Jeanette is from Hayling Island. Her hobbies include . . .' I loved those biographical details, it's a nice little bit of background – fills the story out.

A big memory from this time is going from home to the vast and bustling docks that lined the waterfront. It would be about a half-hour bus journey. The buses in Liverpool at that time were all green, and it would've been a number 80 or an 86, one of the routes that went into town. I was always a top-deck-of-the-bus person because I liked the view better, and great things happened up there. Everyone smoked in those days, and the upper deck was where you smoked. When the bus reached the terminals, me and my friends would pick up the cigarette packets left behind. I know it may seem like a very strange thing to say, but there's a certain joy – at least if you're a kid and just don't know better – in poverty. Especially when you're an adult, you can't say too much about the joy of poverty because people say, 'Oh, no, it's a terrible, terrible thing.' But when you're very young and it's all you've ever seen, it can, in truth, be a joyful thing, because you've got nothing, and starting from there creates all kinds of interesting scenarios that become part of your everyday reality, which becomes totally normal.

So we would collect cigarette packs off the buses and then flatten them just like the baseball cards you find in the US, and that way you could have a great big wad of cigarette packets – Senior Service, Player's Navy Cut, Russian Sobranie, Passing Clouds, Gitanes, Craven A, Robin, Woodbine. There were so many brands of ciggies that they made a great collection. And once your mates did it too, you could say, 'I'll swap you three Woodbines for a Passing Clouds.' It was all advertising cancer, it turned out.

The first time I ever saw John Lennon was on the bus. I didn't know him then, so he was just this slightly older guy with a sort of rocker hairdo, lots of grease, black jacket, sideburns ('sideboards' as we called them; 'sideburns' was American). And I just remember thinking, 'Well, he's a cool guy.' When we did meet, I recognised him as that strange Teddy Boy from the bus. John always managed to be a little bit older than me; I never caught up.

I had no idea who he was at the time, but I'll always remember that very first image.

The first time I ever saw John Lennon was on the bus. I didn't know him then, so he was just this slightly older guy with a sort of rocker hairdo, lots of grease, black jacket, sideburns.

Once Upon a Long Ago

WRITER	Paul McCartney
ARTIST	Paul McCartney
RECORDED	Hog Hill Mill, Sussex; and Abbey Road Studios, London
RELEASED	UK single, 1987

Picking up scales and broken chords
Puppy dog tails in the House of Lords
Tell me darling, what can it mean?

Making up moons in a minor key
What have those tunes got to do with me?
Tell me darling, where have you been?

Once upon a long ago
Children searched for treasure
Nature's plan went hand in hand with pleasure
Such pleasure

Blowing balloons on a windy day
Desolate dunes with a lot to say
Tell me darling, what have you seen?

Once upon a long ago
Children searched for treasure
Nature's plan went hand in hand with pleasure
My pleasure

Playing guitars on an empty stage
Counting the bars of an iron cage
Tell me darling, what can it mean?

Picking up scales and broken chords
Puppy dog tails in the House of Lords
Help me darling, what does it mean?

Once upon a long ago . . .

William S. Burroughs had what he called his 'cut-up technique'. I have from time to time been a devotee of something along those lines – just dragging in words and slinging them around, throwing them up in the air, seeing where they fall. You think, 'Well, that can't mean anything.' But then you read it, and it does seem to mean something.

I know I've told this story before, but when I started painting, I had the idea that what I did must be meaningful, that it had to have some profound significance. That stopped me in my tracks completely. I simply couldn't do anything. Then I met Willem de Kooning, and I asked him about one of his paintings and what it 'meant', and he said, 'I dunno. Looks like a couch, huh?' And I thought, 'Jesus.' That blew my mind open.

In the context of this song, the idea of its not having to mean something was particularly liberating for me. I can make up a story. It takes next to nothing to get me off and running. So, 'Picking up scales and broken chords' refers again to why I never wanted to learn music, because it was 'da-da-da-da-da, da-da-da-da-da' – one five-finger exercise after another. I couldn't stand that. Bored the hell out of me. It put me off learning notation. And with the 'Puppy dog tails in the House of Lords', the idea of there being a bunch of little boys in the House of Lords is what I'm getting at, since, if you recall, little boys are made of puppy dog tails. It's a bit scathing, I know, but I think anything to do with the House of Lords can be a bit stupid.

A lot of the other images in the song are drawn from my childhood, back in the fields near our housing estate. That would be true of 'Blowing balloons on a windy day', whilst the image of 'Desolate dunes with a lot to say' is based on childhood memories of going to the seaside.

As for 'Playing guitars on an empty stage', I don't have performance anxiety per se, but in dreams I do. They say all performers do. Actors arrive on a stage and are about to say their first line and they've no idea which play they're in. They wake up in a cold sweat. I have dreams like that where I'm trying to stop the audience from leaving in droves.

In my dreams if I see people moving around and away from their seats in the audience at a concert, I don't ever think, 'What's wrong with these people? Why don't they sit down and listen?' I always think, 'What's wrong with what we're doing? We're obviously playing the wrong song here.' So I reach for 'Long Tall Sally', thinking, 'That'll get them.' Or, 'Let's do a quick burst of "Yesterday".' On the page or on the stage, I'm always trying to figure out what it's going to take to keep the audience interested.

ONCE UPON A LONG AGO

PICKING UP SCALES AND BROKEN CHORDS.
PUPPY DOG TAILS IN THE HOUSE OF LORDS
TELL ME DARLING — WHAT CAN IT MEAN?

MAKING UP MOONS IN A MINOR KEY,
WHAT HAVE THOSE TUNES GOT TO DO WITH ME?
TELL ME DARLING — WHERE HAVE YOU BEEN?

ONCE UPON A LONG AGO
CHILDREN SEARCHED FOR TREASURE.
NATURE'S PLAN WENT HAND IN HAND
WITH PLEASURE, ... MY PLEASURE ..... SOLO ..

BLOWING BALLOONS ON A WINDY DAY,
DESOLATE DUNES WITH A LOT TO SAY,
TELL ME DARLING — WHAT HAVE YOU SEEN?

PLAYING GUITARS ON AN EMPTY STAGE,
COUNTING THE BARS OF AN IRON CAGE
TELL ME DARLING — WHAT CAN IT MEAN?

ONCE UPON A LONG AGO
CHILDREN SEARCHED FOR TREASURE.
NATURE'S PLAN WENT HAND IN HAND.
WITH PLEASURE .... SUCH PLEASURE ....

'Once Upon a Long Ago'
music video, 1987

A lot of the other images in the song are drawn from my childhood, back in the fields near our housing estate. That would be true of 'Blowing balloons on a windy day', whilst the image of 'Desolate dunes with a lot to say' is based on childhood memories of going to the seaside.

Left: With Willem de Kooning. East Hampton, 1984

Right: *Pintos in the Sky with Desert Poppy* painting by Paul, 1991

When I started painting, I had the idea that what I did must be meaningful, that it had to have some profound significance. That stopped me in my tracks completely. I simply couldn't do anything.

Only Mama Knows

WRITER	Paul McCartney
ARTIST	Paul McCartney
RECORDED	Abbey Road Studios, London
RELEASED	*Memory Almost Full*, 2007

Well I was found in the transit lounge
Of a dirty airport town
What was I doing on the road to ruin?
Well my mama laid me down
My mama laid me down

Round my hand was a plastic band
With a picture of my face
I was crying, left to die in
This godforsaken place
This godforsaken place

Only mama knows why she laid me down
In this godforsaken town
Where she was running to, what she ran from
Though I always wondered, I never knew
Only mama knows
Only mama knows

I'm passing through, I'm on my way
I'm on the road, no ETA
I'm passing through, no fixed abode
And that is why I need to try
To hold on, I've gotta hold on, gotta hold on

Was it planned as a one-night stand
Or did she leave in disgrace?
Well I never, will I ever
See my father's face?
See my father's face?

Only mama knows why she laid me down
In this godforsaken town
Where she was running to, what she ran from
Though I always wondered, I never knew
Only mama knows
Only mama knows

I've gotta hold on
I've gotta hold on
You've gotta hold on

A FRIEND OF MINE WAS ADOPTED WHEN HE WAS A BABY. HE AND his brother were left at an orphanage. They were brought up in the orphanage and never knew their mother. He weathered the experience very well, but his brother struggled. I used this 'true life story' to create an imaginary situation that anchors the song. It's a song written from the point of view of someone who's been left behind. Someone who's been abandoned.

My friend was with me when I wrote this song, just as he was with me when I recorded it. We talked openly about it. He would always wonder why his mother left him. He sort of knew what the story was, that she'd been knocked up by some guy who was just passing through. In those days there was a lot of shame - a woman wasn't supposed to have babies if she wasn't married - and then there was the sheer financial hardship of raising a child.

Here I'm psyching myself, in a way, into the position of the guy who got her pregnant. 'I'm passing through, I'm on my way / I'm on the road, no ETA'. I like those two lines; they sum up a lot of what the touring life is like. 'I'm passing through, no fixed abode'. In the song, it's the kid who's been left and now he's passing through, he's on his way. He's acquired the same habits as his dad, so life is a constant cycle. Once I start writing about that, I obviously come to it from my own perspective. I'm just acknowledging that the kid whose mother left him has got more problems than the average person in life. He's got to hold on, he's got to keep steady. But it's really larger than that. The more I mature, the more I think we all have to hold on. Nobody knows exactly what we're in for, but we're all in it together.

The middle eight gives you an opportunity to approach a subject from a different angle. Because the melody's changed, you've gone somewhere different musically, so it's a good opportunity to go somewhere different lyrically. You can make some sort of important statement that helps the song move along, or you can just make a casual observation; that's the great thing - you're free to do what you want. You're basically trying to just get on the off-ramp for a couple of minutes before re-joining the motorway.

We only ever called this the 'middle eight' because other people called it that, and it did tend to be eight bars, and then of course you want to subvert that, and you don't want eight bars, you want ten. We never quite did what I always wanted to do, which is what the blues players do: They'll do seven bars, and just when you think it's not going to change, it does. Or they'll do nine bars, so when you think, 'Now this is it,' they'll go, 'No, there's a little bit more.'

I like the idea that you're free to do whatever you want. Anyone who writes knows that if you have a following, people get your style. One of my styles is, 'There, there, it's going to be alright', but it's nice to subvert that too. You know what your fans want, so you might try to tease them a bit, try not to give it to them in quite the way they expect. And I think that a lot of my songs, a lot of Beatles songs, did that: you expected it to go here, and it didn't - it went over there. I've had people say that's one of the good things

Memory Almost Full recording sessions, 2007

about our songs. Richard Lester, who directed *A Hard Day's Night* and *Help!*, was one of them, and he's a bit of a jazz fan. He said, 'I like that they don't go where you expect them to go.'

So that became an interesting rule for us: try to go where they don't expect you to go.

ONLY MAMA KNOWS

INTRO

(Emin) (D)

1. I WAS FOUND IN THE TRANSIT LOUNGE
(Emin) (D)
OF A DIRTY AIRPORT TOWN
(Emin) (D)
WHAT I WAS DOING ON THE ROAD TO RUIN
(Emin) (F# min)
WELL, MY MAMA LAID ME DOWN
(Emin) (D)
MAMA LAID ME DOWN

(Emin) (D)
2. ROUND MY HAND WAS A PLASTIC BAND
(Emin) (D)
WITH A PICTURE OF MY FACE
(Emin) (D)
I WAS CRYING, LEFT TO DIE IN
(Emin) (F# min)
THIS GOD FORSAKEN PLACE
(Emin) (D)
GOD FORSAKEN PLACE CHORDS D/A/E B.

(CHORUS) (B) (Ebmin) (C# min)
ONLY MAMA KNOWS, WHY SHE LAID ME DOWN
(Emin) (B)
IN THIS GOD FORSAKEN TOWN
(B) (Ebmin) (C# min)
WHERE SHE WAS RUNNING TO, WHERE SHE RAN FROM
(Emin)
THOUGH I ALWAYS WONDERED, I NEVER KNEW
(Emin) ONLY MAMA KNOWS —

MIDDLE (Emin 7) ——
PASSING THROUGH, IM ON MY WAY
ON THE ROAD, NO E.T.A.
PASSING THROUGH NO FIXED ABODE
AND THAT'S WHY I NEED TO TRY, TO HOLD ON....

(Emin) (D)
3. WAS IT PLANNED AS A ONE NIGHT STAND
(Emin) (D)
OR DID SHE LEAVE IN DISGRACE
(Emin) (D) (Emin) (F# min)
WELL I NEVER, WILL I EVER SEE MY FATHERS FACE
CHORUS (Emin) " " (D) "
(B) (Ebmin) (C# min) (Emin) (B)
ONLY MAMA KNOWS WHY SHE LAID ME DOWN IN THIS GOD FORSAKEN TOWN
(B) (Ebmin) (C# min)
WHERE SHE WAS RUNNING TO, WHERE SHE RAN FROM THOUGH I ALWAYS
(Emin) (Emin)
WONDERED, I NEVER KNEW ONLY MAMA KNOWS.
(Emin 7)

The Other Me

WRITER	Paul McCartney
ARTIST	Paul McCartney
RECORDED	AIR Studios, London
RELEASED	*Pipes of Peace*, 1983

I know I was a crazy fool
For treating you the way I did
But something took a hold of me
And I acted like a dustbin lid

I didn't give a second thought
To what the consequence might be
I really wouldn't be surprised
If you were trying to find another me

'Cause the other me would rather be the glad one
The other me would rather play the fool
I want to be the kind of me
That doesn't let you down as a rule

I know it doesn't take a lot
To have a little self-control
But every time that I forgot
Well I landed in another hole

But every time you pull me out
I find it harder not to see
That we can build a better life
If I can try to find the other me

The other me would rather be the glad one
Yeah the other me would rather play the fool
Said I want to be the kind of me
That doesn't let you down as a rule

But if I ever hurt you
Well you know that it's not real
It's not easy living by yourself
So imagine how I feel

I wish that I could take it back
I'd like to make a different mood
And if you let me try again
I'll have a better attitude

Well I know that one and one makes two
And that's what I want us to be
I really would appreciate it
If you'd help me find the other me

And the other me would rather be the glad one
The other me would rather play the fool
But I want to be the kind of me
That doesn't let you down as a rule

HAD I NOT GOT INTO A GROUP THAT WAS AS SUCCESSFUL as The Beatles - a group that had a long life as groups go - then I might have had to find some other work. I would almost certainly have become an English teacher, that 'other me'.

But the life I've led - as a musician, performer, singer, songwriter - is incredible. I still feel like I'm just *playing at it*. I have a little bit of 'impostor syndrome' - same as, I suppose, many 'successful' people do. This life I've led is something I brought on myself because of the fascination of it, because of the love of some puzzle that can never quite be solved. Every song, then, is part of a solution to it. And it's a solution that I don't necessarily come up with by myself.

We all get into situations where we put our foot in our mouth. We say something we didn't mean to say, or say something that is taken amiss. So this song is an apology: 'I know I was a crazy fool / For treating you the way I did / But something took a hold of me / And I acted like a dustbin lid'. Something took over, and I acted childishly - 'dustbin lid' is Liverpool rhyming slang for a kid. Often after an argument, people walk away with a lot of strong feelings and energy with nowhere for it to go. If you're a songwriter, you can use that. In writing songs like 'The Other Me', you can be your own psychiatrist. You're reviewing your actions, admitting your faults and then looking for the solution which will make it better next time.

Above: Long John and the Silver Beetles audition for Larry Parnes with Stuart Sutcliffe, John Lennon, Johnny Hutchinson and George Harrison. Wyvern Social Club (later the Blue Angel), Liverpool, May 1960

In the very early days of The Beatles, of course, we didn't even think of writing songs, except as a little bit of a side project. We mainly just liked fully formed songs that other people had recorded, so we'd do a Chuck Berry song or we'd do a Carl Perkins song or an Elvis song. When John and I met, the first year of our friendship was spent talking about these cover versions, the records we loved, and then playing them again and again. As we got to know each other, we practised these various covers until one day the conversation went, 'You know, I've written one or two songs.' And he said, 'Yeah, so have I.'

That gave us something in common that was itself wholly uncommon. I went to a school of a thousand boys and I'd never met anyone who said he'd written a song. Mine were just in my head. So were John's. We took each other by surprise. And then the logical extension was, 'Well, maybe we could write one together.' So that's how we started. And we became versions of each other.

We did an audition around 1960 for a London manager and promoter called Larry Parnes, who was quite famous at the time, and he had a stable of young rock boys. He was a reasonable guy, old Larry, and he was coming to Liverpool to hold auditions, so this was really big news, and we were quite excited, you can well imagine. The auditions were at a place called the Wyvern Social Club, which later became the Blue Angel. The Big Three (known as Cass and the Cassanovas at the time), Derry and The Seniors, and Gerry and The Pacemakers, who would become most famous for 'Ferry Cross the Mersey' – we all auditioned that day.

We had Stuart Sutcliffe as a bass player for our own audition. Stuart was a friend of John's from art college who was really a painter, but he'd won an art prize of sixty-five pounds, which was the exact amount of money required to buy a Höfner bass. Stuart basically said, 'No way; I'm not going to do it,' but John could be very persuasive. So, Stuart had this bass that he didn't really know how to play, but as long as it was sort of in A, he would just go doom-doom-doom and lend a bass element to our guitar chords.

George was on lead guitar. John and I were on rhythm guitars. Stuart was turned away from the camera and from Larry because we thought, 'If they see his fingers, they'll know he can't play.' So we'd suggested, very diplomatically, 'Just turn away and look very moody.' So, in early pictures you'll see that Stuart is not facing the camera, and he does look moody.

Larry Parnes said, 'What's your name? What's the name of the group?' And we didn't want to say 'The Quarry Men', so we said, 'We're not sure really.' And he said, 'Well, you've got to have a name.' John was acting like the leader, so Larry asked him, 'What's your name?' And John said, 'Long John Silver'. Then I said my name was 'Paul Ramone'; I'm not quite sure why. 'Ramone', I thought, was, maybe, rather French and sophisticated. Then George said, 'Carl Harrison', after Carl Perkins. Then I think we said, 'We call ourselves "The Beetles",' or something like that, but I think we meant it with double e. And the guy said, 'Oh God, that's a terrible name. We'll call you Long John and the Silver Beetles.' We said, 'Alright.'

So, with Larry Parnes we actually did a tour under the name of The Silver Beetles. Larry's singers all had tumultuous names. There was Billy Fury. There was Marty Wilde. There was Dickie Pride. Kind of like action characters in a comic strip. And we got another of his people to tour with – someone named Johnny Gentle. We thought, 'What the hell is that about?' We

Poster featured in fan magazine *Club Sandwich*, issue 77, 1996

were backing him on a Scottish tour, and we were a bit disappointed not to have someone with a more tempestuous-sounding name.

Johnny Gentle actually came on tour with a young lady, whom he introduced as his wife, and being innocent young Liverpool boys, we would say, 'Why yes, Mrs Gentle.' We really deferred to her, but then scepticism set in. It dawned on us that that's what you could do if you were in Hamburg for a while, or Scotland on tour; you could take a girlfriend and share your hotel room with her and tell your band that she's your wife.

In those early days, Buddy Holly was huge for us. We'd heard him on the radio, and we thought he was a Black American artist. 'That'll Be the Day' was a great song. We just loved it, and it had a great little intro. We tried for years to learn that intro, which we eventually did. Then we looked at the B-side, and at other stuff he was doing. 'Peggy Sue' - wow, we also loved that. 'Maybe Baby' - amazing. And it became clear that he wrote his own songs, which hardly anybody else did. We were young, but we always looked at the writing credits because we were very interested in the whole process. That's one of the great things about The Beatles: we never missed a trick; we knew who wrote things, and we'd try and find out who they were.

Under quite a few hits that we liked we saw the name 'Goffin/King'. We thought this could be two guys, but it turned out to be a woman and a man: Carole King and her first husband, Gerry Goffin. They were working out of the Brill Building in Manhattan. We'd see 'Holly' under Buddy Holly's songs, and we'd think, 'Wow, he wrote it.' Then we saw him on telly at the London Palladium, and he played guitar and sang. But Elvis didn't write his own songs, and he couldn't really play guitar; we watched his fingers and saw that he couldn't play too well. In 'Love Me Tender' we could really tell he wasn't playing. He was, of course, an amazing performer, but he was playing only a few basic chords.

So, we liked Buddy and The Crickets for those reasons. We liked his band, but we truly loved Buddy, his voice and his guitar playing - not to mention those glasses - and the fact that he wrote. And if you think about it, that's what The Beatles did: we did our own writing, we played guitars up front, and we sang. That's how we became who we were meant to be.

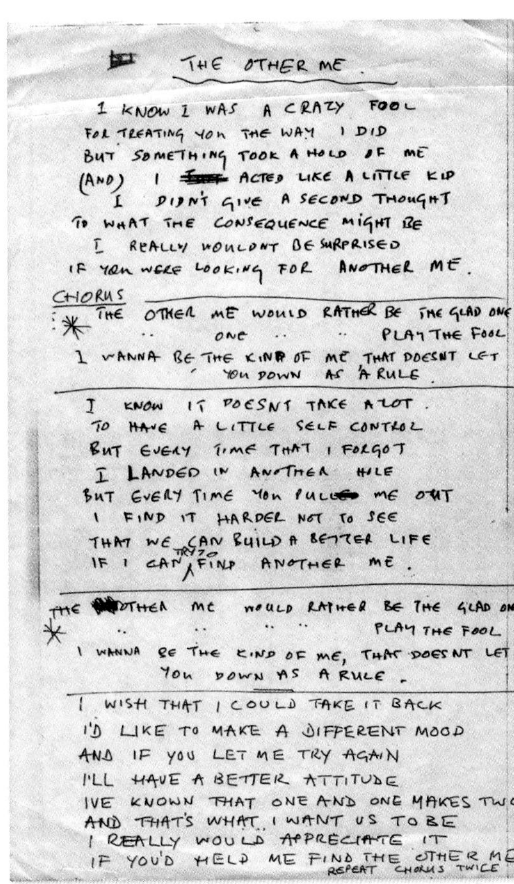
THE OTHER ME.

I KNOW I WAS A CRAZY FOOL
FOR TREATING YOU THE WAY I DID
BUT SOMETHING TOOK A HOLD OF ME
(AND) I ACTED LIKE A LITTLE KID
I DIDN'T GIVE A SECOND THOUGHT
TO WHAT THE CONSEQUENCE MIGHT BE
I REALLY WOULDNT BE SURPRISED
IF YOU WERE LOOKING FOR ANOTHER ME.

CHORUS
THE OTHER ME WOULD RATHER BE THE GLAD ONE
" ONE " " PLAY THE FOOL
I WANNA BE THE KIND OF ME THAT DOESNT LET
YOU DOWN AS A RULE.

I KNOW IT DOESNT TAKE A LOT.
TO HAVE A LITTLE SELF CONTROL
BUT EVERY TIME THAT I FORGOT
I LANDED IN ANOTHER HOLE
BUT EVERY TIME YOU PULL ME OUT
I FIND IT HARDER NOT TO SEE
THAT WE CAN BUILD A BETTER LIFE
IF I CAN TRY TO FIND ANOTHER ME.

THE OTHER ME WOULD RATHER BE THE GLAD ONE
" " " " PLAY THE FOOL
I WANNA BE THE KIND OF ME, THAT DOESNT LET
YOU DOWN AS A RULE.

I WISH THAT I COULD TAKE IT BACK
I'D LIKE TO MAKE A DIFFERENT MOOD
AND IF YOU LET ME TRY AGAIN
I'LL HAVE A BETTER ATTITUDE
IVE KNOWN THAT ONE AND ONE MAKES TWO
AND THAT'S WHAT I WANT US TO BE
I REALLY WOULD APPRECIATE IT
IF YOU'D HELP ME FIND THE OTHER ME
REPEAT CHORUS TWICE

THE OTHER ME.

1. I KNOW I WAS A CRAZY FOOL
FOR TREATING YOU THE WAY I DID
BUT SOMETHING TOOK A HOLD OF ME
(AND) I ~~[illegible]~~ ACTED LIKE A LITTLE KID
I DIDN'T GIVE A SECOND THOUGHT
TO WHAT THE CONSEQUENCE MIGHT BE
I REALLY WOULDNT BE SURPRISED
IF YOU WERE LOOKING FOR ANOTHER ME.

CHORUS THE OTHER ME WHO'D RATHER BE THE GLAD ONE
" " ME WHO WOULDN'T ~~PLAY~~ BE THE FOOL
I WANNA BE THE KIND OF ME THAT DOESNT LET
YOU DOWN AS A RULE.

2. I KNOW IT DOESNT TAKE A LOT.
TO HAVE A LITTLE SELF CONTROL
BUT EVERY TIME THAT I FORGOT
I LANDED IN ANOTHER HOLE
AND EVERY TIME YOU PULL[illegible] ME OUT
I FIND IT HARDER NOT TO SEE
THAT WE CAN BUILD A BETTER LIFE
IF I CAN TRY TO FIND ~~AN~~ THE OTHER ME.

CHORUS.
THE ~~AN~~OTHER ME ~~WHO'D~~ RATHER BE THE GLAD ONE.
" " WHO WOULDN'T BE ~~PLAY~~ THE FOOL
I WANNA BE THE KIND OF ME, THAT DOESNT LET
YOU DOWN AS A RULE.

MIDDLE. ~~AND IF I EVER HURT YOU~~, PLEASE IMAGINE HOW ~~I~~ FEEL
~~LIVING WITH~~
~~ITS NOT EASY TO RESPECT YOURSELF WHEN [illegible]~~
~~WHEN YOU NEVER~~ TO MAKE A DEAL ~~YOUR [illegible]~~.

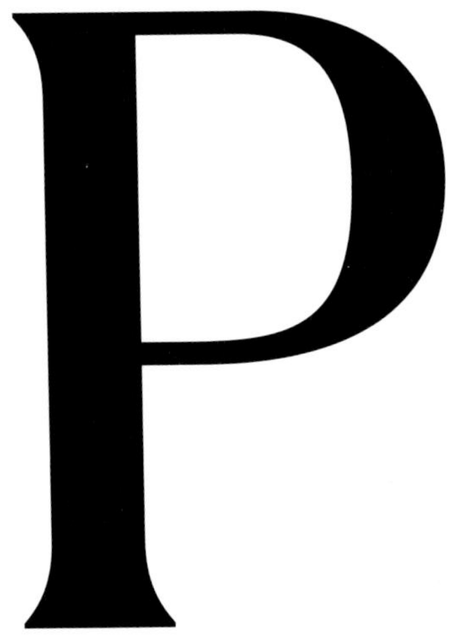

Paperback Writer

WRITERS	Paul McCartney and John Lennon
ARTIST	The Beatles
RECORDED	Abbey Road Studios, London
RELEASED	Single, 1966

Paperback writer
(Paperback writer)

Dear Sir or Madam, will you read my book?
It took me years to write will you take a look?
It's based on a novel by a man named Lear
And I need a job so I want to be a
Paperback writer, paperback writer

It's a dirty story of a dirty man
And his clinging wife doesn't understand
His son is working for the Daily Mail
It's a steady job but he wants to be a
Paperback writer, paperback writer

Paperback writer
(Paperback writer)

It's a thousand pages give or take a few
I'll be writing more in a week or two
I can make it longer if you like the style
I can change it round and I want to be a
Paperback writer, paperback writer

If you really like it you can have the rights
It could make a million for you overnight
If you must return it you can send it here
But I need a break and I want to be a
Paperback writer, paperback writer

Paperback writer
(Paperback writer)

THE TRUTH OF IT IS THAT WE DISCOVERED POT, AND – JUST AS had been promised on the label – it expanded our minds. Things opened up. We realised that it didn't just have to be 'thank you girl, from me to you, she loves you . . .' It didn't have to be that simple anymore. We were on the lookout for the kind of subject that hadn't really been the stuff of popular song.

This realisation coincided with the fact that I was now bumping into writers on the cocktail circuit. Kingsley Amis, John Mortimer, Penelope Mortimer, Harold Pinter, to name a few. These were the very people I was reading, and the people I was reading about. When I was younger, I used to go to Philip Son & Nephew, our local bookstore in Liverpool. The London bookshops were almost as good as the guitar shops; there was so much to discover inside.

I had this idea of being an aspiring writer, and I imagined writing a letter to the publishing company to extol my own virtues and try to sell myself. That's why the song starts 'Dear Sir or Madam'. That was the way you opened letters then. I set that to music. I had bought a new electric guitar, an Epiphone Casino. It's the one I still use on stage, and I plugged it into my Vox amp and turned it up nice and loud, and I got this riff. It's quite a nice, easy riff to play. In fact, with most of my musical compositions, there's a simple trick, because I'm not massively proficient. For example, I couldn't always go and hit the right notes on the piano. So, there's nearly always some sort of holding position. I just vary that. I move around a little bit on the surface, but I don't move too far from the anchor.

The Beach Boys were an immediate influence on the sound of the song. We were particularly turned on by their harmonies. But much earlier, in fact, my dad had sat us down and taught my brother and me the basics of harmony. Long before The Beach Boys, The Everly Brothers had sung in harmony, so my brother Mike and I did too. We even performed at a Butlin's holiday camp talent competition. I was about fifteen at the time, and we sang 'Bye Bye Love', which we had heard from The Everly Brothers. Didn't win, of course. We weren't talented enough for the Butlin's crowd!

We may have taken a leaf or two from The Beach Boys' harmony book, but we'd change things up like the naughty schoolboys we were. We would tell people we were singing 'dit, dit, dit, dit', but our little smirks should have given away the fact that we were singing 'tit, tit, tit, tit'.

We loved puns above all forms of wordplay. We loved the absurd. We loved the nonsensical, particularly the writings of Edward Lear. That's why he is name-checked in 'Paperback Writer'.

Left: With brother Mike at Butlin's holiday camp, 1940s

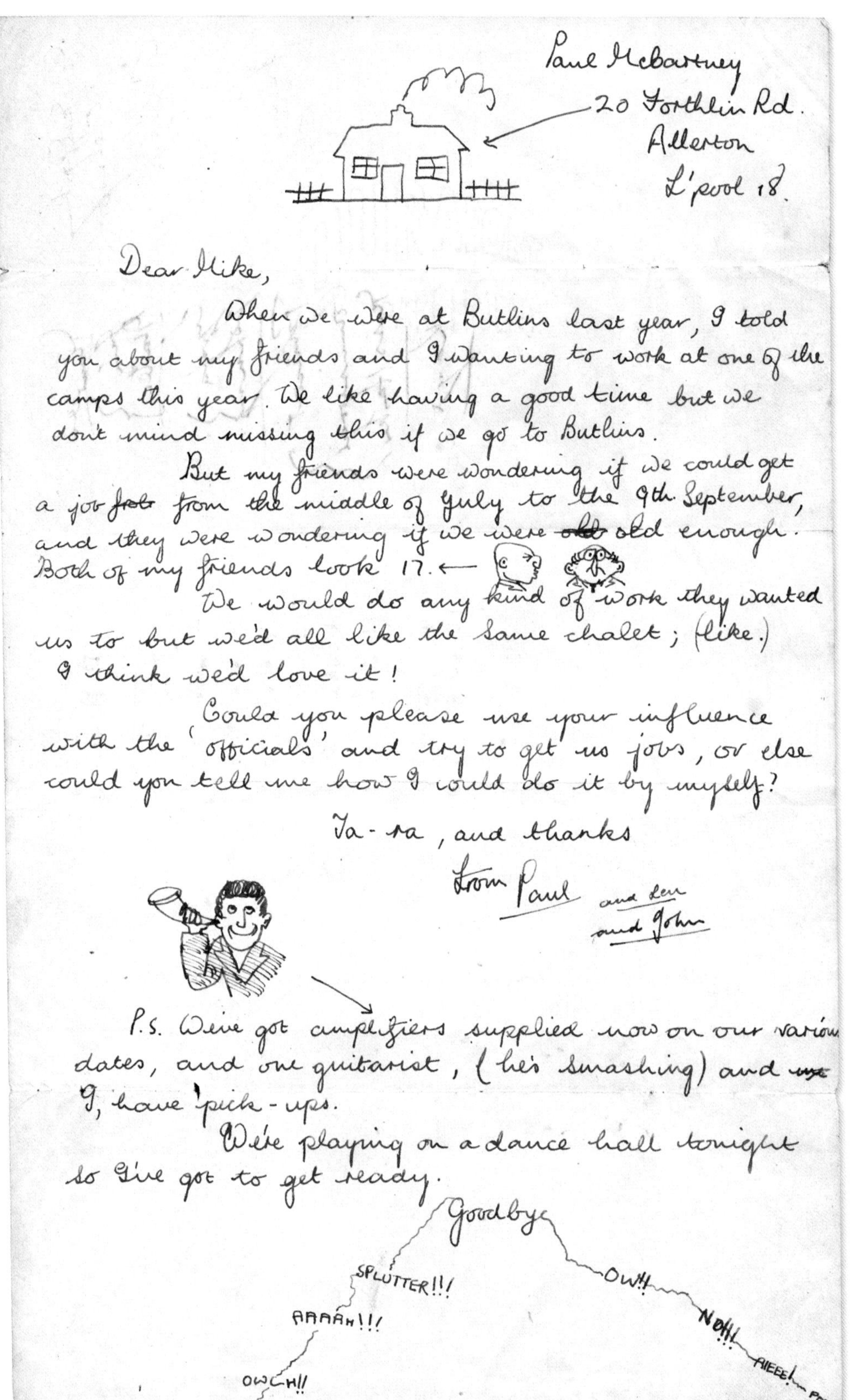

Paul McCartney
20 Forthlin Rd.
Allerton
L'pool 18.

Dear Mike,

When we were at Butlins last year, I told you about my friends and I wanting to work at one of the camps this year. We like having a good time but we don't mind missing this if we go to Butlins.

But my friends were wondering if we could get a job ~~fob~~ from the middle of July to the 9th September, and they were wondering if we were ~~old~~ old enough. Both of my friends look 17. ←

We would do any kind of work they wanted us to but we'd all like the same chalet; (like.) I think we'd love it!

Could you please use your influence with the 'officials' and try to get us jobs, or else could you tell me how I could do it by myself?

Ta-ra, and thanks

From Paul
and Len
and John

P.S. We've got amplifiers supplied now on our various dates, and one guitarist, (he's smashing) and ~~we~~ I, have 'pick-ups.

We're playing on a dance hall tonight so I've got to get ready.

Goodbye

The Beatles performing 'Paperback Writer' on *Top of the Pops*, 1966

Playing the Epiphone Casino at the Robin Hood Benefit. New York, 2015

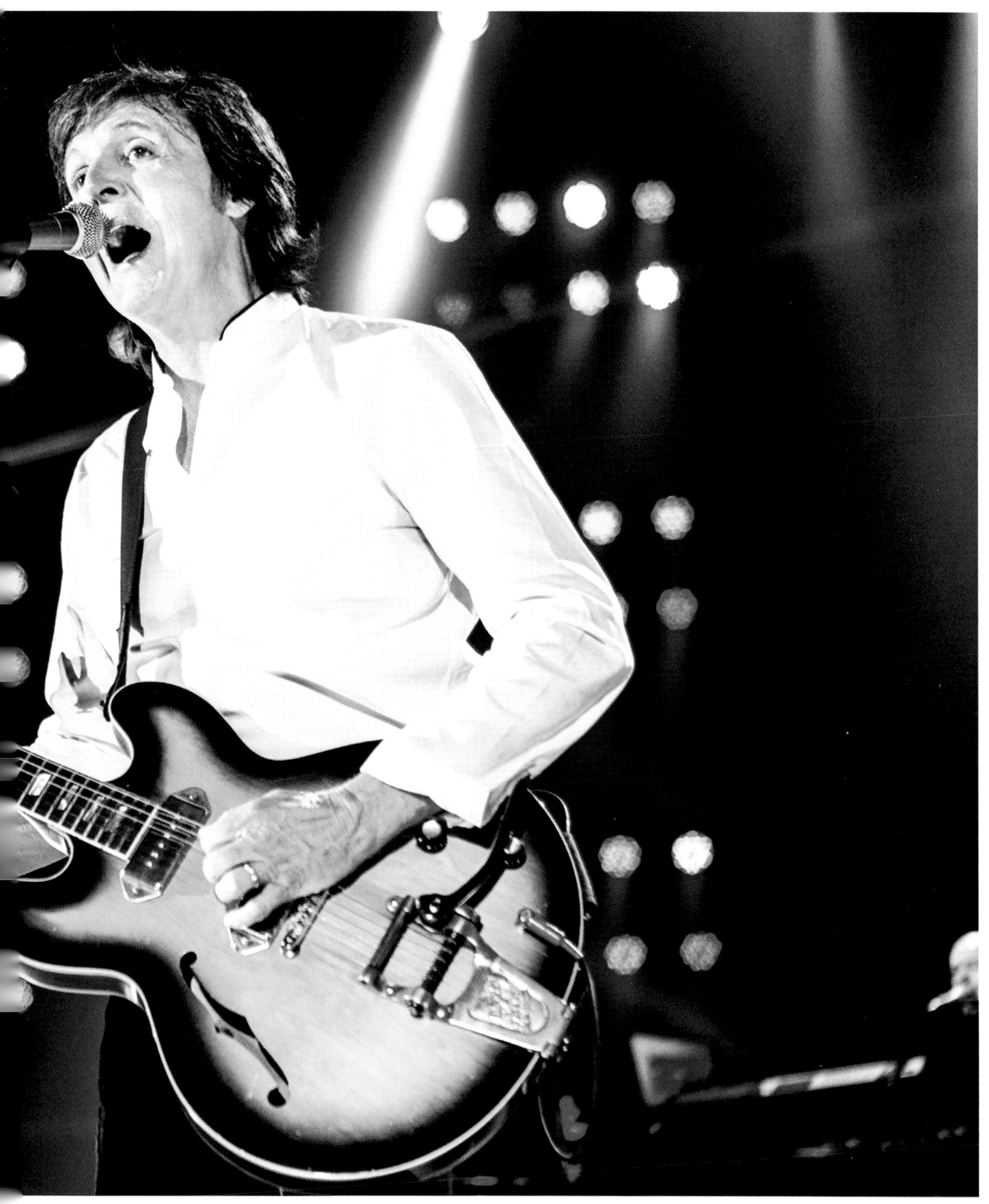

Penny Lane

WRITERS	Paul McCartney and John Lennon
ARTIST	The Beatles
RECORDED	Abbey Road Studios, London
RELEASED	'Penny Lane'/'Strawberry Fields Forever' double A-side single, 1967

In Penny Lane there is a barber showing
photographs
Of every head he's had the pleasure to know
And all the people that come and go
Stop and say hello

On the corner is a banker with a motorcar
The little children laugh at him behind his back
And the banker never wears a mac
In the pouring rain, very strange

Penny Lane is in my ears and in my eyes
There beneath the blue suburban skies
I sit and meanwhile back

In Penny Lane there is a fireman with an hourglass
And in his pocket is a portrait of the Queen
He likes to keep his fire engine clean
It's a clean machine

Penny Lane is in my ears and in my eyes
A four of fish and finger pies
In summer, meanwhile back

Behind the shelter in the middle of the roundabout
The pretty nurse is selling poppies from a tray
And though she feels as if she's in a play
She is anyway

In Penny Lane the barber shaves another customer
We see the banker sitting waiting for a trim
And then the fireman rushes in
From the pouring rain, very strange

Penny Lane is in my ears and in my eyes
There beneath the blue suburban skies
I sit and meanwhile back

Penny Lane is in my ears and in my eyes
There beneath the blue suburban skies
Penny Lane

THERE'S A DOCUMENTARY ASPECT TO 'PENNY LANE', though it's best viewed perhaps as a docudrama. Which is not so strange, since, when I was going to John's house in Liverpool, I would change buses at the Penny Lane roundabout, where Church Road meets Smithdown Road. As well as being a bus terminal, and a place that featured very much in my life and in John's life - we would often meet there - it was near St Barnabas Church, where I was a choirboy. So it resonates in several ways; it's still 'in my ears and in my eyes'.

The line about 'a barber showing photographs' is still amusing to me, because it's as if the barbershop is a gallery that shows paintings. There's an exhibition in his window. You'd look at the photos in the barber's window and then go in and say, 'I'll have a Tony Curtis' or 'I'll have a crew cut.' I thought 'showing photographs' was a good choice of words. All I'm saying is there's a barbershop and the barber has photos of haircuts in his window, but that would be too mundane.

The shop in Penny Lane was owned by Harry Bioletti. It was an Italian barbershop complete with the striped pole outside it. All the members of The Beatles had our hair cut there at one time or another. 'Of every head he's had the pleasure to know' is a line that uses a device my old English teacher would refer to as 'free indirect speech'. You can hear the barber say, 'It's been a pleasure to know you' or something like that. So it's a wonderfully succinct way of delivering information. It crams a lot in.

I'm certain Dylan Thomas's *Under Milk Wood* was a big influence too. It was a radio drama, a portrait of a Welsh town through a cast of characters. It was first done in 1953, but there had been a new radio version of it in 1963 and a television version in 1964. So it was very much in the air.

The characters in 'Penny Lane' are still very real to me. I drive past it to this day, showing people the barbershop, the bank, the fire station, the church I used to sing in, and where the girl stood with the tray of poppies as I waited for the bus. That pretty nurse. I remember her vividly. It was Remembrance Day, and she had a tray full of paper poppies and badges. Funnily enough, a lot of Americans thought she was selling puppies, which is another interesting image, a tray full of *puppies*. But no, she's selling poppies, and 'she feels as if she's in a play / She is anyway'.

The 'She is anyway' is very sixties - it's a commentary on its own method. If I were going to write a play about these characters, I'd rather have it be like a Harold Pinter play than something a bit straighter. I like the idea that they're a bit wonky, all these characters. There's something a bit strange about them. And, of course, I'd not only seen Pinter on stage but had been to his house in Regent's Park. We went round once for a party, and the bathtub was filled with bottles of champagne.

Pages 584–585: Paul and John's handwritten lyrics to 'Penny Lane'

1. In Penny ~~Lane~~ there is a barber showing photographs
of every head he's had the pleasure to know
A & all the people that come and go
stop and say hello

On the corner
2. ~~In Penny Lane there~~ is a banker with a motor car
the ~~and~~ little children laugh at him behind his back
A and ~~for~~ the banker never wears a mac
in the pouring rain, very strange

Penny Lane, is in my ears, and in ~~my~~ eyes,
B ~~Penny Lane~~
There beneath the blue suburban skies I sit and
Meanwhile back in Penny Lane.
A
~~There is a fireman with an hour glass~~
A ~~And in his pocket is a portrait of the Queen~~
B He likes to keep his fire engine clean
A Its a clean machine (Ah Ah etc)
A ~~Penny Lane~~ is in my ears and in my eyes
~~A Four of fish and finger pies in Summer~~
B (THEN B IN C)

In Penny Lane there was a barber
Showing photographs
Of every head he'd had the pleasure to know
It was easy not to go - he was very slow

Meanwhile back behind the shelter
in the middle of the roundabout
A pretty nurse is selling poppies from a tray
And though she feels as if she's in a play
She is anyway.

In Penny Lane the barber shaves another customer
We see the banker sitting for a trim
And then the fireman rushes in
From the pouring rain - very strange
Penny Lane is in my ears and in my eyes
There beneath the blue suburban skies I sit
And meanwhile back at:
Penny Lane is in my ears and in my eyes
There beneath the blue suburban skies Penny Lane

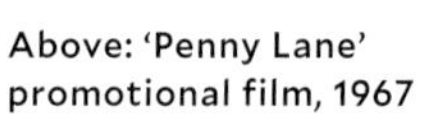

Above: 'Penny Lane' promotional film, 1967

Right: Suit worn in 'Penny Lane' promotional film designed by costumier Monty Berman.

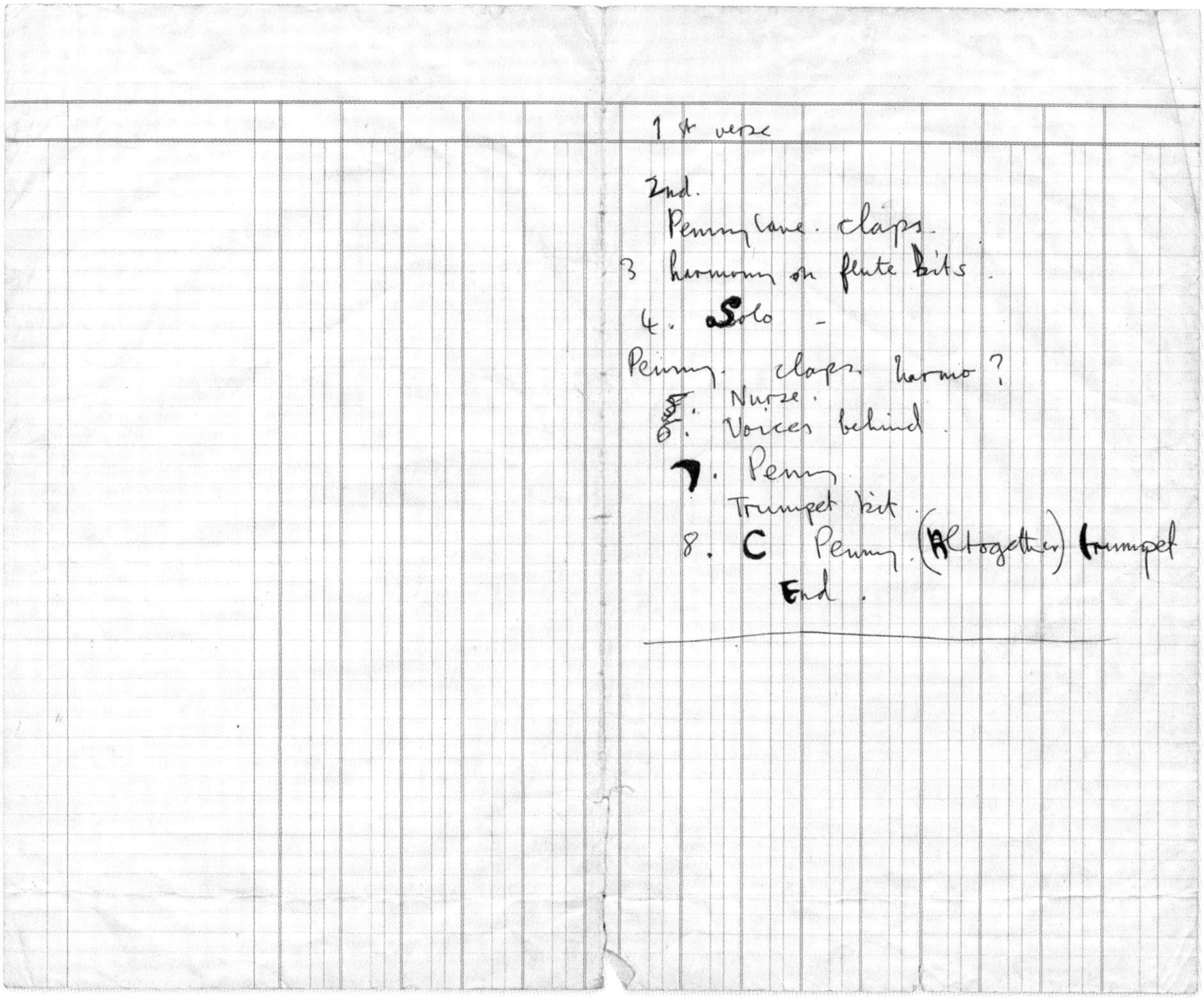

1st verse

2nd.
Penny Lane. claps.
3 harmony on flute bits.
4. Solo –
Penny. claps. harmo?
5. Nurse.
6. Voices behind.
7. Penny.
Trumpet bit.
8. C Penny. (Altogether) trumpet
End.

Above: Paul's recording notes

Right: Bioletti's barbershop as featured in the 'Penny Lane' promotional film, 1967

Picasso's Last Words (Drink to Me)

WRITERS	Paul McCartney and Linda McCartney
ARTIST	Paul McCartney and Wings
RECORDED	EMI Studios, Lagos; ARC Studio, Lagos; and AIR Studios, London
RELEASED	*Band on the Run*, 1973

The grand old painter died last night
His paintings on the wall
Before he went, he bade us well
And said goodnight to us all

Drink to me, drink to my health
You know I can't drink any more
Drink to me, drink to my health
You know I can't drink any more

Three o'clock in the morning
I'm getting ready for bed
It came without a warning
But I'll be waiting for you, baby
I'll be waiting for you there

So drink to me, drink to my health
You know I can't drink any more
Drink to me, drink to my health
You know I can't drink any more

‘PICASSO’S LAST WORDS’ STARTED AS A DARE. I’D MET DUSTIN Hoffman because he was filming *Papillon* in Jamaica, and we’d gone round to his house in Montego Bay.

He said to me, ‘Can you write a song about anything?’ I said, ‘Well, I don’t know, maybe.’ He said, ‘Just a minute,’ and he ran upstairs and came back down with a *Time* magazine article about the death of Picasso.

He then said, ‘See what Picasso’s last words were?’ The article reported that when Picasso died in April 1973, there were friends with him and his last words to his friends were, ‘Drink to me. Drink to my health. You know I can’t drink any more.’

Dustin asked, ‘Could you write a song about that?’ I didn’t know, but I had my guitar with me, so I hit a chord and started singing a melody to those words, and he was flabbergasted. He said to his then wife Anne, ‘Come here! Listen to this! I just gave Paul this, and he’s already got the song.’ The whole thought here was just the challenge of doing it for Dustin, so I was just concentrating on the words he’d stuck in front of me. And I think what was nice is that he’d obviously seen those words as melodic himself. He’s an actor, so he understands the rhythm of words, and I think when he read the quote, he might have thought, ‘This flows beautifully.’ It was a pleasure to do it, just to show off a little bit. I am lucky that it’s something that comes naturally to me.

I think the rhythm of the words itself influences how the melody might turn out. You want to get something that rolls along naturally and that’s interesting at the same time, but that also fits with the music you’re hearing. Sometimes you have to alter a word because it just doesn’t quite work with the metre, so you’ll look for something that says more or less the same thing but with an alternate word. Maybe now it’s a two-syllable word instead of the one-syllable word that didn’t work, or the other way round. It’s very important that the rhythm sounds natural. When it doesn’t, it sticks out like a sore thumb.

You really don’t think of these specific things when you’re forming the words, it’s not so self-conscious, but when Dustin dared me, I thought to myself, ‘Well, I’ve got to set it up’: ‘The grand old painter died last night / His paintings on the wall / Before he went, he bade us well / And said goodnight to us all’. Then it strays from the point, which is what a lot of my songs do, for who will ever know what Picasso did at three in the morning, but the lines sounded good: ‘Three o’clock in the morning / I’m getting ready for bed / It came without a warning / But I’ll be waiting for you, baby / I’ll be waiting for you there’. And then I could use his words: ‘Drink to me’.

In normal speech, which is presumably what Picasso was doing, it’s just something ordinary that was said earnestly: ‘Drink to me!’ But once it’s set down in a magazine, it’s halfway to becoming a poem, and someone like Dustin will read it and think, ‘Picasso’s last words. That’s a great quote.’ And I agreed. I’m always pleased when things happen like that.

Left: Dustin Hoffman with a 'rag bag' on his head. Jamaica, 1973

Pages 592–593: Handwritten score for 'Picasso's Last Words (Drink to Me)'

Dustin asked, 'Could you write a song about that?' I didn't know, but I had my guitar with me, so I hit a chord and started singing a melody to those words, and he was flabbergasted.

PICASSOS LAST WORDS (DRINK TO ME...)

The grand old painter died last night
His paintings on the wall
Before he went he bade us well
And said goodnight to us all

CHORUS Drink to me, drink to my health,
You know I cant drink any more
Drink to me, drink to my health,
You know I can't drink any more
MIDDLE 3 oclock in the morning
I'm getting ready for bed
It came without a warning
But I'll be waiting for you baby
I'll be waiting for you there
So Drink to me drink to my health
You know I cant drink any more
Drink to me drink to my health
You know I cant drink any more

FRENCH INTERLUDE.
(TEMPO CHANGE)
JET —— Drink to me CHORUS
(TEMPO) DRUNKEN CHORUS
FRENCH (TEMPO) Drink to me - HO HEY HO

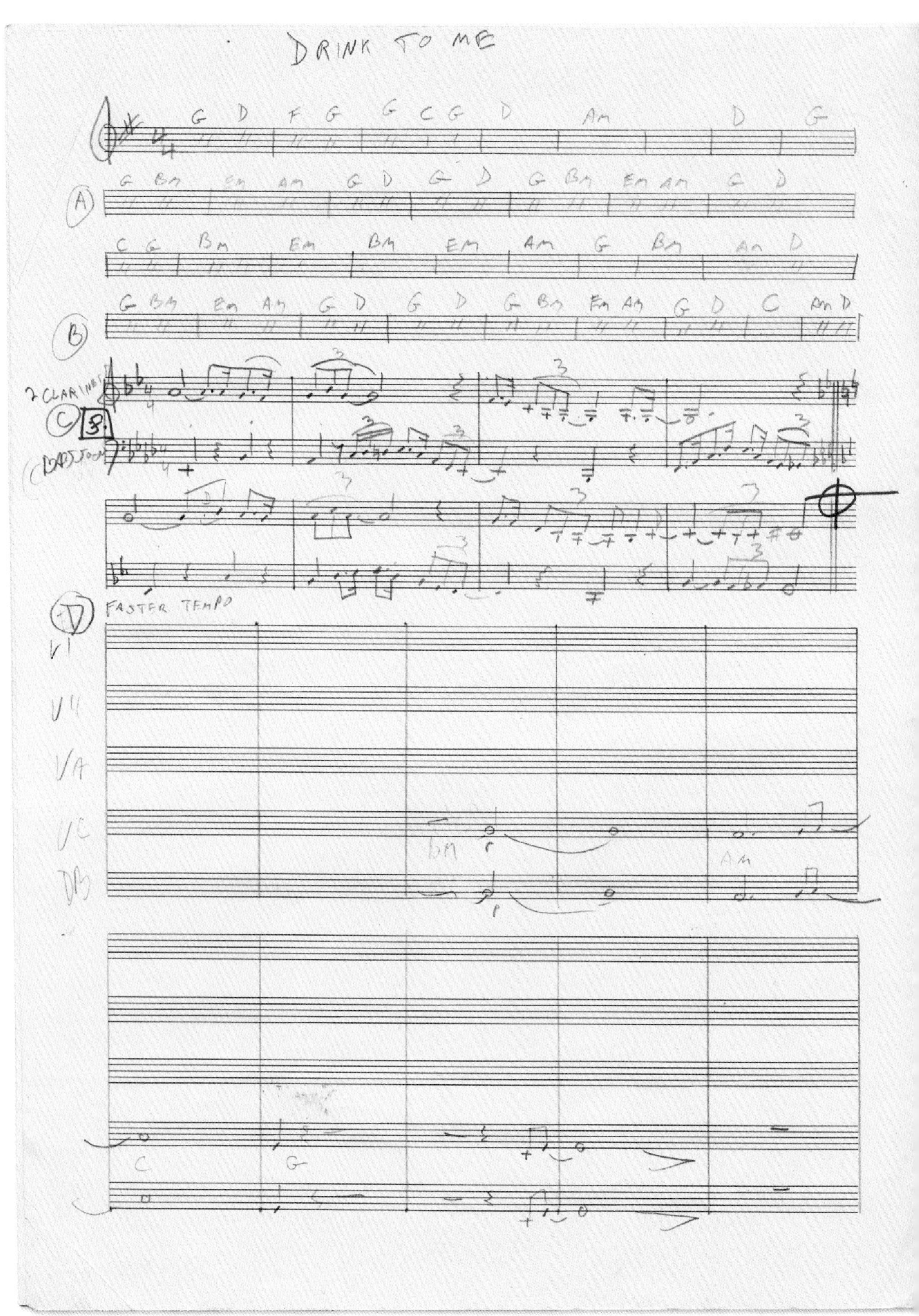
DRINK TO ME
A
B
2 CLARINETS
C
BASSOON
D
FASTER TEMPO
VI
VII
VA
VC
DB

DRINK TO ME P. 2
Bm
Am
C
G
E
8VA
mf
G
Bm
mf
Em
Am
G
D
G

Pipes of Peace

WRITER	Paul McCartney
ARTIST	Paul McCartney
RECORDED	AIR Studios, London
RELEASED	*Pipes of Peace*, 1983
	Single, 1983

I light a candle to our love
In love our problems disappear
But all in all we soon discover
That one and one is all we long to hear

All round the world
Little children being
Born to the world
Got to give them all we can
Til the war is won
Then will the work be done

Help them to learn
Songs of joy instead of
Burn baby burn
Let us show them how to play
The pipes of peace
Play the pipes of peace

Help me to learn
Songs of joy instead of
Burn baby burn
Won't you show me how to play
The pipes of peace
Play the pipes of peace

What do you say?
Will the human race
Be run in a day?
Or will someone save
This planet we're playing on
Is it the only one?
What are we going to do?

Help them to see
That the people here
Are like you and me
Let us show them how to play
The pipes of peace
Play the pipes of peace

I light a candle to our love
In love our problems disappear
But all in all we soon discover
That one and one is all we long to hear

THE QUAINTLY, IF ACCURATELY, NAMED PHILIP SON & NEPHEW WAS the bookshop in Liverpool in which I spent quite a lot of time. I've always liked bookshops, since I was a kid. I love the smell of them. I love the fact that all this work is collected together under one roof.

Around the time 'Pipes of Peace' was being written at the beginning of the eighties, I was in another favourite bookshop, Daunt Books on Marylebone High Street, and I found a book by the Bengali poet Rabindranath Tagore, who won a Nobel Prize. One of Tagore's poems had a line 'light a candle' or something similar, and I just moved it around a bit. That was the start of this song. Tagore, with his sunken eyes and long, flowing beard, looks interesting in photographs, so that might've attracted me to him, but I really liked his poetry, so I nicked this one line.

I might've misremembered the line. It might've just been the idea of lighting a candle to love, but that was what I remembered. It's what we all long to hear: getting together, love for one another, 'Little children being / Born to the world', giving all we can till the war - the war that is life, as well as the war, wherever it may be today, that is maiming our planet - is won. 'Songs of joy instead of / Burn baby burn' was a phrase that became famous after the disturbances in Watts that destroyed much of downtown Los Angeles. So this song, written years later, became a sort of anthem for peace, which was very heartening. Heartening, too, that it was number one in the UK in December 1983.

My upbeat attitude really goes back to my Liverpool upbringing. After the war the people there were amazingly optimistic; they were just so glad to get out of that hole. Our family's annual New Year's Eve party was a joyous thing where everyone sat around singing. It was all optimistic songs - 'Roll out the barrel / We'll have a barrel of fun' - tunes like that. My dad was on the piano, and everyone was having a grand old time. I'm very lucky to have been born into such a happy family.

Above: Dad Jim with Auntie Jin at the piano. Liverpool

As a boy, I thought everyone's family was like that, until I met people like John and realised that wasn't true, and perhaps it was the contrast of our different outlooks that produced a kind of magic. But I was born into that way of thinking, that it'll be okay in the end. Tragedy can happen but the page will turn, and I love that. Realising that I have a reach in the world, that people listen to my stuff, I feel a responsibility (though perhaps I wouldn't put it quite so boldly as that), to be optimistic till I no longer can be. That attitude naturally creeps into my songs because I know that these songs are going to go somewhere, and I think it would be nice if they make people take a positive path. I'm going to be optimistic until it's no longer possible, and the situation would have to be pretty *Blade Runner*, pretty bad, for me to not be able to think, 'Let's sing a song . . .'

It was also great fun making the video for this song. It was directed by a guy called Keith McMillan, with whom I'd made some other things. He had worked for the BBC, then he'd left and gone freelance. He and I were talking about 'Pipes of Peace', and I remembered a piece of film that was shown on the telly when I was a kid, about soldiers in the trenches greeting each other in No Man's Land and having a game of football on Christmas Day 1914. That's where we started visually, so in the video I play both a British and a German soldier.

Above: On the set of the 'Pipes of Peace' music video. Clobham Common, Surrey, 1983

PIPES OF PEACE

I light a candle to our love
In love our problems disappear
But all in all we soon discover
That one and one is all we want to hear.

1. All round the world
Little children being born to the world
Got to give them all we can till the war is won
Then will the work be done.

CHORUS. ~~Help~~ Help them to learn, songs of joy instead of burn, baby, burn,
Let us show them how to play — the pipe of peace.
— Repeat — (SINGLE END)
— Instrumental —

CHORUS. Help me to learn songs of joy instead of burn baby burn,
Won't you show me how to play — the p. o. p.
— Repeat — (DOUBLE END.)

2. What do you say? will the human race be run in a day
Or will someone save ~~this~~ the planet we're playing on
Is it the only one?

Help them to see, that the people hear are like you and me,
Let us show them how to play the p. o. p.
— Repeat — (DOUBLE END.)

~~I~~ I light a candle to our love
In love our problems disappear
And all in all we soon discover
That one & one is all we want to hear

C. — p. o. p. riff.
A min. — E. END.

Poster for the 'Pipes of Peace' single, 1983

PEACE
THE SINGLE
AND GOOD WILL TO ALL MEN

Please Please Me

WRITERS	John Lennon and Paul McCartney
ARTIST	The Beatles
RECORDED	Abbey Road Studios, London
RELEASED	Single, 1963
	Please Please Me, 1963
	Introducing...The Beatles, 1964

Last night I said these words to my girl
I know you never even try, girl

Come on (come on)
Come on (come on)
Come on (come on)
Come on (come on)
Please please me
Whoa yeah like I please you

You don't need me to show the way, love
Why do I always have to say, love

Come on (come on)
Come on (come on)
Come on (come on)
Come on (come on)
Please please me
Whoa yeah like I please you

I don't wanna sound complaining
But you know there's always rain in my heart
(in my heart)
I do all the pleasin' with you
It's so hard to reason with you
Whoa yeah why do you make me blue?

Last night I said these words to my girl
I know you never even try, girl

Come on (come on)
Come on (come on)
Come on (come on)
Come on (come on)
Please please me
Whoa yeah like I please you
(Please me)
Whoa yeah like I please you
(Please me)
Whoa yeah like I please you

Above: Schoolbook drawings by John Lennon, mid-1950s

WE WROTE WITH TWO GUITARS, JOHN AND I. AND, AS I've mentioned previously, the joy of that was that I was left-handed while he was right-handed, so I was looking in a mirror and he was looking in a mirror.

We would always tune up, have a ciggie, drink a cup of tea, start playing some stuff, look for an idea. Normally, one or the other of us would arrive with a fragment of a song. 'Please Please Me' was a John idea. John liked the double meaning of 'please'. Yeah, 'please' is, you know, pretty please. 'Please have intercourse with me. So, pretty please, have intercourse with me, I beg you to have intercourse with me.' He liked that, and I liked that he liked that. This was the kind of thing we'd see in each other, the kind of thing in which we were matched up. We were in sync.

There is an old Bing Crosby song called 'Please', and the opening line is 'Please lend your little ear to my pleas'. Even if you'd never heard the song before, you would hear – aha, okay – two meanings at work. We both enjoyed wordplay. I recently bought a lot of drawings and writings by John. I have them on the wall so I get to look at them all the time, and it's just pun city. That was part of John's cleverness. Anything that could be distorted, was.

'Please Please Me' arrived as a very slow song when John brought it in. I heard it and straightaway said, 'Orbisonesque.' In fact, Orbison should have sung it. I don't know if he ever did, but it has Roy written all over it. If you slow it down and do an impression of him, it fits exactly.

But then our producer, George Martin, changed it. George liked the song when we brought it in, but he said, 'Do you think we could do it faster?' We were like, 'No, no, no,' but George, being very persuasive, said, 'Let's just try it. If you don't like it, we don't have to.' He said, 'I think this could be your first number one.' So, grudgingly, we lifted the tempo, and it was, indeed, our first number one.

That was one of the great things about working in collaboration. I could bring something in that John would spot needed alteration. He would bring something in that I would spot needed alteration. Then, if neither of us spotted the problem, George Martin would. That collaboration made The Beatles a very lucky little group to be in.

Left: George Martin at the piano during *The Beatles* recording sessions. Abbey Road Studios, London, 1968

Right: With John Lennon in the dressing room before The Beatles' appearance on *Thank Your Lucky Stars*. Birmingham, 1963

Pretty Boys

WRITER	Paul McCartney
ARTIST	Paul McCartney
RECORDED	Hog Hill Mill, Sussex
RELEASED	*McCartney III*, 2020

Look into my lens
Give me all you got
Work it for me, baby
Let me take my best shot

Meet the Pretty Boys
A line of bicycles for hire
Objects of desire
Working for the squire
You can look but you'd better not touch

'Cause here come the Pretty Boys
They're gonna set your world on fire
Objects of desire
Preaching to the choir
They can talk but they never say much

Strike another pose
Try to feel the light
Hey the camera loves you
Don't put up a fight

There go the Pretty Boys
A row of cottages for rent
For your main event
They're what the angels sent
You can look but you'd better not touch

Look into my lens
Try to feel the light
Hey the camera loves you
It's gonna be alright

Oh here come the Pretty Boys
A line of bicycles for hire
Objects of desire
When they're working for the squire
You can look but you'd better not touch

The Pretty Boys
(But you'd better not touch)
The Pretty Boys

Above: New York, 2020

IT'S ABOUT MALE MODELS. I'D READ AN ARTICLE ABOUT A GROUP of male models who were suing one or two photographers because they'd been abused and humiliated by them.

Some of the photographers they were talking about I knew. Now, I didn't actually know what they got up to in those particular sessions, but because I'd been photographed by them, I did know that the modus operandi of these photographers was to say, 'Come on, baby. Come on, give it to me. Come on, fuck me. Oh, show me that tit . . .'

In other words, they tended to be extremely vulgar. It used to come with the territory. You'd say, 'That's just him.' He'd say, 'Come on, pretend you're fucking some chick.' This is the way some of those guys worked, to get you to not just stand there looking boring. They were trying to excite something. Like people in so many professions – pop stars, cops – they'd become caricatures of themselves.

That's why I wondered whether some of these models just didn't understand the murky territory they'd entered. It may also be that the photographers went further and touched the models inappropriately. That I don't know, but this song is fictional, and I was imagining the models getting upset simply because of the vulgar attitude that these photographers had.

The song starts off with the photographer saying, 'Look into my lens / Give me all you got / Work it for me, baby / Let me take my best shot'. That's a mild representation of how the photographers worked back in the sixties and seventies – only now they would be ten times more vulgar. I was imagining a line of male models, and they are a line of bicycles for hire and objects of desire. They're trying to get you to desire them in the pages of a magazine, but they're working for the squire. In the magazine world, the photographers are a pretty big deal.

'They can talk but they never say much'. Models aren't traditionally known to be the most intellectual people going - disclaimer! - although I know some who are extremely intelligent, and it's always tricky to generalise with any profession. 'There go the Pretty Boys / A row of cottages for rent'. I'm imagining the sort of little sheds you can rent on seafronts. I've come to understand that "cottaging" refers to gay sex in a public toilet, but that meaning wasn't in my mind at the time I wrote the song.

I've got this very simple little guitar line - just two fingers on the strings, and then the other notes are all open. That's all it is.

'You can look but you'd better not touch'. You'll see a model giving you a come-hither look from a magazine. That's what they're supposed to be doing, because you're supposed to want to buy the clothes they've got on or the product they're selling. This song focuses on the experience of male models, but it's the same with female models and the bra they're wearing; you're supposed to think, 'My girlfriend would look good in that.' Models are used to selling commodities, and I suspect they've also commodified themselves.

It was interesting to put 'Pretty Boys' together, as it's a perspective I don't often write from. But that's one of the joys of being a writer. A lot of people might have a similar thought - in this instance, about the treatment of models - but don't have an outlet for it. I'm lucky to have the opportunity to crystallise these thoughts into a song. The idea of a model being treated as a commodity raises interesting comparisons to The Beatles too. We were musicians, not models, but at the height of Beatlemania, people wanted to put our names and faces on all manner of things, and it felt out of control sometimes.

So, that was part of the reasoning behind setting up Apple and then, later on in my case, MPL. It was a liberation for us from the men in suits who had been in charge before. We no longer had to work for the squire. Now, we could take control of our destinies. And MPL celebrated its fiftieth birthday in 2019, so it seems to have worked out pretty well.

Right: Photographed by daughter Mary. Sussex, 2020

Left: With Magic Alex, John Lennon and Neil Aspinall promoting Apple Corps. Hans Christian Andersen statue, Central Park. New York, 1968

Below: The 'Apple Jacket' designed by fashion boutique Dandie Fashions, as worn to the launch of Apple Corps. New York, 1968

So, that was part of the reasoning behind setting up Apple and then, later on in my case, MPL. It was a liberation for us from the men in suits who had been in charge before.

PRETTY BOYS

(Intro riffs)

(A) Look into my lens
Give me all you've got
Work it for me baby
Let me take my best shot

(1) Meet the Pretty Boys
A line of bicycles for hire
Objects of desire
Working for the Squire
You can look but you'd better not touch
(short riffs)

(2) Here come the Pretty Boys
They gonna set your world on fire
Objects of desire
Preaching to the choir
They can talk but they never say much

(B) Strike another pose
Try to feel the Light
Hey - the camera loves you
Don't put up a fight

(A2)
Look into my lens
Try to feel the light
Hey the camera loves you
It's gonna be alright

SOLO (Verse)
(short riffs)

(3) There go the Pretty Boys
A row of cottages to rent
For your main event
They're what the angels sent
You can look but you'd better not touch
The Pretty Boys
Repeat A2/ Verse (1) END.

Pretty Little Head

WRITERS	Paul McCartney and Eric Stewart
ARTIST	Paul McCartney
RECORDED	Hog Hill Mill, Sussex
RELEASED	*Press to Play*, 1986 UK single, 1986

Hillmen, hillmen, hillmen, hillmen
Oh, oh, oh, oh
Hillmen come down from the lava
Forging across the mighty river flow
Always forever
Only so you don't worry
Your pretty little head

Ursa Major
Ursa Minor
Ursa Major
Ursa Minor

Hillmen, hillmen, hillmen, hillmen
Oh, oh, oh, oh
Hillmen bring garments, spices
Carrying trinkets, silk and precious stones
Exotic legends
Only so you don't worry
Your pretty little head

Hillmen, hillmen, hillmen, hillmen
Oh, oh, oh, oh
Hillmen are sworn to allegiance
Living a life of silent dignity
For your protection
Only so you don't worry
Your pretty little head

Ursa Major
Ursa Minor
Ursa Major
Ursa Minor

The hillmen
Living in the higher reaches

'HILLMEN' IS A WORD I REMEMBER THINKING ABOUT LONG AND hard. Sometimes when I'm blocking out a song, I just sort of hear a word and I think, 'Well, that doesn't mean anything,' and I keep trying to change it but it just keeps coming back, and in the end I go, 'Oh, sod it, it doesn't matter. It fits. I don't know what it means.' This 'hillmen' is a case in point. I've no idea where it came from.

I remember having a lot of fun thinking about tribesmen, and I'm calling them 'hillmen'; I'm getting a bit Neanderthal here, even a bit Viking. I've become a sucker for Egyptology and the study of ancient civilisations, and I do read a lot about that and watch a lot of it on TV, so the idea of creating my own tribe and my own ancient civilisation must have appealed to me.

Next thing you know, it cross-fades into a love song. I've just created a big tribal picture and then thrown in that little line that just trips it up: '. . . don't worry / Your pretty little head', which was very modern and very eighties, but actually quite a contrast to the rest of the song. I'm sure the Vikings would have had an equivalent term.

I suppose that is what different civilisations are about; all of this palaver – the Chinese palaver, American palaver, British palaver, South American palaver – is just to make sure that we're taken care of. It's to protect us. In a way, civilisation exists so that we don't have to worry our 'pretty little heads'. In itself, that simple reason for existence is not without its dangers, of course.

I may be looking for a tribe that doesn't exist anymore. It's just a fanciful tribe, and I enjoy creating my own history for them. It's getting a bit spiritual, like the Aztecs, but definitely Northern Hemisphere. How do I see them? Sort of Viking-like, but without the helmets. They're fording the mighty river flows and looking at the stars, and they're trading goods. So in that respect, I'm making up my own Vikings and ferrying them over to Britain.

'Living in the higher reaches'. What I'm thinking about is the higher reaches of spirituality, but higher can also be interpreted as taking the higher road. The moral high ground. Or looking at it another way, it could be a druggie thing. It's fanciful, but one thing I've discovered, going through all of my lyrics, is that I've got quite a broad style and I'll allow myself almost anything – including the techno feel of this song, techno being very big at the time.

Above: Hog Hill Mill, Sussex, 1984

ON THE MOVE
Tribe
"...Stampede"...
dust· C.U.

PRETTY LITTLE HEAD.

(Intro) in a palace troubadour / girl (reflected in ornate mirror mood lighting)
tells story / reacts.

① lava. (caravan, dust, C.U.'s)

(danger →). mighty river
drownings / fast current

(p. l. h.)
troubadour — girl.

"logo" Δ
blue (woad.)
great faces
horses, motor
cattle, bikes
Stampede, dust
spray, water
crossing

Bridge.

② garments, spices, trinkets
Δ

Exotic legends. (beards oiled
things tied in...
(..small ribbons)

(p. l. h.)

INT. tent
jewellery,
clothes.
T.V.
card game
("stick".)
Charm bracelet.
african tribal
make-ups.

Bridge (troubadour / twirl.)

storytelling
kids at feet.

③ palace attack (danger)
allegiance. ("new" martial arts moves.)
("branded" with Δ)

... silent dignity (guards.)

"new" hieroglyphics

(p. l. h.)
troub. walks off → OFF-SET director walks in
mime CUT — freeze cast — walk off
"take care of you".

bracelet
on wrist

Hillmen Uniquerace.

Tribe of Hill people. Traders. Warriors. Priests.

Style. — mixture of many past tribes (plus "modern aspect") (bikes / TVs (portables))

ie. Cossacks

Egyptians

Afghanistans

Celtic races

Druids

Buddhist ("oranges") (– greens)

Red Indian.

Quest for fire primitives.

Hippy colony

Have "raided" best of all cultures.
meditation. vegetarian (spices)
Candles

Wall hangings

painters / paintings

abstract –

tattoos

"giraffe neck" women.

gold.

triangle "charm" bracelet

Army on the move ——
African materials
moroccan
dreadlocks
American Indian

HILLMEN.

mud make-ups.

Tribe includes .....

All types · female/male

old / young

dignified / bawdy

Put It There

WRITER	Paul McCartney
ARTIST	Paul McCartney
RECORDED	Hog Hill Mill, Sussex
RELEASED	*Flowers in the Dirt*, 1989
	Single, 1990

Give me your hand, I'd like to shake it
I want to show you I'm your friend
You'll understand if I can make it clear
It's all that matters in the end

Put it there if it weighs a ton
That's what a father said to his young son
I don't care if it weighs a ton
As long as you and I are here, put it there
Long as you and I are here, put it there

If there's a fight, I'd like to fix it
I hate to see things go so wrong
The darkest night and all its mixed emotions
Is getting lighter, sing along

Put it there if it weighs a ton
That's what a father said to his young son
I don't care if it weighs a ton
As long as you and I are here, put it there
Long as you and I are here, put it there

Above: With brother Mike, mum Mary and dad Jim. Liverpool, late 1940s

'PUT IT THERE' IS AN EXPRESSION MY DAD JIM OFTEN USED. HE was loaded with colourful expressions, as so many Liverpool people still are today. He loved to play with words, juggle them in his head, and he had loads of little sayings that were sometimes nonsensical, sometimes functional, but always rather lyrical. When he was shaking your hand he would say, 'Put it there if it weighs a ton.'

It's been pointed out more than enough times that the capital of Ireland is really Liverpool, and Liverpool certainly has a huge Irish component. Our humour is essentially Irish. We tend to see the fun in things. That's partly because of the bleakness that so often hung over people's lives.

My dad's generation had just been through a war, and although they'd won it, there was a lot of heartache and a lot of physical rebuilding, but at the same time an emotional optimism that was everywhere in the air. My dad and my uncles - Uncle Jack came round a lot - would always have a new joke, and it would be a good joke. He'd say, 'Here, son, have you heard the one about the mannequin?' and he'd tell some great joke, then he'd give you two and six, or half a crown, and say, 'Here you are, son. You treat yourself.' So, I really count myself very lucky to have been at that party because, looking back, it was pretty sensational. But now it's over. That party's over.

Anyway, my dad had a million of these funny phrases, and often I thought they were so good that I wanted to write a song about them. Another one of these expressions was, 'There's no hairs on a seagull's chest.' Your guess is as good as mine as to what it really means, but it's such a beautiful line that I'm pretty sure I'm going to feature it in a song one of these days.

It's strange, since I'm now in my seventies, but I was thinking the other day about how my dad spanked us on the legs if we were naughty boys, which we were. Mostly inadvertently, we'd screw with the rules, and he

Right: Dad Jim photographed by Paul. Heswall, 1966

would spank us on the legs and say, 'This hurts me more than it hurts you.' We never dared say it, of course, but we'd be thinking, 'Well, then stop, if it's hurting you.' Now I get it. As a parent, I get what he meant.

'Put it there if it weighs a ton.' I'm not sure I thought of it at the time, even though this was well after The Beatles disbanded, but I can't help connecting the oppressiveness associated with that phrase to the oppressiveness that coincided with the end of The Beatles. Not that The Beatles are over exactly. It's not like we were some little band that never had another record; even though half of us have died, the phenomenon continues stronger than ever. Everything I do seems to be painted with 'Beatle', and there is always some sort of echo that comes from that echo chamber. My daughter Mary jokes, 'I can't get away from you,' because she'll see me on the underground - a picture of me, or some advert of The Beatles or something - or she'll turn on the radio and they're playing a Beatles song. Some might regard this as a burden, and some celebrities, like Greta Garbo, have become hermits, but I'm very happy about it all because I think it was a great thing we achieved and I'm very proud of it. Rather than secluding myself, I feel a genuine responsibility to give back to all those fans what they've given to us over the years.

I cannot help but realise that so much of what I do is still entangled with the fact that I was in The Beatles. In fact, I say to people that I still am in The Beatles. Well, maybe not *in* The Beatles, but I'm still 'a Beatle'. The philosophy we had was, and remains, very attractive; it's a whole-world picture - an insistence on the freedom of creative thought that we discovered and that I still love. You'll never see a photo of Ringo without him giving the peace sign and saying, 'Peace and love'. It's an old philosophy, but always timely. And a lot of the Beatles stuff still is amazingly timely, so I'm happy to bathe in it.

I wonder whether I wanted to direct this song towards John - whether it's not, in its own way, a peace offering to a man who died way too early. 'If there's a fight, I'd like to fix it / I hate to see things go so wrong'. But then I'm an eternal optimist: 'The darkest night and all its mixed emotions / Is getting lighter, sing along'. The ending of 'Put It There' is particularly upbeat: 'As long as you and I are here, put it there'. A little wordplay at the end.

Mostly inadvertently, we'd screw with the rules, and he would spank us on the legs and say, 'This hurts me more than it hurts you.' We never dared say it, of course, but we'd be thinking, 'Well, then stop, if it's hurting you.' Now I get it. As a parent, I get what he meant.

PUT IT THERE.

Put it there
if it weighs a ton
That's what a father said
to his young son.
I don't care if it weighs a ton,
As long as you and I are here
Put it there
long as you and I are here
Put it there!

Paul McCartney.

Drawing by Paul used for the 'Put It There' single, 1990

It's been pointed out more than enough times that the capital of Ireland is really Liverpool, and Liverpool certainly has a huge Irish component. Our humour is essentially Irish. We tend to see the fun in things.

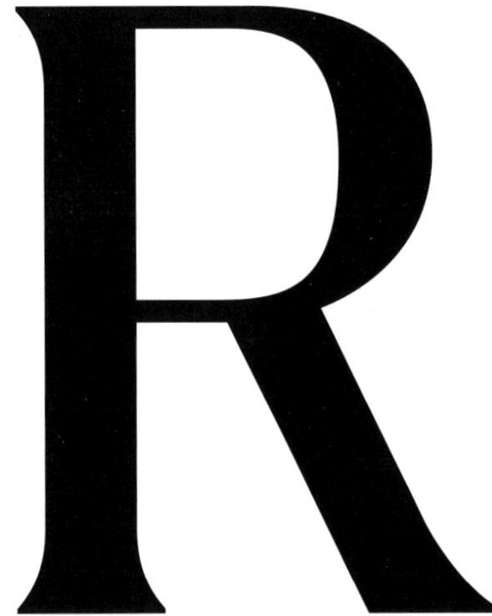

Rocky Raccoon

WRITERS	Paul McCartney and John Lennon
ARTIST	The Beatles
RECORDED	Abbey Road Studios, London
RELEASED	*The Beatles*, 1968

Now somewhere in the black mountain
hills of Dakota
There lived a young boy named Rocky Raccoon
And one day his woman ran off with another guy
Hit young Rocky in the eye
Rocky didn't like that
He said, I'm gonna get that boy
So one day he walked into town
Booked himself a room in the local saloon

Rocky Raccoon checked into his room
Only to find Gideon's Bible
Rocky had come equipped with a gun
To shoot off the legs of his rival
His rival, it seems, had broken his dreams
By stealing the girl of his fancy
Her name was Magill and she called herself Lil
But everyone knew her as Nancy

Now she and her man who called himself Dan
Were in the next room at the hoedown
Rocky burst in and grinning a grin
He said, Danny boy, this is a showdown
But Daniel was hot he drew first and shot
And Rocky collapsed in the corner

Now the doctor came in stinking of gin
And proceeded to lie on the table
He said, Rocky, you met your match
And Rocky said, Doc, it's only a scratch
And I'll be better, I'll be better, Doc, as soon as I am able
Now Rocky Raccoon he fell back in his room
Only to find Gideon's Bible
Gideon checked out and he left it no doubt
To help with good Rocky's revival

ONE OF THE GREAT THINGS ABOUT THIS SONG IS THAT IT WORKS perfectly well with just me on the guitar. Come to think of it, that's how it was written!

When you're sitting around with an acoustic guitar, often the natural thing to do is to get a bit folky. I was doing a bit of a spoof on records I'd heard, kind of talking blues songs. Bob Dylan was doing that kind of thing, so I just started imagining the Black Hills in South Dakota. I knew of an old song, 'The Black Hills of Dakota', which begins, 'Take me back to the black hills / The black hills of Dakota.' That was Doris Day in *Calamity Jane*. So, we were doing this rap, and I just dreamt up a character called 'Rocky Raccoon', because of Davy Crockett and his raccoon cap. I'd watched *Davy Crockett* on telly, starring Fess Parker, when I was a kid. I saw the TV show, but my main thing was the song: 'Davy Crockett, King of the Wild Frontier'. It was quite a cool song.

I just started imagining this little story, and for me it's like going on a train ride or something - a train ride of the mind. And because I was doing it sort of tongue-in-cheek, it was quite pleasant to write and sing. There were poems that people - a drunken uncle perhaps? - would recite at parties, like Robert Service's 'The Shooting of Dan McGrew' or Marriott Edgar's 'The Lion and Albert', made famous by Stanley Holloway's stage recitation, in which the lion eats Albert and the parents complain to the zookeeper. It's that kind of black humour.

Above: With George Harrison, Ringo Starr and John Lennon during *The Beatles* recording sessions. Trident Studios, London, 1968

In 'Rocky Raccoon', his woman runs off with another guy, and Rocky doesn't like that. Then he books himself a room, only to find the Gideon Bible. Well, those were in every hotel in America. Probably still are. We'd never seen that in England. So I just thought about that image - checking into a room, looking in the desk, opening the drawer and there's a Bible. Rocky's girlfriend's name was Magill: '. . . she called herself Lil / But everyone knew her as Nancy'. And it's nice that I've ended up married to a Nancy.

The doctor stinking of gin? I did once have an accident in Liverpool where I fell off a moped and busted my lip open, and we had to get the doctor round to my cousin Betty's house. That was around this same time, when I was twenty-something and going out on the moped from my dad's house to Betty's house. I was taking a friend, Tara Guinness. He died later in a car accident. He was a nice boy. I wrote about him in 'A Day in the Life': 'He blew his mind out in a car / He didn't notice that the lights had changed'. Anyway, I was with Tara and had an accident – fell off my moped, busted my lip, went to Betty's, and she said, 'Get a doctor, get a doctor. It needs stitches.'

So they got this guy, and he arrived stinking of gin. This guy was so drunk. 'Hello, Paul. How are you?' 'Great.' 'Oh yes, that's going to need stitches. I've brought my bag.' So he brings his black bag and now he's got to try and thread a little needle, a curved surgical needle, but he's seeing three needles at least.

I think I said, 'Let us do it.' And we threaded it for him. I said, 'You're just going to do this with no anaesthetic?' He said, 'Well, I haven't got any.' I think I might have had a slug of scotch or something. He just put the needle in and pulled it round. And then the thread came out and he said, 'Oh, I'm sorry, I have to do that again.'

So he had to do it a second bloody time, and I was trying not to scream. To be honest, he really didn't do a marvellous job, and I had this bump in my lip for a good while after. I can still feel it. And I was black and blue and really quite a mess. So I decided to grow a moustache. Then the other Beatles saw it and liked it, so they all grew moustaches too. John got so into it that I think somebody bought him a moustache cup with a little lid that sort of stops the moustache from getting wet when you drink. That's where I think this 'stinking of gin' image came from – from this little painful memory.

I keep meaning to do this song in concert, since a lot of people request it. Maybe I will one of these days.

So they got this guy, and he arrived stinking of gin. This guy was so drunk. 'Hello, Paul. How are you?' 'Great.' 'Oh yes, that's going to need stitches. I've brought my bag.' So he brings his black bag and now he's got to try and thread a little needle, a curved surgical needle, but he's seeing three needles at least.

(7)

ROCKY RACOON.

1. Rocky Racoon checked into his room
Only to find Gideons bible.

2. Rocky had come, equipped with a gun,
To shoot off the legs of his rival,

3. His rival it seems had broken his dreams
By stealing the girl of his fancy.

4. Her name was McGill, she called herself
Lil,
But everyone knew her as Nancy

5. She and her man, who called himself
Dan,
Were in the next room at the hoedown,

(8)

6. Rocky burst in, + grinning a grin
Said Danny boy. this is a Showdown,

7. Daniel was hot, he drew first + shot
+ Rocky collapsed in the corner.
SCREAM.... SOLO ....

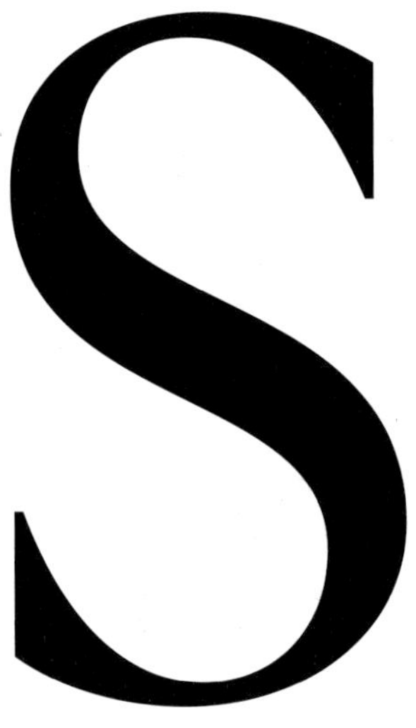

San Ferry Anne

WRITERS	Paul McCartney and Linda McCartney
ARTIST	Wings
RECORDED	Abbey Road Studios, London
RELEASED	*At the Speed of Sound*, 1976

You've got a lot
And from what you've got
I'd say you're doing well, dear

Dressed like a dream
And if things are what they seem
You're looking swell, dear

Your little man
Brings you trinkets when he can
But he can't stay, dear

That's very well
But inside your shiny shell
You dance all day, dear

So go, be gay
Let your feelings leap away
Into the laughter

San Ferry Anne
And the world keeps turning
Happy ever after

YOU DIDN'T HEAR AN AWFUL LOT OF GERMAN MUSIC AFTER THE war. Maybe there was a good reason for that! But French songs got over to Britain, not only because we had been allies but because France was so close, and there were some lovely melodies. As a boy in those early post-war years, I remember hearing Édith Piaf and Maurice Chevalier, Jacques Brel and Juliette Gréco. We fancied Juliette, very much.

But I didn't study French in school. Most British kids did. John did; he wasn't very good at it, mind you. I chose Spanish, German and Latin, but because of the big hits that came over from France, almost any kid of my generation – including me – knew certain phrases, and in saying those words and in hearing them, my imagination almost unconsciously played with them. In this regard, 'San Ferry Anne' was a pun on *ça ne fait rien* ('it doesn't matter'). 'San Ferry Anne' was an instance of my trying to write a French song, as I had done with 'Michelle'. So here's San Ferry Anne, and she's a doll. She looks good, she's got a sugar daddy, a 'little man', who's buying her trinkets and things, but inside her shiny shell it seems like all's not right. *Ça ne fait rien*.

I have another one that I haven't written yet: 'Sausage on Show', or *saucisson chaud*. It would be a sausage in a theatre, a sausage wearing a boater. Come on, roll up, and see the sausage on show. We may have to wait a while for that one!

Above: *At the Speed of Sound* recording sessions. Abbey Road Studios, London, 1975

East Hampton, 1975

you get a lot
and from what you've got
I'd say you're doing well, dear

Dressed like a dream
And if things are what
they seem ~~you're looking~~ swell, dear
your looking

Your little man
Brings you trinkets when
he can but he can't stay dear

Thats very well, ~~but~~
t inside your shiny shell
you dance all day, dear

So go be gay
let your feelings leap away
into the laughter
an ferry ann
and the world keeps turning
happy ever after.

Say Say Say

WRITERS	Paul McCartney and Michael Jackson
ARTIST	Paul McCartney and Michael Jackson
RECORDED	AIR Studios, London; Odyssey Studios, London; Cherokee Studios, Los Angeles; and Sigma Sound Studios, New York
RELEASED	Single, 1983 *Pipes of Peace*, 1983

Say say say
What you want
But don't play games
With my affection
Take take take
What you need
But don't leave me
With no direction

All alone
I sit home by the phone
Waiting for you, baby
Through the years
How can you stand to hear
My pleading for you, dear?
You know I'm crying

Now go go go
Where you want
But don't leave me
Here forever
You you you
Stay away
So long, girl, I
See you never

What can I do
Girl, to get through to you
'Cause I love you, baby
Standing here
Baptised in all my tears
Baby, through the years
You know I'm crying

You never ever worry
And you never shed a tear
You're saying that
My love ain't real
Just look at my face
These tears ain't drying

You you you
Can never say
That I'm not the one
Who really loves you
I pray pray pray
Every day
That you'll see things
Girl, like I do

What can I do
Girl, to get through to you?
'Cause I love you, baby
Standing here
Baptised in all my tears
Baby, through the years
You know I'm crying
Say say say

IT WAS CHRISTMASTIME. SOMEBODY RANG ME UP, AND THIS HIGH voice I didn't recognise said, 'Hi, Paul.' I thought, 'This is a girl fan, and how the hell did she get my number?' I was quite annoyed. Then the voice said, 'It's Michael,' and suddenly it dawned on me. It wasn't a girl; it was Michael Jackson, and he basically said, 'Do you want to make some hits?' And I said, 'Well, yeah, sure. Come over here.' Our paths had crossed a few times before. Michael covered the Wings song 'Girlfriend' on his album *Off the Wall*, and I'd known his producer, Quincy Jones, for a long time. Quincy had picked up the Oscar for The Beatles when we won for best Original Song Score with *Let It Be* in 1971.

So, Michael flew to England and came to my office in London. We went up to the top floor, where I have a piano, and just started doing 'Say Say Say'. I let him lead quite a bit, and I think a lot of the sensibility of the song was Michael's. 'Baptised in all my tears' - that's a line I wouldn't have used. I would help with the tune, and he'd be throwing in the lyrics. We were both quite excited to work together, and the song came together pretty quickly; we were bouncing off each other. I wrote the lyrics down, and by the time we left the office we had 'Say Say Say'. I think the first time we recorded it as a demo, it was just the two of us singing and me on guitar.

For me, writing a song is just following a trail and then diverging from it and beating a new path. I set down a map of sorts, some rough coordinates, and then go there and find stuff on the way, just picking up little objects that happen to be lyrics or melodies. It's a time of discovery, and that's what I love about it. Before I write a song there's a sense of something missing, and I pick up my guitar or go to the piano, and afterwards - say, three hours later, if I'm in a productive mood - there won't be a hole anymore; there'll be a new object. It's a very satisfying feeling. You've created a car or a piece of furniture, or in my case a song. And it's not just something that takes up space in the world. With any luck, it helps define the world.

Above: With George Martin and Michael Jackson. AIR Studios, London, 1983

(1)
SAY SAY SAY what you want
but don't play games with my affections

TAKE TAKE TAKE what you need
but don't leave me with no direction
cos all alone I sit home by
the phone, waiting for you baby
All these years, how do you stand
to hear, my pleading for you dear
and hear me crying ooh oohooh
ooh ooh

(2) go go go where you want
But don't leave me here forever
But you you you stay away so long
girl I see you never.
it's plain to see girl that you
leaving me, for some other baby
so here's a tear for a souvenir
cause if he's not sincere
you'll know I'm crying
ooh ooh ooh ooh ah -

For me, writing a song is just following a trail and then diverging from it and beating a new path.

SAY SAY SAY.

1) PAUL 22
Say say say what you want
But don't play games with my affection.
Take take take / what you need 20 +13.
But don't leave me with no direction!
8. MICHAEL 15. All alone, I sit home by the phone.
Waiting for you .... Baby... 22
15 Through the years how can you stand to hear
My pleading for you dear – you know I'm crying... OOH.. PAUL EN

2) PAUL 20 22
Go go go / where you want
But don't leave me.. here forever
But you you you stay away 77.
So long girl – I .... see you never
What can I do ... girl to get through to you
17 Cos I love you ... baby...
Standing here – baptized in all my tears
Faithful through the years ... ~~Ooh~~ .....
You know I'm crying – ooh ...

= SOLO =

Sgt. Pepper's Lonely Hearts Club Band

WRITERS	Paul McCartney and John Lennon
ARTIST	The Beatles
RECORDED	Abbey Road Studios, London
RELEASED	*Sgt. Pepper's Lonely Hearts Club Band*, 1967

It was twenty years ago today
Sergeant Pepper taught the band to play
They've been going in and out of style
But they're guaranteed to raise a smile
So may I introduce to you
The act you've known for all these years
Sergeant Pepper's Lonely Hearts Club Band

We're Sergeant Pepper's Lonely Hearts Club Band
We hope you will enjoy the show
Sergeant Pepper's Lonely Hearts Club Band
Sit back and let the evening go
Sergeant Pepper's Lonely
Sergeant Pepper's Lonely
Sergeant Pepper's Lonely Hearts Club Band

It's wonderful to be here
It's certainly a thrill
You're such a lovely audience
We'd like to take you home with us
We'd love to take you home

I don't really want to stop the show
But I thought you might like to know
That the singer's going to sing a song
And he wants you all to sing along
So let me introduce to you
The one and only Billy Shears
And Sergeant Pepper's Lonely Hearts Club Band

ONE OF THE THINGS ABOUT THE BEATLES IS THAT WE noticed accidents. Then we acted upon them. When we had a tape playing backwards by accident, we would stop and go, 'What is that?' A lot of other people would go, 'Oh God, what is that bloody noise?' But we always loved being sidetracked by these ideas.

In this case, I'd gone to the US to see Jane Asher, who was touring in a Shakespeare production and was in Denver. So I flew out to Denver to stay with her for a couple of days and take a little break.

On the way back, I was with our roadie Mal Evans, and on the plane he said, 'Will you pass the salt and pepper?' I misheard him and said, 'What? Sergeant Pepper?'

We had recently played Candlestick Park. That was a show where we couldn't even hear ourselves; it was raining, we were nearly electrocuted and when we got off stage we were chucked into the back of a stainless steel minitruck. The minitruck was empty, and we were sliding round in it, and we all thought, 'Fuck, that's enough.'

That day we decided we wouldn't tour again. The idea was that we would make records, and the records would tour. We'd once heard that Elvis Presley had sent his gold-plated Cadillac on tour, and we thought that was just brilliant. So we thought, 'We'll make a record, and that'll be our gold-plated Cadillac.'

On the way back from Denver I suggested to the guys that we take on alter egos. The concept was that we'd stopped being The Beatles. We were now this other band.

I did a sketch in which the four of us were pictured in front of a floral clock. It was as if time stood still, because the clock was made of flowers. There was something lovely about that. The idea was that the band were going to be presented with a trophy by the Lord Mayor of London, or someone like that. So, we agreed on the cover idea, then went down to the costumier Monty Berman, in Soho, to be fitted with the band's outfits.

I must admit I'd taken some acid in Denver, and this was all a kind of game I was playing after that trip. I had drawn the sketch to show the guys what this new project might be like. They loved it. And it really freed us up. It gave us a kind of anonymity and a new lease on life.

Above: The Beatles at the *Sgt. Pepper's Lonely Hearts Club Band* press launch. London, 19 May 1967

Left: Suit designed by costumier Monty Berman, 1967

Right top: Alternative design for the drum skin featured on the cover of *Sgt. Pepper's Lonely Hearts Club Band*

SGT PEPPERS
LONELY HEARTS
CLUB BAND

M. Berman Ltd.
18 IRVING ST.
LEICESTER SQ. W.C.2
Paul

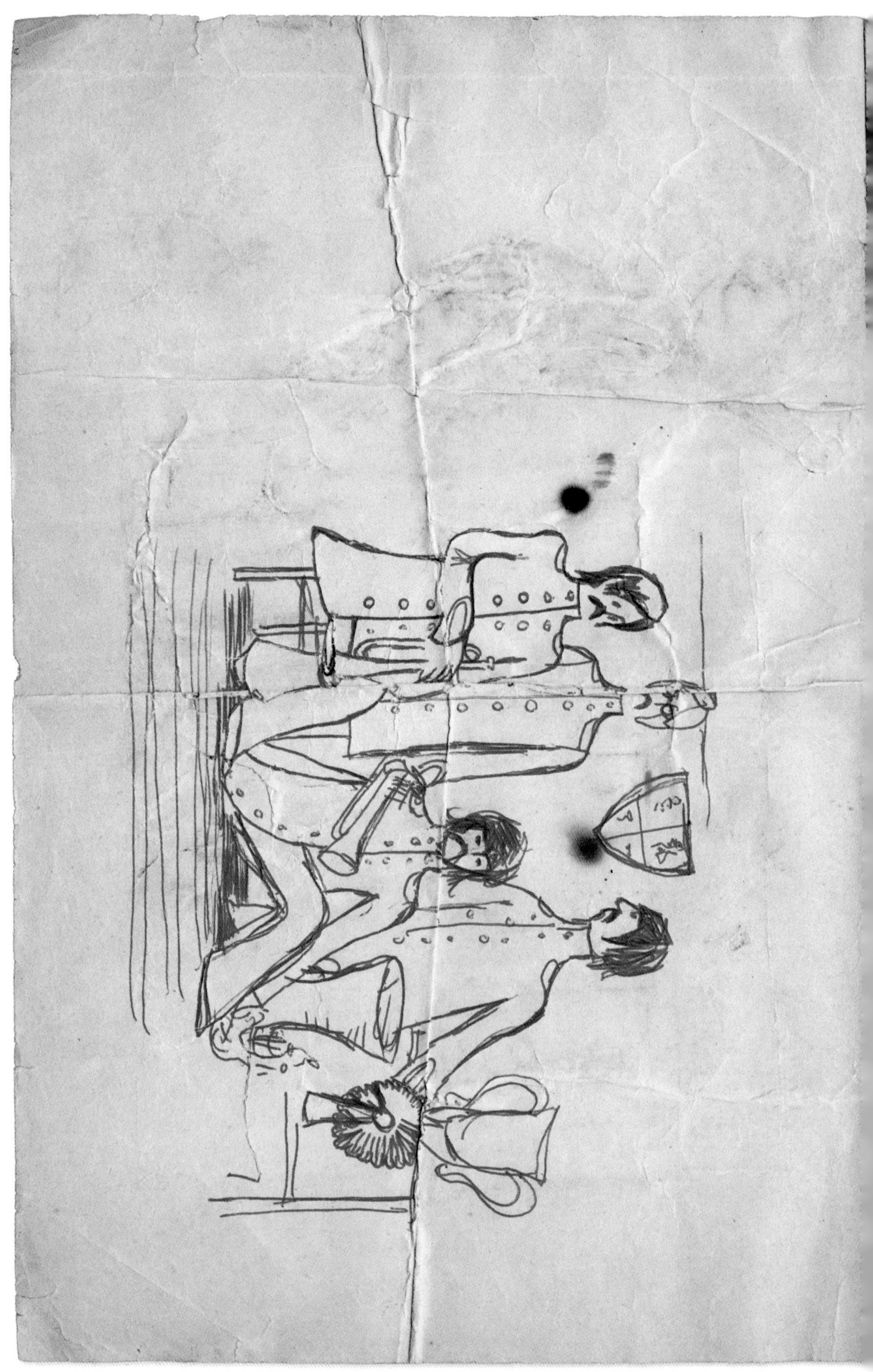

It was 20 yrs ago today
When Sgt. Pepper taught the band to play
They've been going in and out of style.
But they're guaranteed to raise a smile,
So may I introduce to you
The act you've known for all these years.
Sgt. Peppers Lonely hearts club band
Applause. Band – laughter mid solo
CHORUS. We're Sgt. Pepper ......
We hope you will enjoy the show
Sgt. Peppers l........
Sit back & let the evening go. Sgt. Peppers lonely
THEN DRUMS

~~really want to~~
I Don't ~~to~~ me stop the show
but I thought you might like to know
That the singers going to sing a song
And he wants you all to sing along,
So let me introduce to you,
The one & only Billy Shears,
AND SGT. PEPPERS LONELY HEARTS CLUB BAND.
Applause ... (different) into song.

It's wonderful to be here,
~~It's~~ certainly a thrill.
You're such a lovely audience,
We'd like to take you home with us,
we'd like to take you home

END
We Sgt Peppers lonely hearts club band
we hope you've all enjoyed the show
Sgt. Peppers etc .. but once again we've got to go.

She Came in Through the Bathroom Window

WRITERS	Paul McCartney and John Lennon
ARTIST	The Beatles
RECORDED	Abbey Road Studios, London
RELEASED	*Abbey Road*, 1969

She came in through the bathroom window
Protected by a silver spoon
But now she sucks her thumb and wonders
By the banks of her own lagoon

Didn't anybody tell her?
Didn't anybody see?
Sunday's on the phone to Monday
Tuesday's on the phone to me

She said she'd always been a dancer
She worked at fifteen clubs a day
And though she thought I knew the answer
Well I knew what I could not say

And so I quit the police department
And got myself a steady job
And though she tried her best to help me
She could steal but she could not rob

Didn't anybody tell her?
Didn't anybody see?
Sunday's on the phone to Monday
Tuesday's on the phone to me, oh yeah

MY MUM WAS A NURSE AND MY DAD LOVED WORDS, SO I was the only one in my class who could spell 'phlegm'. And even though she was never anything more than a nurse, or midwife, and my dad never anything more than a cotton salesman, we always thought of ourselves as posh working class. It's a mental attitude. Our attitude was posh. We aspired to do better in every department.

We usually associate the idea of being 'born with a silver spoon in your mouth' with nobility, but even in my (albeit posh) working-class family, I was given a silver spoon at the time of my christening. I knew nothing about it until, years later, my Auntie Dyl told me that she had kept it safe for me.

Literally and metaphorically, until my mum died, I had quite a lucky childhood. I was 'protected by a silver spoon'. Mind you, I did have some out-of-the-ordinary ideas. For example, I used to see the days of the week in colours. Monday was black, Tuesday was yellow, Wednesday was green, Thursday was dark blue, Friday was red, Saturday was orange, Sunday was white. When I saw the name of the day of the week, I pictured them like that. It's a form of synaesthesia.

So the lines 'Sunday's on the phone to Monday / Tuesday's on the phone to me' are particularly resonant for me. I use essentially the same device in 'Lady Madonna', where I have 'Friday night arrives without a suitcase' and 'Sunday morning, creeping like a nun'. It seems to be fruitful ground for me.

I think music can be a very visual art really. It's image driven. We can see the 'dancer' working 'fifteen clubs a day'. We can see the character 'quit the police department'. There's a story about that which I've told a few times but I still love. It's about my riding in a New York cab whose driver had 'Eugene Quits, New York Police Department' on his ID. I like that little dig at the police. Naughty! And I'm still amused by the description of the woman who 'could steal but she could not rob'. A nice distinction if ever there was one.

And that, of course, goes back to the fact that a woman did actually sneak into my house through the bathroom window that was a bit ajar. A fan, apparently - one of a group called the 'Apple scruffs'. She found a ladder lying outside my house in London. As far as I recall, she stole a picture of my cotton salesman dad. Or robbed me of it. But I got the song in return.

Left: At home. London, 1969

Above: Fans waiting outside. London, 1969

And that, of course, goes back to the fact that a woman did actually sneak into my house through the bathroom window that was a bit ajar. A fan, apparently – one of a group called the 'Apple scruffs'. She found a ladder lying outside my house in London. As far as I recall, she stole a picture of my cotton salesman dad. Or robbed me of it. But I got the song in return.

APPLE CORPS LIMITED
3 SAVILE ROW LONDON W1
TELEPHONE 01-734 8232
CABLES APCORE LONDON W1

BATHROOM WINDOW.

(1) She came in through the bathroom window
Protected by a silver spoon
But now she sucks her thumb & wonders
By the banks of her own lagoon.

CHORUS
Didn't anybody tell her?
" " see?
Sunday's on the phone to Monday,
Tuesday's on the phone to me.

(2) She said she'd always been a dancer
She worked at 15 clubs a day
And though she thought I knew the answer
I just knew what I could not say.

CHORUS.

(3) And so I quit the police department
And got myself a steady job
And though she tried her best to help me
She could steal but she could not rob.

CHORUS. and out.

Another Lennon & McCartney original.

DIRECTORS N ASPINALL D O'DELL H PINSKER

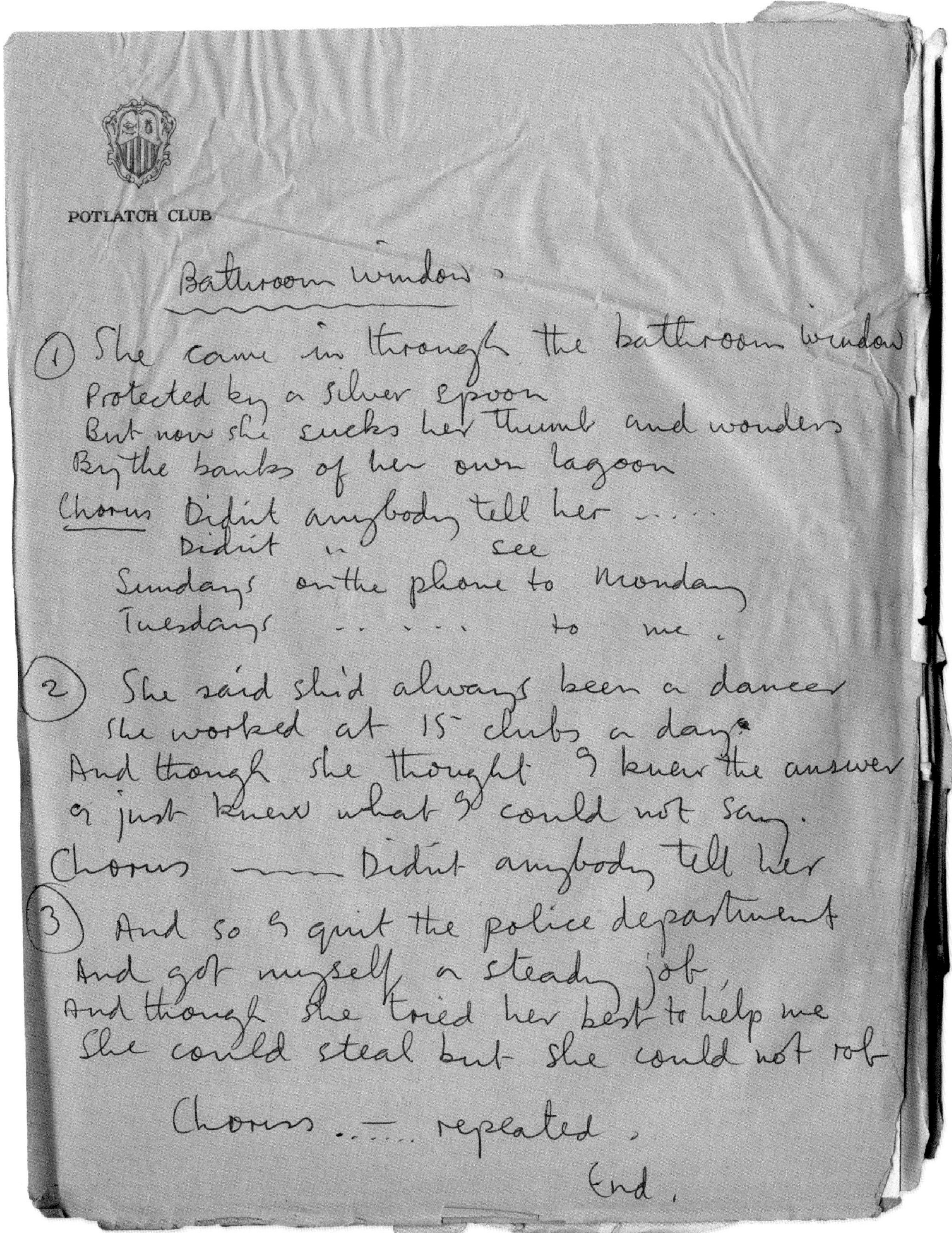
POTLATCH CLUB

Bathroom window.

(1) She came in through the bathroom window
Protected by a silver spoon
But now she sucks her thumb and wonders
By the banks of her own lagoon
Chorus Didn't anybody tell her ....
Didn't " see
Sundays on the phone to Monday
Tuesdays . . . . . to me.

(2) She said she'd always been a dancer
She worked at 15 clubs a day.
And though she thought I knew the answer
I just knew what I could not say.
Chorus ——— Didn't anybody tell her
(3) And so I quit the police department
And got myself a steady job,
And though she tried her best to help me
She could steal but she could not rob

Chorus ..... repeated.
End.

She Loves You

WRITERS	Paul McCartney and John Lennon
ARTIST	The Beatles
RECORDED	Abbey Road Studios, London
RELEASED	Single, 1963
	The Beatles' Second Album, 1964

She loves you
Yeah, yeah, yeah
She loves you
Yeah, yeah, yeah
She loves you
Yeah, yeah, yeah, yeah

You think you've lost your love
Well I saw her yesterday
It's you she's thinking of
And she told me what to say
She says she loves you
And you know that can't be bad
Yes she loves you
And you know you should be glad

She said you hurt her so
She almost lost her mind
But now she says she knows
You're not the hurting kind
She says she loves you
And you know that can't be bad
Yes she loves you
And you know you should be glad

She loves you
Yeah, yeah, yeah
She loves you
Yeah, yeah, yeah
And with a love like that
You know you should be glad
You know it's up to you
I think it's only fair
Pride can hurt you too
Apologise to her
Because she loves you
And you know that can't be bad
She loves you
And you know you should be glad

She loves you
Yeah, yeah, yeah
She loves you
Yeah, yeah, yeah
With a love like that
You know you should be glad
With a love like that
You know you should be glad
With a love like that
You know you should be glad

Yeah, yeah, yeah
Yeah, yeah, yeah, yeah

WE STARTED COMPOSING 'SHE LOVES YOU' AFTER A concert in Newcastle upon Tyne, where we shared a bill with Roy Orbison and Gerry and The Pacemakers. John and I were sitting on twin beds in a Newcastle hotel room. We finished it in the dining room at my dad's house in Forthlin Road. My father, who had been in the next room smoking his pipe and watching TV, complained about our singing 'yeah, yeah, yeah' and wondered if we shouldn't sing 'yes, yes, yes'. He was concerned about too many Americanisms creeping into UK English. If we'd done that, I'm not sure it would have become our biggest-selling single in the UK.

One idea that lay behind 'She Loves You' was the song by Bobby Rydell called 'Forget Him', which was based on the call-and-response structure. That's how it started out. The idea was that one person would sing, 'She loves you', and the other ones would answer, 'Yeah, yeah, yeah'. That idea got lost along the way.

Like many of our first songs, the title of 'She Loves You' was framed around the use of personal pronouns. What's different here is that the speaker of the song is a middleman, an agent, a go-between. I can't say for sure whether I'd heard of L. P. Hartley's novel *The Go-Between* at the time. But I might well have had some sense of Hartley, who was very well known then, and this familiarity with Hartley may well have influenced the writing of the song.

We did a version in German, 'Sie liebt dich', with Odeon Records, the German arm of EMI. The feeling was that if we put out a record in Germany, it would have to be in German. That was amusing in its way, given our relationship with Germany. We'd been working a long time in Liverpool, essentially as a bunch of rockers with quiff hairdos and everything. We'd gone over to Hamburg as a lot of rockers did, and we'd got a little bit 'leatherified' there. Later, one of these guys from Hamburg cut our hair in the style he wore. So we were developing an image, and then we moved from leather to suits, at the request of our manager, Brian Epstein. We all went over to Beno Dorn, the Polish tailor in Birkenhead. We'd never been to a tailor, certainly not en masse. We all went over and got suits.

More important than the look, though, was all the musical experience we had in Hamburg in the early 1960s. That's where we did a lot of our ten thousand hours – the ten thousand hours that Malcolm Gladwell made famous in his book *Outliers*. Apparently, we played nearly 300 times in Hamburg between 1960 and 1962. So, the German version of 'She Loves You' really brought things back full circle in a strange way.

Above: Early Beatles line-up with Pete Best, George Harrison and John Lennon. Liverpool, 1961

Right: In the garden with dad Jim. Forthlin Road, Liverpool

GIRLS

She's a Woman

WRITERS	Paul McCartney and John Lennon
ARTIST	The Beatles
RECORDED	Abbey Road Studios, London
RELEASED	B-side of 'I Feel Fine' single, 1964
	Beatles '65, 1964

My love don't give me presents
I know that she's no peasant
Only ever has to give me
Love forever and forever
My love don't give me presents
Turn me on when I get lonely
People tell me that she's only foolin'
I know she isn't

She don't give boys the eye
She hates to see me cry
She is happy just to hear me
Say that I will never leave her
She don't give boys the eye
She will never make me jealous
Gives me all her time as well as lovin'
Don't ask me why

She's a woman who understands
She's a woman who loves her man

My love don't give me presents
I know that she's no peasant
Only ever has to give me
Love forever and forever
My love don't give me presents
Turn me on when I get lonely
People tell me that she's only foolin'
I know she isn't

She's a woman who understands
She's a woman who loves her man

My love don't give me presents
I know that she's no peasant
Only ever has to give me
Love forever and forever
My love don't give me presents
Turn me on when I get lonely
People tell me that she's only foolin'
I know she isn't

She's a woman
She's a woman

WE ALL LIKED A CERTAIN KIND OF R & B. THESE DAYS R & B IS sort of hip-hop, but back then it was proper rhythm and blues. And early on, we all loved Black music. We loved the spontaneity, or seeming spontaneity, of it.

The songs we listened to often seemed to refer to 'a woman'. A song like 'I Got a Woman' by Ray Charles, or Little Richard's hymns to 'Long Tall Sally' and 'Good Golly, Miss Molly'. A lot of what we were listening to was already there, but I think what we did was to take it in, send it through the tumble dryer, distil it and push it out the other end.

'She's a Woman' extols the virtues of a girl of mine, and let's be clear, she's not a girl, she's a *woman*. Because this was the interesting thing: when does a girl become a woman? To us, they'd been girls till we were around twenty-one. And they were still sort of girls, but now we could dare to think of ourselves as men, and could think of girls as women.

Often one of us would come up with something that put a spark in the recording, and I think the spark on the recording of 'She's a Woman' was the combination of John's backbeat guitar and my bass.

I've never composed on the bass. Never. Not to this day. So how did I end up playing the bass in this band? Well, after my cheap Rosetti Solid 7 guitar fell apart in Hamburg, I had to find a new instrument. We already had two guitars, a drummer and Stuart Sutcliffe, the bass player. There happened to be a piano on the stage where we played, so I took to that and just sort of worked all the songs out on piano. So, I became the pianist in the group. What was quite funny was that Stuart didn't have any spare bass strings, so if one of his bass strings broke, he would raid my piano. He'd take a pair of pliers and cut out a string.

When we were in Hamburg, Stuart fell in love with a local girl called Astrid and decided he was leaving the group. So we were now without a bass player. We couldn't have three guitars and no bass. Nobody wanted to be the bass player in those days because it was always the fat guy playing bass. There seemed to be some sort of stigma attached to it. Anyway, I bought a Höfner bass, a lovely violin-shaped thing that appealed to me because, being left-handed, I knew I was going to turn it upside down. Its symmetry was a big attraction for me. And it was light as a feather.

I have to smile at the fact that I turned out to be a bass player, because my dad always used to point out the bass in songs we heard. He was a musician with Jim Mac's Jazz Band, playing piano and trumpet, and he educated me and my brother in music appreciation. We'd be listening to something on the radio, and he'd say, 'Hear that? That's the bass!'

Nobody wanted to be the bass player in those days because it was always the fat guy playing bass. There seemed to be some sort of stigma attached to it. Anyway, I bought a Höfner bass, a lovely violin-shaped thing that appealed to me because, being left-handed, I knew I was going to turn it upside down. Its symmetry was a big attraction for me. And it was light as a feather.

Below: Performing with George Harrison, John Lennon, Pete Best and Stuart Sutcliffe. Indra Club, Hamburg, 1960

Right: Early 1960s

She's Given Up Talking

WRITER	Paul McCartney
ARTIST	Paul McCartney
RECORDED	Henson Studios, Los Angeles
RELEASED	*Driving Rain*, 2001

She's given up talking
Don't say a word
Even in the classroom
Not a dickie bird
Unlike other children
She's seen and never heard
She's given up talking
Don't say a word

You see her in the playground
Standing on her own
Everybody wonders
Why she's all alone
Someone made her angry
Someone's got her scared
She's given up talking
Don't say a word

But when she comes home
It's yap-a-yap-yap
Words are running freely
Like the water from a tap
Her brothers and her sisters
Can't get a word in edgeways
But when she's back at school again
She goes into a daze

She's given up talking
Don't say a word
Even in the classroom
Not a dickie bird
Unlike other children
She's seen and never heard
She's given up talking
Don't say a word

She's given up talking
She don't say a word
Don't say a word
Don't say a word

THE PHENOMENON OF 'SELECTIVE MUTISM' FASCINATES ME. There's a family I got to know over the years. I saw them have kids, and I saw the kids grow up, and sometimes I'd give one of the kids a ride on my horse if I was out on my horse.

One day, one of these kids just stopped speaking. In school she wouldn't speak or answer. The idea that one day someone would just decide not to talk - it's kind of crazy, but it's brave. So this is just me imagining what it might be like. 'Not a dickie bird' is cockney rhyming slang. We used it in Liverpool. It's nice to come across that when the previous line is 'Don't say a word'.

I love the way ordinary people won't go for fancy words, so they adapt them to their own satisfaction. They refuse to say it the way it should be said, so they just say it another way. There's an old monument on the south coast of England, near where I live, which is French, from Ypres. It's a tower, like a little castle, and it's called the Ypres Tower. The locals, who are not about to use the French pronunciation, call it 'The Wipers'.

I didn't really talk to the girl about her silence, but I talked to her family, and then I said I'd written a song about it. Years later they told me it was just a phase. She's grown up, and she talks now.

Just another phase, perhaps.

Above: Ypres Tower with Spike Milligan in the foreground, Sussex

SHE'S GIVEN UP TALKIN'

(1) SHE'S GIVEN UP TALKIN'
(SHE) DONT SAY A WORD
EVEN IN THE CLASSROOM
NOT A DICKIE BIRD
UNLIKE OTHER CHILDREN
SHE'S SEEN AND NEVER HEARD
(SHE) GIVEN UP TALKIN'
DONT SAY A WORD

(2) YOU SEE HER IN THE PLAYGROUND
STANDIN' ON HER OWN
EVERYBODY WONDERS
WHY SHE'S ALL ALONE
SOMEONE MADE HER ANGRY
SOMEONE GOT HER SCARED
(SHE) GIVEN UP TALKIN'
DON'T SAY A WORD

AH BUT WHEN SHE COMES HOME
ITS YAP-A-YAP-YAP
WORDS ARE RUNNING FREELY
LIKE THE WATER FROM A TAP
HER BROTHERS AND HER SISTERS
CANT GET A WORD IN EDGE WAYS
BUT WHEN SHE'S BACK AT SCHOOL AGAIN
SHE GOES INTO A DAZE

REPEAT (1)

Driving Rain album cover taken using a Casio wrist camera watch, 2001

I love the way ordinary people won't go for fancy words, so they adapt them to their own satisfaction. They refuse to say it the way it should be said, so they just say it another way. There's an old monument on the south coast of England, near where I live, which is French, from Ypres. It's a tower, like a little castle, and it's called the Ypres Tower. The locals call it 'The Wipers'.

She's Leaving Home

WRITERS	Paul McCartney and John Lennon
ARTIST	The Beatles
RECORDED	Abbey Road Studios, London
RELEASED	*Sgt. Pepper's Lonely Hearts Club Band*, 1967

Wednesday morning at five o'clock as the day
begins
Silently closing her bedroom door
Leaving the note that she hoped would say more
She goes downstairs to the kitchen clutching her
handkerchief
Quietly turning the backdoor key
Stepping outside she is free

She
(We gave her most of our lives)
Is leaving
(Sacrificed most of our lives)
Home
(We gave her everything money could buy)
She's leaving home
After living alone
For so many years
(Bye-bye)

Father snores as his wife gets into her dressing
gown
Picks up the letter that's lying there
Standing alone at the top of the stairs
She breaks down and cries to her husband,
Daddy, our baby's gone
Why would she treat us so thoughtlessly?
How could she do this to me?

She
(We never thought of ourselves)
Is leaving
(Never a thought for ourselves)
Home
(We've struggled hard all our lives to get by)
She's leaving home
After living alone
For so many years
(Bye-bye)

Friday morning at nine o'clock she is far away
Waiting to keep the appointment she made
Meeting a man from the motor trade

She
(What did we do that was wrong?)
Is having
(We didn't know it was wrong)
Fun
(Fun is the one thing that money can't buy)
Something inside
That was always denied
For so many years
(Bye-bye)

She's leaving home
(Bye-bye)

OTHER THAN *WEST SIDE STORY*, JOHN HATED MUSICALS. *West Side Story* we went to see together – a touring production in Liverpool. We saw the film, of course, with that famous opening shot of New York from a helicopter. We liked that and thought it was ballsy enough for us. But John walked out on *South Pacific* – too corny, too prissy and sweet. Even though 'Lennon and McCartney' sounded like 'Rodgers and Hammerstein', it was pretty clear from early on that we were never going to be writing musicals.

We did, however, write story songs. This one is based somewhat on a newspaper report of a missing girl. The headline was something like 'A-Level Girl Dumps Car and Vanishes'. So, I set out to imagine what might have happened, the sequence of events. The detail of leaving a note that she 'hoped would say more' is one of the strongest moments in the song. (Like many writers, I'm fascinated by what's missing in a piece. I used to love how you'd be listening to the radio and you'd hear an audience laugh for no obvious reason. The comedian hadn't made a joke, but maybe he'd pulled a funny face. You would never know exactly what he'd done.)

In addition to the newspaper report, I'm pretty sure another influence was *The Wednesday Play*. It was a weekly television play that often addressed 'big' social issues. It's the kind of thing people would be discussing at the bus stop on Thursday morning. It was a very important part of the week. One of the most famous of these plays was *Cathy Come Home*, directed by Ken Loach. It's a play about homelessness that a quarter of the UK population watched the night it was broadcast in November 1966.

When we recorded 'She's Leaving Home' it was almost like a shooting script for *The Wednesday Play*. 'Clutching her handkerchief / Quietly turning the backdoor key'. On one hand we have the narrator who's describing the action ('She's leaving home'), and then there are a couple of people in the spotlight, a mini Greek chorus, who fade in and out ('We gave her most of our lives'). There was a line in that style – 'Is this all the thanks that we get?' – which somehow didn't make the final cut.

I realise now that you can easily imagine a 'man from the motor trade' showing up in a Philip Larkin poem with all those travelling salesmen. Is she meeting a man from the motor trade to buy a car or for a romantic liaison? It's left wide open.

I'm not sure whether a song like this could be written nowadays. Funnily enough, a musical theatre setting is where this kind of story song gets written now. So, maybe Lennon and McCartney did write musicals after all.

SHE IS LEAVING HOME.

Wednesday morning at 5 o'clock as the day begins
Silently closing her bedroom door
Leaving the note. that she hoped would say more
She goes down stairs to the kitchen clutching her handkerchief
Quietly turning the back door key
Stepping outside she is free

SHE, we gave her most of our lives
IS LEAVING sacrificed most of our lives
HOME, we gave her everything money could buy
She's leaving home after living alone for so many years

Father snores as his wife gets into her dressing gown
Picks up the letter thats lying there
Standing alone at the top of the stairs
She breaks down and cries to her husband
Daddy our baby's gone
Why would she treat us so thoughtlessly
How could she do this to me,

SHE (Is this the thanks that we get) (We never thought of ourselves)
IS LEAVING (All of the thanks that we get (Never a thought for ourselves)
HOME, We struggled hard all our lives to get by

Friday morning at 9 o'clock she is far away
Waiting to keep the appointment she made
Meeting ~~the man~~ A MAN from the motor trade

SHE What did we do that was wrong?
IS HAVING We didn't know it was wrong
FUN Fun is the one thing that money can't buy
Something inside that was always denied for so many years.

MIKE Iwa 5605

Early sketch for *Sgt. Pepper's Lonely Hearts Club Band* album cover on reverse of lyric, 1967

Silly Love Songs

WRITERS	Paul McCartney and Linda McCartney
ARTIST	Wings
RECORDED	Abbey Road Studios, London
RELEASED	*At the Speed of Sound*, 1976
	Single, 1976

You'd think that people
Would have had enough
Of silly love songs
But I look around me
And I see it isn't so
Some people want to fill the world
With silly love songs
And what's wrong with that?
I'd like to know
'Cause here I go again

I love you

Ah I can't explain
The feeling's plain to me
Now can't you see?
Ah she gave me more
She gave it all to me
Now can't you see?
What's wrong with that?
I need to know
'Cause here I go again

I love you

Love doesn't come in a minute
Sometimes it doesn't come at all
I only know that when I'm in it
It isn't silly
No it isn't silly
Love isn't silly at all

How can I tell you about my loved one?

I love you

Ah I can't explain
The feeling's plain to me
Say can't you see?
Ah he gave me more
He gave it all to me
Say can't you see?

You'd think that people
Would have had enough
Of silly love songs
But I look around me
And I see it isn't so, oh no
Some people want to fill the world
With silly love songs
And what's wrong with that?

THERE WERE ACCUSATIONS IN THE MID-1970S – INCLUDING ONE from John – that I was just writing 'silly love songs'. I suppose the idea was that I should be a bit tougher, a bit more worldly. But then I suddenly realised, that's exactly what love is – it's worldly. 'Some people want to fill the world / With silly love songs'. I'd been given that reputation, and I had to stand up for it. Instead of abandoning songs about love, just get on with it, get into it and don't be embarrassed, because even though you might say this is a soppy subject, it's actually the opposite: this thing people can feel for each other that makes life better. I think that's the crux of it, and if you want to be cynical, it's easy, you can. 'Love doesn't come in a minute / Sometimes it doesn't come at all'. I think a lot of people who are cynical about love haven't been lucky enough to feel it.

It's easier to get critical approval if you rail against things and swear a lot, because it makes you seem stronger. If you say, 'Oh, it's a lovely day; everything's nice; I like the rain,' then you're a soppy bastard. But if you say, 'Oh, this fucking weather! It's fucking unbelievable! I fucking hate thunder! I fucking hate lightning! What the hell is God doing this for?' the critic might say, 'That's marvellous!'

Anyone who knows my performances must realise that I don't use a lot of 'bad language' onstage, and not much in life either. When we were younger, we used to swear a lot more. Let's be realistic, when you're younger you're more apt to do that because you've been let off the leash. But then when you have kids, you think, maybe not. So it's a life cycle that becomes almost predictable. But I've still had periods when I've sworn – 'fucking this and fucking that' – and I remember shocking my dinner guests and thinking, 'What am I doing?' It's bravado, trying to be cool, man.

John always had a lot of that bluster, though. It was his shield against life. We'd have an argument about something, and he'd say something particularly caustic; then I'd be a bit wounded, and he'd pull down his glasses and peer at me and say, 'It's only me, Paul.' That was John. 'It's only me.' Oh, alright, you've just gone and blustered and that was somebody else, was it? It was his shield talking.

He'd say, 'My dad left home when I was three, and my mother got run over and killed by an off-duty policeman outside the house, and my Uncle George died. Yeah, I'm bitter.' He told me once he thought he was a curse on the male line of the family because his dad had run away, and then he went to live with Auntie Mimi and Uncle George. Then George, whom he'd really liked, died. His mum was run over after she'd visited him, while walking to the bus stop down the street where he lived. He idolised her. Just having to accommodate all that would make you want to put up a few defences.

The point is that most people don't tend to show their emotions unless they are in private, but deep down, people *are* emotional, and all I'm really saying in this song is, 'Love isn't silly at all'.

Wings at Checkpoint
Charlie. Berlin, 1976

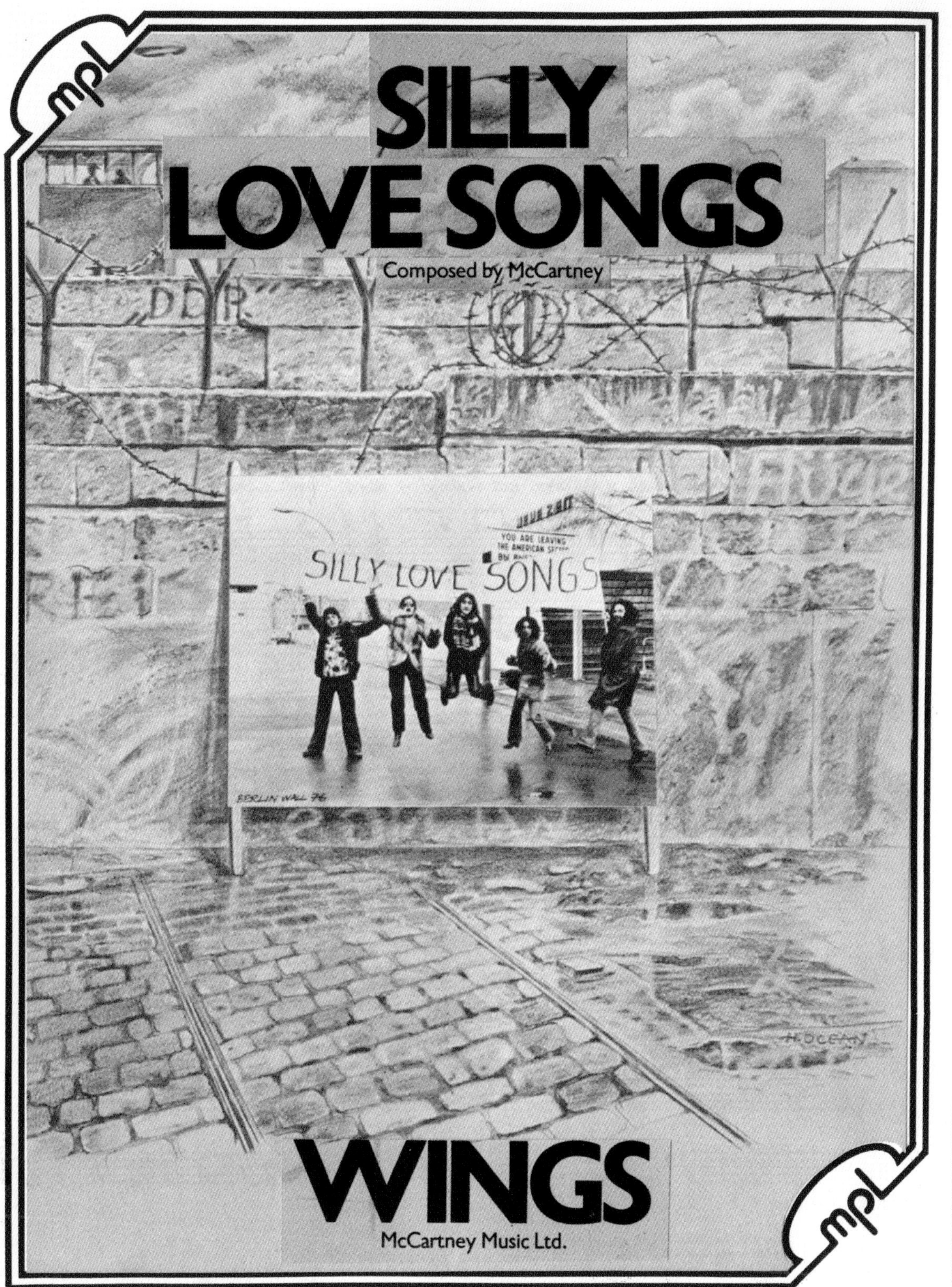
mpl
SILLY
LOVE SONGS
Composed by McCartney
DDR
YOU ARE LEAVING
SILLY LOVE SONGS
BERLIN WALL 76
WINGS
McCartney Music Ltd.
mpl

SILLY LOVE SONGS

You'd think that people
would have had enough
of silly love songs

HUSTLE
BEAT.

But I look around me
and I see it isn't so

"OH YEAH"

HOOK

Some people want to fill
the world with silly love songs

and what's wrong with that
I need to know (OR I'M ONE
OF THEM!)
(AND) cos here I go
again.

Chorus
FIRST LINE
I love you

VERSE SECOND LINE.
Ah – I can't explain
the feelings plain to me.
say – can't you see?

Ah she gave me more
she gave it all to me.
~~say can't you see~~

THIRD
LINE.
How can I tell you about
my loved one?

Chords

You'd think that people would have
had enough of silly love songs

But I look around me
and I see it isn't so

Some people want to fill the world
with silly love songs
and what's wrong with that?
I need to know cos here I go - again

(1) I — love — you
I — love — you
I - love - you
I — love — you

INSTRUMENTAL ~~and~~ what's wrong with that?
I need to know cos here I go - again!

BREAK
(2) Ah I cant explain the feelings plain to me
say cant you see
Ah she gave me more she gave it all to me Say cant you see!

whats wrong with that -
INSTRUMENTAL going into E —
out.

(1)+(2)

Simple as That

WRITER	Paul McCartney
ARTIST	Paul McCartney
RECORDED	Hog Hill Mill, Sussex
RELEASED	*The Anti-heroin Project: It's a Live-in World*, 1986

I know it isn't easy to refuse
A lot of thoughts are flying through your head
Tell me this before you have to choose
Would you rather be alive or dead?

It's as simple as that
Would you rather be alive or dead?
It's as simple as that
It's so simple
It makes you wanna cry

They ask you if you wanna join in
You linger for a minute or so
Well now's a perfect time to begin
Are you gonna say yes or no?

It's as simple as that
Are you gonna say yes or no?
It's as simple as that
It's so simple
It makes you wanna cry

And if you love your life
Everybody will love you too
Yes if you love your life
Everybody will love you too

It's harder when you start to get around
I want you to remember what I said
I know you never like to let them down
But would you rather be alive or dead?

It's as simple as that
Would you rather be alive or dead?
It's as simple as that
It's so simple
It makes me wanna cry
So simple
It makes you wanna cry

Yes if you love your life
Everybody will love you too
And if you love your life
Everybody will love you too

Would you rather be alive or dead?
Would you rather be alive or dead?
It's as simple as that
It's as simple as that
It's as simple as that

And if you love your life
Everybody will love you too
Yes if you love your life
Everybody will love you too

IN THE MID-1980S THE BBC ASKED ME TO DO SOMETHING for an anti-heroin charity. They wanted a song to give young people the sense that maybe heroin isn't such a good idea. This is what I came up with: 'It's as simple as that!'

The style is one of my favourites - reggae. I remember vividly the first occasion I really got interested in reggae. It was when I was painting my roof in Scotland. It was summer and we had a reggae record on - *Tighten Up* - one of the original albums with various artists on it, what they used to call a compilation album. It was really good, and it suited the atmosphere: a sunny Scotland day, up on the roof painting it green, reggae playing. It made me feel great.

As a family, we used to go quite often to Jamaica on holiday. There was a hotel in Montego Bay that we liked, so we'd go and stay there and listen non-stop to the radio. Jamaica had a great radio station called RJR, and it played reggae all day long.

In town, there was a little shop called Tony's Record Shop on Fustic Road, and it was very funky. You'd leaf through the 45s and you'd see something that you liked the look of. Often it was just an acetate disc, a demo disc; they didn't necessarily have proper labels from a company. So I would ask the assistants, 'What's this one like?' 'Oh yeah, man, that's great.' I remember one that I bought. The song was called 'Lick I Pipe', and I just thought, 'That's great. Whoever made that up, and whatever the hell it means, it's good.' Lick I pipe!

So I'd get a little pile, and we'd take them home, and we discovered some fabulous little songs. Once we saw an album with a song on it called 'Poison Pressure' written by Lennon and McCartney, so I got it and listened to it, and it was nothing remotely like one of our songs. But then I thought, well, it could be Bob Lennon and Charlie McCartney; who was I to argue? 'Poison Pressure' by Lennon and McCartney. A hit!

When Bob Marley came along, he solidified the genre of reggae and brought it to the mainstream. I never met Marley, unfortunately. I came very close once or twice. One night he was playing at the Lyceum Theatre in London, and we got halfway there and just changed our minds. I was thinking I might get a bit noticed in the crowd. It's stupid really, because it would have been worth it to see him live and then to meet him.

It was one of our little family traditions to make a record sometimes for Linda's dad. So I had a fabulous group of backup singers on this song: my kids. It was always such fun when the whole family went down to the studio and we mucked in. The kids would sing on it; everyone would get a line, and they would enjoy that. So I said, 'Look, this is for a charity, and it's a great charity.' I thought getting kids involved in an anti-heroin project wouldn't be a bad idea.

Left: Jamaica, 1974

Top right: Jamaica, 1972

Bottom right: Painting the roof. Scotland, 1971

I remember one that I bought. The song was called 'Lick I Pipe', and I just thought, 'That's great. Whoever made that up, and whatever the hell it means, it's good.' Lick I pipe!

Single Pigeon

WRITERS	Paul McCartney and Linda McCartney
ARTIST	Paul McCartney and Wings
RECORDED	Olympic Sound Studios, London
RELEASED	*Red Rose Speedway*, 1973

Single pigeon through the railings
Did she throw you out?
Sunday morning fight about Saturday night

Single seagull gliding over
Regent's Park canal
Do you need a pal for a minute or two?
You do?
Me too (me too, me too)

I'm a lot like you
Me too (me too, me too)
I'm a lot like you

Did she turf you out in the cold morning rain
Again?
Me too (me too, me too)

I'm a lot like you
Me too (me too, me too)
I'm a lot like you

Sunday morning fight about Saturday night

ONE OF MY HOBBIES IS ORNITHOLOGY. IN FACT, I'M A KEEN ORNIthologist and always have been. As I've mentioned before, one of my favourite pastimes as a child was to take my *Observer's Book of Birds*, sit in the fields and lose myself in nature. I like me birds, as they say.

I had seen a single pigeon, just pecking around - a blue-grey pigeon on its own near some railings – and I thought the combination of those words was quite winning: 'single pigeon'. I began to think about why the pigeon might be single.

The minute you decide to make up a story about a pigeon, it's not just a pigeon. It's a character in a play. It's a guy who's had an argument with his girl the night before, and he's got chucked out of the house. So here he is. He's single now. All because of the 'Sunday morning fight about Saturday night'.

Second verses are always interesting because you're going somewhere else but you want to retain the feeling of the first verse. Now that I've established the single pigeon, the second verse introduces a 'single seagull' - another character in my little play. I'd often see a seagull gliding over Regent's Park canal, but it's also possible he flew in from Chekhov. The seagull in Chekhov's play isn't just a seagull but a symbol of a character, Konstantin, and his relationship to Nina.

The idea that the protagonist of the song is 'a lot like you' suggests that he, too, has been chucked out. He's relating to the pigeon and seagull because he, too, has been turfed out into the cold morning rain. So, I've changed it from being just an ornithological observation to a representation of me. That pigeon is me, or that seagull is me, or a version of me.

The irony is that this song was written at a time when I was actually very happy in my personal life. People listening to the song might have recognised that the corner of my mouth was raised ever so slightly in a smile because my relationship with Linda was a very happy one. That's why it was so lovely to have her singing backup on 'Me too / I'm a lot like you'.

I've said it before, but I'll say it again: a lot of songwriters draw merely on their day-to-day autobiographical thoughts, but I like to take flights of fancy. That's one of the great things about being an artist of any kind. I like songs and poetry that take off in unexpected ways. It's probably one of the reasons I admire Bob Dylan so much. You never know what he's going to do or which way he's going to jump.

Linda and Mary.
Marrakesh, 1973

The idea that the protagonist of the song is 'a lot like you' suggests that he, too, has been chucked out. He's relating to the pigeon and seagull because he, too, has been turfed out into the cold morning rain.

Somedays

WRITER	Paul McCartney
ARTIST	Paul McCartney
RECORDED	Hog Hill Mill, Sussex; and AIR Studios, London
RELEASED	*Flaming Pie*, 1997

Somedays I look
I look at you with eyes that shine
Somedays I don't
I don't believe that you are mine

It's no good asking me what time of day it is
Who won the match or scored the goal
Somedays I look
Somedays I look into your soul

Sometimes I laugh
I laugh to think how young we were
Sometimes it's hard
It's hard to know which way to turn

Don't ask me where I found that picture
  on the wall
How much it cost or what it's worth
Sometimes I laugh
I laugh to think how young we were

We don't need anybody else
To tell us what is real
Inside each one of us is love
And we know how it feels

Somedays I cry
I cry for those who live in fear
Somedays I don't
I don't remember why I'm here

No use reminding me, it's just the way it is
Who ran the race or came in first
Somedays I cry
I cry for those who fear the worst

We don't need anybody else
To tell us what is real
Inside each one of us is love
And we know how it feels

Somedays I look
I look at you with eyes that shine
Somedays I don't
I don't believe that you are mine

It's no good asking me what time of day it is
Who won the match or scored the goal
Somedays I look
Somedays I look into your soul

THE TITLE CAME FROM JUST THE FIRST LINE, 'SOMEDAYS I LOOK', which is followed by the repetition of 'I look'. 'Somedays I look / I look at you with eyes that shine / Somedays I don't / I don't believe that you are mine'. It's that little trick of repeating the phrase, of reinforcing it, that makes the lyric work. It drives it like a little dynamo. My grammar school education taught me that it's a rhetorical device apparently known as anadiplosis, but essentially, it's repetition. You think you're going one way, and then there's a little surprise and it takes you another. I like playing with phrases, dancing round words, shuffling them like a deck of cards.

I often think that when I'm writing a song, I'm following a trail of bread crumbs. Someone's thrown out these bread crumbs and I see the first few, and 'Somedays I look' and see the next one. I'm following the song rather than writing it. I will think of the line that's coming and think of how to get into it, like following stepping-stones. My thinking process goes like this: I've got to do that to get to there, and so it continues. I quite enjoy that; it's an interesting process. I often liken it to doing crossword puzzles. My dad was a big fan of crosswords and was a very wordy man. I think I inherited that love of words and crossword puzzles from him. That's often what songs are - puzzles. Trying to figure how one word fits with another word. So if you put this together with that and you twist that word around, the answer is . . .

It's then all about filling in the gaps.

George Martin called this song 'deceivingly simple'. He would have known, because he was one of the best at making the complex seem simple. That's why he was always my arranger of choice. I'd known him a long time - most of my professional life, in fact - since The Beatles did our artist test with him for EMI when I was a few days shy of my twentieth birthday. I'd worked with him so much that I knew if I wanted a nice arrangement on something, it would be a delight to ring him up and say, 'Hey, George, are you interested in doing a thing together?' He was a true gentleman, and like

Above: With George Martin. AIR Studios, London, 1982

a second father to me, and always the grown-up in the room, with that delightfully plummy English accent of his. If I had the opportunity to work with him rather than anyone else, I always would - until it came to classical stuff, like the *Liverpool Oratorio*, when I worked with people who had a bit more knowledge in that field. But from that June day in 1962 when he gave us our first recording contract, right up to the last time we saw each other, George was just the most generous, intelligent and musical person I've had the pleasure to know.

'Somedays' is a good little song. For me, it's very meaningful. Looking into a soul; it's what you try to do in a relationship, yet don't often succeed at. The lyric contains some contradictory ideas, but its purpose is to support the song rather than be a lyric on its own, so it's quite liberating. I know this might sound odd, but the lyric and the song are two slightly different things.

Once I've managed to isolate myself (in this case it was another little room while Linda was doing a cooking assignment elsewhere in the house), once I'm actually writing the song, I'm off on that trail. I really don't know what the goal is, or even where I'm heading, but I do like to get there and find things out on the way. You can experiment as you go along, so there's a crack between the headlong and the halting where, if you're lucky, a few things might slip out: 'I look at you with eyes that shine / Somedays I don't'. That's like a thought that could come out in a session with a psychiatrist. I follow it up with 'I don't believe that you are mine', but there's now a wonderful ambiguity there.

With George Martin.
AIR Studios, London, 1982

(B min — A) ①
SOMEDAYS I LOOK
(B min - A)
I LOOK AT YOU
WITH EYES THAT SHINE (G)
(E min)
(B min - A)
SOME ~~TIMES~~ DAYS I DONT
I DONT BELIEVE
THAT YOU ARE MINE
ITS NO GOOD ASKING ME
WHAT TIME OF DAY IT IS
WHO WON THE MATCH
OR SCORED THE GOAL
SOMEDAYS I LOOK
LOOK AT YOU WITH EYES THAT SHINE

SOMETIMES I LAUGH ②
I LAUGH TO THINK
HOW YOUNG WE WERE
SOMETIMES ITS HARD
ITS HARD TO KNOW
WHICH WAY TO TURN
DONT ASK ME WHERE
I FOUND THAT PICTURE
ON THE WALL
HOW MUCH IT COST
OR WHAT ITS WORTH
SOMETIMES I LAUGH
I LAUGH TO THINK
HOW YOUNG
WE WERE.

MIDDLE. ③
WE DONT NEED
ANYBODY ELSE
TO TELL US WHAT IS REAL
INSIDE EACH ONE
OF US IS LOVE
AND WE KNOW
HOW IT FEELS.

~~F#~~ F# E C#,
D C# B A F#
G A B C# A D

repeat

F# B C# D ④
SOMEDAYS I CRY
F# B C# D
I CRY FOR THOSE
C# B A B
WHO LIVE IN FEAR
(same)
SOMEDAYS I DONT
I DONT REMEMBER
WHY IM HERE
E E E E E E
NO USE REMINDING ME
E D B B B B
WHAT TIME OF DAY IT IS
(same)
WHO RAN THE RACE
OR CAME IN FIRST
SOMEDAYS I CRY
I CRY FOR THOSE
WHO LIVE IN FEAR.

SOMEDAYS

SOMEDAY'S I LOOK,
I LOOK AT YOU WITH EYES THAT SHINE
SOMEDAY'S I DON'T,
I DON'T BELIEVE THAT YOU ARE MINE
IT'S NO GOOD ASKING ME WHAT TIME OF DAY IT IS.
WHO WON THE MATCH OR SCORED THE GOAL
SOMEDAY'S I LOOK,
SOMEDAY'S I LOOK INTO YOUR SOUL.

SOMETIMES I LAUGH,
I LAUGH TO THINK HOW YOUNG WE WERE
SOMETIMES IT'S HARD,
IT'S HARD TO KNOW WHICH WAY TO TURN
DON'T ASK ME WHERE I FOUND THAT PICTURE ON THE WALL
HOW MUCH IT COST OR WHAT IT'S WORTH
SOMETIMES I LAUGH
I LAUGH TO THINK HOW YOUNG WE WERE.

WE DON'T NEED ANYBODY ELSE
TO TELL US WHAT IS REAL
INSIDE EACH ONE OF US IS LOVE
AND WE KNOW HOW IT FEELS

SOMEDAY'S I CRY
I CRY FOR THOSE WHO LIVE IN FEAR,
SOMEDAY'S I DON'T,
I DON'T REMEMBER WHY I'M HERE
NO USE REMINDING ME WHAT TIME OF DAY IT IS,
WHO RAN THE RACE OR CAME IN FIRST,
SOMEDAY'S I CRY,
I CRY FOR THOSE WHO LIVE IN FEAR.

SOMEDAY'S I LOOK,
I LOOK AT YOU WITH EYES THAT SHINE

WE DON'T NEED ANYBODY ELSE
TO TELL US WHAT IS REAL
INSIDE EACH ONE OF US IS LOVE
AND WE KNOW HOW IT FEELS.

SOMEDAY'S I LOOK
I LOOK AT YOU WITH EYES THAT SHINE
SOMEDAY'S I DON'T
I DON'T BELIEVE THAT YOU ARE MINE
IT'S NO GOOD ASKING ME WHAT TIME OF DAY IT IS
WHO WON THE MATCH OR SCORED THE GOAL
SOMEDAY'S I LOOK
SOMEDAY'S I LOOK INTO YOUR SOUL.

SOMEDAY'S I LOOK,
I LOOK AT YOU WITH EYES THAT SHINE.......

George Martin's handwritten score for 'Somedays', 1996

Spirits of Ancient Egypt

WRITERS	Paul McCartney and Linda McCartney
ARTIST	Wings
RECORDED	Sea-Saint Recording Studio, New Orleans
RELEASED	*Venus and Mars*, 1975

You're my baby
And I love you
You can take a pound of love
And cook it in the stew
When you've finished doing that
I know what you'll want to do
'Cause you're my baby
And I love you

I'm your baby
Do you love me?
I can drive a Cadillac
Across the Irish Sea
But when I've finished doing that
I know where I'll want to be
'Cause I'm your baby
And you love me

Spirits of ancient Egypt
Shadows of ancient Rome
Spirits of ancient Egypt
Hung on the telly
Hung on the telly
Hung on the telephone

You're my baby
I know you know
You could sell an elevator
To Geronimo
And when you're finished doing that
I know where you'll want to go
'Cause you're my baby
I know you know

Spirits of ancient Egypt
Echoes of sunken Spain
Spirits of ancient Egypt
Hung on the phone
A-hung on the phone
A-hung on the phone again

WE KNEW GEORGE MELLY FROM LIVERPOOL. GEORGE WAS A very posh Liverpudlian, and he used to be the vocalist with a band called the Merseysippi Jazz Band. He was a very nice man, flamboyant, slightly eccentric. He had a big collection of paintings by René Magritte, the Belgian surrealist. In the seventies I was very into surrealism too, and Magritte in particular. It goes some way to explain the wacky nature of some of these songs.

I always thought I didn't do quite enough with the title. 'Spirits of Ancient Egypt' could have been intriguing and mystical, yet I somehow went the opposite way. 'You're my baby / And I love you / You can take a pound of love / And cook it in the stew.' There are very lyrical moments – 'Spirits of ancient Egypt / Shadows of ancient Rome' . . . 'Echoes of sunken Spain' – all great epic legends, but then set against those moments you've got just a love song. It's the ordinary pitched against the extraordinary. On one hand you've got the spirits of ancient Egypt, but suddenly there's a Cadillac and someone cooking up a pound of love, and then there's Geronimo. What's he doing in Egypt? Or Rome? Or Spain? How does a Cadillac drive across the Irish Sea? It's a surrealist picture. I had this belief that you could throw words together and they would attain some meaning, that you didn't need to think it out too much, that it might just be better to chuck it out there and see what happens.

I'd always half glimpsed Egyptian history: 'Oh yeah, pyramids; that's nice.' But, growing up, I was never really that interested. Then we rented a farm near Nashville for six weeks to work, but also to ride horses and spend the summer in the country with the family. Linda and I befriended Chet Atkins and his wife, and they invited us round for dinner. It was lovely. He had his guitar; I had mine. I played a couple of my songs. He asked me to play 'Yesterday'. (He inspired me to record a song that my dad had written, which we did end up doing and Chet played on, but that's another story.)

Anyway, after dinner he suddenly turned to me and said, 'Are you interested in Egyptian mythology?' It was abrupt, a real non sequitur, but I'm not easily fazed, so I said, 'Well, kind of,' and he started talking about it.

Above: With Linda and George Melly celebrating Buddy Holly Week. Peppermint Club, London, 1978

Left: With Linda. Nashville, 1974

Right: With Chet and Leona Atkins. Nashville, 1974

He then gave me this book by Peter Tompkins, *Secrets of the Great Pyramid*, and it was fascinating. There were some great theories in it, including that the Egyptians knew much more than people thought they did, and that the measurements around the base of the pyramid are somehow connected to the circumference of the Earth. How did they know the circumference of the Earth? You couldn't go around it with a tape measure, but they'd figured it out. So I devoured the book, and I treasured it all the more because it had Chet Atkins's *ex libris*.

14. SPIRITS OF ANCIENT EGYPT.

~~

Youre my baby, and I love you
You can take a pound of love
And cook it in the stew....

When youive finished doing that
I know what you'll want to do

Cos youire my baby and I love you

~~

~~Youre~~ Im your baby
do you love me?
I can drive a cadillac
across the Irish sea
– but when Ive finished doing that
I know where I'll want to be
Im your baby, do you love me?

~~

15. SPIRITS OF ANCIENT EGYPT.

Spirits of ancient Egypt
Shadows of ancient Rome
Spirits of ancient Egypt
hung on the telly
hung on the telly
hung on the telephone.....

You're my baby
I know you know
You could sell an elevator
To Geronimo
And when you're finished doing that
I know where you'll want to go
Cos' you're my baby
I know you know.
Spirits of Ancient Egypt
Echoes of sunken Spain
Spirits of ancient Egypt
Hung on the phone - a - hung on the
phone a - hung on the phone
....again .....

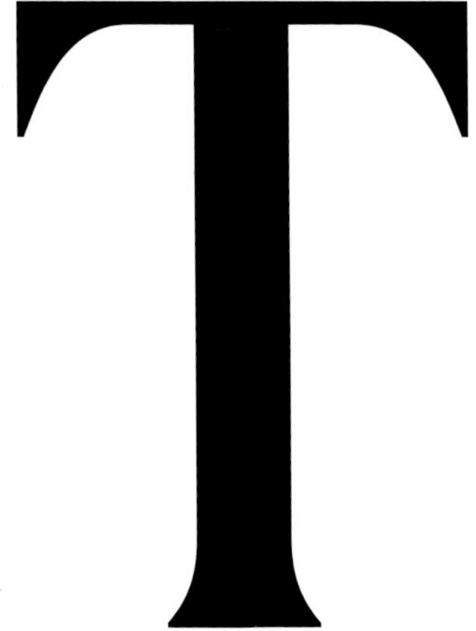

Teddy Boy

WRITER	Paul McCartney
ARTIST	Paul McCartney
RECORDED	At home, London; and Morgan Studios, London
RELEASED	*McCartney*, 1970

This is the story of a boy named Ted
If his mother said
Ted, be good, he would

She told him tales about his soldier dad
But it made her sad
Then she'd cry, oh my

Ted used to tell her he'd be twice as good
And he knew he could
'Cause in his head, he said

Momma, don't worry now
Teddy Boy's here
Taking good care of you
Momma, don't worry your
Teddy Boy's here
Teddy's gonna see you through

Then came the day she found herself a man
Teddy turned and ran
Far away, okay

He couldn't stand to see his mother in love
With another man
He didn't know, oh no

He found a place where he could settle down
And from time to time
In his head, he said

Momma, don't worry now
Teddy Boy's here
Taking good care of you
Momma, don't worry your
Teddy Boy's here
Teddy's gonna see you through

She said, Teddy, don't worry now
Mummy is here
Taking good care of you
Teddy, don't worry your
Mummy is here
Mummy's gonna see you through

This is the story of a boy named Ted
If his mother said
Ted, be good, he would

TEL. MOUNTWOOD 3391

THE MIKE ROBBINS AGENCY
(ENTERTAINMENTS)

171 MOUNT ROAD,
HIGHER BEBINGTON,
WIRRAL, CHESHIRE.

D. M. ROBBINS

MY SECOND COUSIN TED IS THE SON OF MY COUSIN BETTY DANher, who was a big influence on me musically. She loved singing and introduced me to songs like 'My Funny Valentine' and 'Till There Was You', which I later performed with The Beatles. She was married to a guy called Mike Robbins. They brought their kids up surrounded by a lot of music.

Ted was their first boy, so that's partly why I refer to him as 'Teddy Boy'. It's an affectionate term, as I'm just over ten years older than him. But the Teddy Boys were also the ruffians of my youth, the guys who wore long frock coats with velvet collars, drainpipe trousers and crepe-soled shoes. Their shoes were known as 'beetle crushers' or 'brothel creepers'. These Teddy Boys were notable in the UK for hanging around street corners waiting for a little aggro.

So, Ted is the jumping-off point for the song, but as usual, it takes its own cues and puts on its own show. The 'tales about his soldier dad' are pure imagination. The lines 'Teddy boy's here / Teddy's gonna see you through' are what I imagined Teddy saying to his mum when he was trying to support her.

It's not too much of a stretch to connect this psychodrama to two sources. One is the terrible sense of loss I still feel about my mother. Teddy is then a version of myself, trying to console myself while purportedly consoling my mother. The other is that 'Teddy Boy' was written during that oddly productive time we spent in India in 1968. The Beatles actually did several takes of it in early 1969 for the *Let It Be* film. They were mostly acoustic takes with a little electric guitar from George Harrison, but there was a bit of tension between us all and it wasn't released until I included it in my first solo record, *McCartney*, which came out in 1970.

Ted actually went on to have a successful career as an entertainer, like his dad. The whole family is steeped in showbiz.

(10) Momma Miss America. instrumental.

(11) Teddy Boy

This is the story of a boy named Ted
If his mother said, Ted be good, he would,
She told him tales about his soldier dad,
but it made her sad, and she'd cry, oh my!
Ted ~~used~~ to tell her he'd be twice as good,
and he knew he could, 'cos in his head,
he said
CHORUS ~~Teddy~~ momma don't worry your Teddy Boy's here,
Taking good care of you
Momma don't worry now Teddy is here,
Teddy's gonna see you through.

Then came the day she found herself
a man, Teddy turned and ran, far
away – O.K.
He couldn't stand to see his mother in love
~~with~~ another man, he didn't know
oh no!

(11) Teddy Boy continued.

He found a place where he could settle down, and from time to time, in his head, he said .....

CHORUS
Mamma don't worry . . .

.... and she said,

Teddy don't worry, your mummy is here, taking good care of you . . .
Teddy don't worry now mummy is here, mummy's gonna see you through.

— This is the story of a boy named Ted, if his mother said, Ted be good, he would ......

(12) Singalong Junk
instrumental.

Photos from Paul's childhood scrapbook

The Teddy Boys were also the ruffians of my youth, the guys who wore long frock coats with velvet collars, drainpipe trousers and crepe-soled shoes.

TEDDY BOY.

This is the story of a boy named Ted,
if his mother said, "Ted, be good!" he would
B She told him tales about his soldier dad
but it made her sad, and she'd cry, oh my!

—

Ted used to tell her he'd be twice as good
and he knew he could, 'cos in his head,
he said.

Mommy don't worry, your Teddy boy's here
DT Taking good care of you,
Mommy don't worry your Teddy boy's here
Teddy's going to see you through.

Then came the day she found herself a man
Teddy turned and ran far away, ~~oh hey~~ OK.
He couldn't stand to see his mother in love
with another man he didn't know oh. ~~oh~~ No!
He found a place where he could settle down
+ from time to time, in his head, he said..
Mommy don't worry, your Teddy Boy's here..
etc...
And she said — Teddy don't worry...etc..
& he said — Mommy don't worry. End.

Tell Me Who He Is

Unrecorded song. The lyrics were found in a notebook suggesting the song was written in the late 1950s or early 1960s.

Tell me who he is
Tell me that you're mine not his
He says he loves you more than I do
Tell me who he is

Tell him where to go
Tell him that I love you so
He couldn't love you more than I do
Tell me who he is

I BARELY REMEMBER THIS SONG. IT'S PROBABLY EARLY SIXTIES. BUT it may have started with me coming to John with an idea for a lyric. It's as if there's only a certain set of subjects. Love is one of them. Desire. Breakups. Revenge. That covers an awful lot of territory! So, I would have sat down with the idea of a girl having been unfaithful, or the suggestion she's being unfaithful. It's terrifically fertile ground.

Next thing you know, you get into a little story. I have always liked to do that. I remember George Harrison saying to me, 'How do you do that?' He could only write (or at least he *said* he could only write) from his personal experience. Something had happened to him and he felt lousy and then things got better, and then he would write 'Here Comes the Sun' or 'Something'.

For me it was all about making it up. It's not that I don't write autobiographically, but it's also great to write in the way Charles Dickens would have. Dickens would have written from the perspective of a girl, a poor girl. He would have been remembering his childhood. Remembering his dad being in jail. Remembering people he'd seen. There's necessarily an autobiographical component in everything, but the *merely* autobiographical is not always so scintillating. You're doing all that, but you just pull 'historical' characters into your song and play with them - give them a funny hat, a red hat. Red? Can I find a better word?

One of the great things about the lifestyle when we first went to London was our recording hours. You normally go in at ten o'clock and get yourself together. You start at ten thirty; you work three hours. At one thirty you have an hour break. Then you work from two thirty to five thirty, and that's it. In those two periods of three hours we expected to do two songs. But the great thing about it was you were done for the day by five thirty.

That meant you could go to the theatre at night. You had the Royal Court bopping away, you had the National Theatre bopping away at the Old Vic, you had the West End. Lots of great things. So, after the recording day, I would go and see *Juno and the Paycock*, say, with Colin Blakely, a very fine actor. You always had your copy of the weekly listings, magazines like *Time Out*, and you'd scour it and pick out all the things you wanted to see. And not only would you have the time to go to the theatre, but what you went to see would then inform your work. If I've just seen a National Theatre production of *Juno and the Paycock*, the next day when I'm writing a song or recording a song, that's in my mind. I want to try to achieve that kind of standard.

Tell me who he is

tell me that you're mine not his
he says he loves you more than I do
tell me who he is.

Tell him where to go
tell him that I love you so

he couldn't love you more than I do
tell me who he is.

Early Beatles postcard with John Lennon, George Harrison, Stuart Sutcliffe and Pete Best, circa 1960

Temporary Secretary

WRITER	Paul McCartney
ARTIST	Paul McCartney
RECORDED	Lower Gate Farm, Sussex
RELEASED	*McCartney II*, 1980
	Single, 1980

Mister Marks, can you find for me
Someone strong and sweet fitting on my knee
She can keep her job if she gets it wrong
Ah but Mister Marks, I won't need her long

All I need is help for a little while
We can take dictation and learn to smile
And a temporary secretary
Is what I need for to do the job

I need a
Temporary secretary
Temporary secrétaire
Temporary secretary
Temporary secretary

Mister Marks could you send her quick
'Cause my regular has been getting sick

I need a
Temporary secretary
Temporary secretary

Mister Marks, I can pay her well
If she comes along and can stay a spell
I will promise now that I'll treat her right
And will rarely keep her til late at night

I need a

She can be a belly dancer
I don't need a true romancer
She can be a diplomat
But I don't need a girl like that
She can be a neurosurgeon
If she's doin' nothin' urgent
What I need's a temporary
Temporary secretary

I need a
I need a
Temporary secretary
Temporary secrétaire
Temporary secretary
Temporary secretary
Temporary secretary
Temporary secrétaire

Now Mister Marks, when I send her back
Will you please make sure she stays on the right track

Well, I know how hard it is for young girls these days
In the face of everything to stay on the right track

Temporary secretary
(I need a)
Temporary secrétaire
Temporary secretary
Temporary secrétaire
(I need a)
Temporary secretary
Temporary secretary
Temporary secretary

THE MELLOTRON WAS A TAPE SAMPLE PLAYBACK KEYBOARD THAT The Beatles had used back in the mid-sixties on 'Strawberry Fields Forever'. I remember being in Abbey Road, and we were introduced to this big, grey Mellotron that looked like something out of wartime, though it was spanking new. EMI was a very good organisation. A very smart organisation. They made their own tape for their artists, and today it's still the best tape; it doesn't shed its oxide. They were a high-quality operation.

So, they put this Mellotron in the middle of Studio Two for our use, and we went, 'Ooh.' We were all over it. 'Wow, amazing!' So that was fascinating, just seeing if we could use it in our songs. We were always looking for new sounds and elements.

Then the Moog synthesizer came along, and it was about the size of this room. Robert Moog himself came over to demonstrate it to EMI, around 1968 or '69. A very nice boffinish inventor guy in a room with millions of knobs and devices. He showed us how to use it, and I ended up playing it on 'Maxwell's Silver Hammer'. We loved how futuristic it sounded, and it still does. A few years ago I worked on a project with Skype to create the world's first audio emojis – 'Love Mojis', they called them, because they were launched for Valentine's Day. I wrote these very short pieces of music, around five or six seconds long, to represent different emotions. It was a fun challenge, and something I hadn't done before. Then Skype added animations, and people sent them to each other in their chats. I wanted a futuristic sound for them, and the Moog was the starting point.

I used to experiment then with whatever came in, to see whether we could do anything with each new instrument. So, once these synths started to come in, around the late sixties, we would mess with them and see what each of the different controllers did, to create sounds you couldn't get else-

Above: *McCartney II* recording sessions. Lower Gate Farm, Sussex, 1979

where. Then, eventually, sequencers came along with that whole synth thing, starting whole new genres of music. These sequencers were fascinating because they would allow you to create an endless permutation of notes. So I would just fiddle around till I got something interesting, then build a song around it.

Many years later, towards the end of the seventies, I had set up a little room on the farm in Sussex with instruments and things I would just play with, and I found this sequence and thought, 'Well that's a good one.' That became the basis, the sonic bed, and then I wrote this song inspired by it.

Not a lot of people today know or remember who Alfred Marks was, but there used to be agencies around London called Alfred Marks Bureaus - not to be confused with Alfred Marks the old-time comedian, of course. The bureaus would be advertised in newspapers and various directories. And I thought, 'Well, I'll just address it to Mr Marks.'

People often say, 'Oh, you work so hard,' and I say, 'We don't work; we play.' I try to keep that in the front of my brain when things are getting tiresome. 'Jesus, we've worked too hard. No, we've *played* too hard.' The idea of needing a secretary, but only a temporary one, just made me smile. So I played with the idea.

A few years ago we started performing this song again because a DJ in Brighton had unearthed it. It was going down really well, so I wondered if I could do it too. I worked with Wix Wickens, our keyboard player, and he programmed it so he could play it live on tour.

Could you write a song like this today, with MeToo? I doubt it, and I wouldn't want to. But this was a different time, and the world has rightly progressed since then. Today, you'd think twice, if at all, before you'd suggest that you wanted to keep the secretary or assistant late at night. A good thing with this song, though, is that there's nothing overtly sexual; it's just very tongue-in-cheek. Any inference that the protagonist is keeping the secretary late at night to do other things would be in the mind of the listener.

Right: 'Temporary Secretary' track sheet

Could you write a song like this today, with MeToo? I doubt it, and I wouldn't want to. But this was a different time, and the world has rightly progressed since then.

ARTIST	TAPE BOX No. 2
TITLE 7 TEMPORARY SECRETARY.	JOB No.

1	SEQUENCER.			
2	B/D			
3	SNARE .	DRY.		
4	ECHO SNARE (O/D)			
5	SYNTH (Secretary Bits.)			
6	BASS.			
7	BASS SYNTH	(Secretary Bits)		
8	VOICE (~~Harmony~~ CHORUS.)			
9	VOICE	(Chorus)		
10	VOICE	(Lead Chorus.)		
11	ACOUSTIC	Gtr.		
12	OVATION Elec. "			
13	TOMS			
14	VOICE	Lead		
15	VOICE	Lead D/T.		
16	BANJO.			
17				
18				
19				
20				
21				
22				
23				
24				

REMARKS

Ref. No. 12527

ARE YOU BRIGHT, HARDWORKING, INTELLIGENT AND AMBITIOUS, WITH A KEEN INTEREST IN CONTEMPORARY MUSIC, A FRIENDLY PERSONALITY AND A SMART APPEARANCE?

Then what are you doing reading this?

If you are bright then you'll probably have realised that this is an advertisement for Paul McCartney's new single 'Temporary Secretary'.

Only available as a limited edition 12" record, the B-Side is the 10½ minute, previously unavailable "Secret Friend".

No previous experience necessary.

Apply in person at your local record store.

Top right: Mellotron Mark II

Bottom right: Minimoog synthesizer

Left: 'Temporary Secretary' advertisment, 1980

People often say, 'Oh, you work so hard,' and I say, 'We don't work; we play.' I try to keep that in the front of my brain when things are getting tiresome. 'Jesus, we've worked too hard. No, we've *played* too hard.'

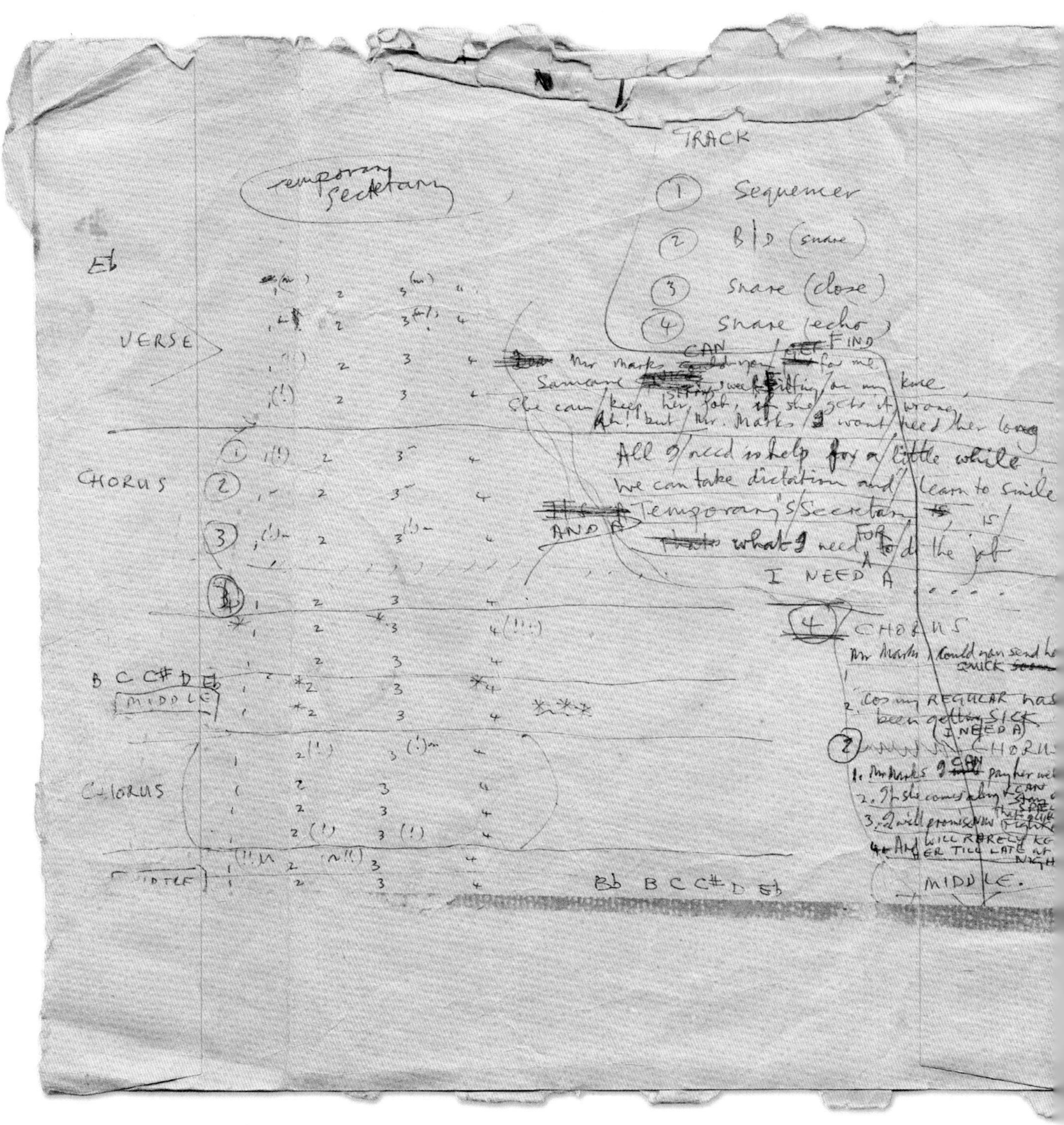
temporary secretary
TRACK
1 Sequencer
2 B/D (snare)
3 Snare (close)
4 Snare (echo)
Eb
VERSE
CHORUS
MIDDLE
CHORUS
Someone sitting on my knee
She can keep her job, if she gets it wrong
Ah! but Mr. Marks I won't need her long
All I need is help for a little while
We can take dictation and learn to smile
Temporary Secretary
I NEED A . . . .
CHORUS
MIDDLE.
Bb B C C# D Eb

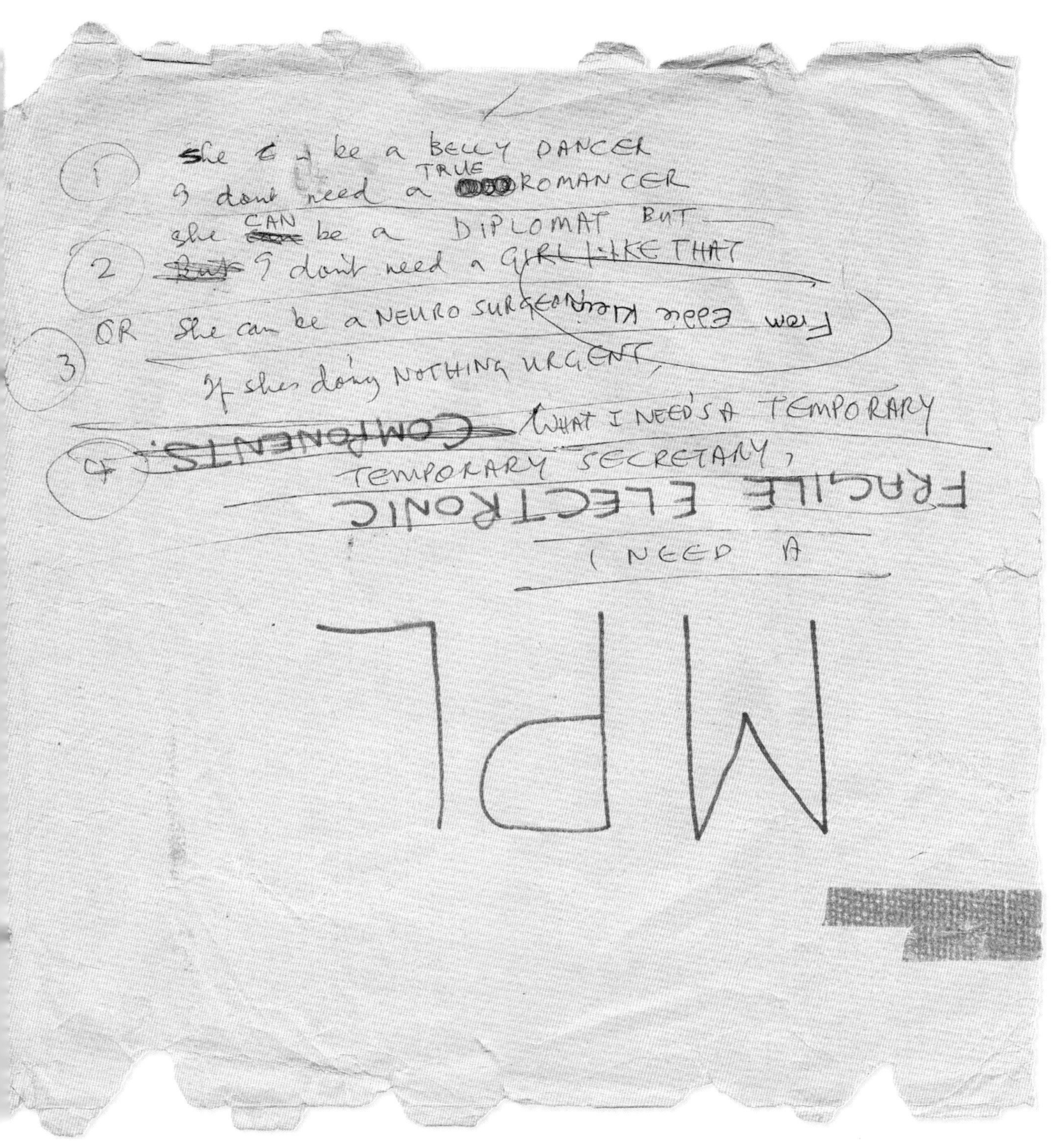

Lyrics and recording notes to 'Temporary Secretary'

Things We Said Today

WRITERS	Paul McCartney and John Lennon
ARTIST	The Beatles
RECORDED	Abbey Road Studios, London
RELEASED	B-side of 'A Hard Day's Night' UK single, 1964
	A Hard Day's Night, 1964

You say you will love me
If I have to go
You'll be thinking of me
Somehow I will know

Someday when I'm lonely
Wishing you weren't so far away
Then I will remember
Things we said today

You say you'll be mine, girl
Til the end of time
These days, such a kind girl
Seems so hard to find

Someday when we're dreaming
Deep in love, not a lot to say
Then we will remember
Things we said today

Me, I'm just the lucky kind
Love to hear you say that love is love
And though we may be blind
Love is here to stay and that's enough

To make you mine, girl
Be the only one
Love me all the time, girl
We'll go on and on

Someday when we're dreaming
Deep in love, not a lot to say
Then we will remember
Things we said today

Me, I'm just the lucky kind
Love to hear you say that love is love
And though we may be blind
Love is here to stay and that's enough

To make you mine, girl
Be the only one
Love me all the time, girl
We'll go on and on

Someday when we're dreaming
Deep in love, not a lot to say
Then we will remember
Things we said today

'THINGS WE SAID TODAY' WAS WRITTEN ON A BOAT, ON HOLIday in the Virgin Islands, with Ringo and Maureen, his then wife, and me and Jane Asher. Now that we were in The Beatles, we could afford a boat holiday! It was very nice, except when I got a major case of sunburn. One thing the working class like us didn't know about was sunblock. My auntie used to put on vinegar and oil.

However agreeable the boat might have been, I liked to go down to my cabin. Somewhere where no one could get to me. I could lock the world out, and I'd sit there and strum away for a little while and see if anything came.

By this stage I had a really good Epiphone guitar. When we were kids, we fantasised about the guitars our heroes had. The Gibson, the Gretsch, the Fender. But these were expensive instruments, and we had to scale down our aspirations. I scaled mine down a lot: when I was around eighteen I bought this terrible little thing, a Rosetti Solid 7 - basically just a plank of wood with a neck. It wasn't a good instrument at all, but it was red; it looked shiny. I got it from Frank Hessy's in Liverpool.

I bought it on hire purchase, though my dad was very against never-never payment plans, probably because he'd been burned or he'd known a lot of people who had been burned. So I went to Hamburg in 1960 with this Rosetti Solid 7, which lasted me a month or two and then fell apart. That's why I moved to piano; that's why I played more piano than the other guys in the group. But later, when we had a bit of money, I got myself an Epiphone acoustic, so by 1964 I had a pretty good guitar.

That particular day on the boat, I started with an A minor chord. A minor to E minor to A minor, which gave me a sort of folksy, whimsical world. And then in the middle, on 'Me, I'm just the lucky kind', it goes to the major and gets hopeful. The thing I always loved and still love about writing a song is that, at the end of two or three hours, I have a newborn baby to show everyone. I want to show it to the world, and the world at that moment was the people on the boat.

I had to remember it, of course, because I didn't write it down. I didn't write down music - because I couldn't. It was all in the head. I have wondered since why it was easy for me to remember these things. When I've used a little cassette recorder or some other recording device, I find it hard to remember songs because I haven't made myself remember them. Looking back, I love the fact that my circumstances were as they were. Years later, as I try to explain why I don't read music or write it down, I blame my Celtic tradition, the bardic tradition. The people I come from trained themselves to rely on their memories.

(1)

YACHT HAPPY DAYS
Yacht Haven
St. Thomas, U. S. Virgin Islands

Dear Dad and Mike,

I've been meaning to write but you know how it is.

Well, as you will have noticed the press got us, but apart from that one incident we've been left alone.

We are, of course, having a great time the boat is nice, and weather etc.. is lovely.

We've been doing quite a bit of snorkelling and I've seen one ~~or~~ or two barracudas (they're the ones that sometimes get you – mind you, the ones I saw were about 1½ feet long.

P.T.O.

Right: Payment book entry for Paul's Rossetti Solid 7 guitar. Frank Hessy's, Liverpool, 1960

FRANK HESSY LTD.

62 STANLEY STREET

and

20 MANCHESTER STREET

Liverpool 1.

Telephone: CENtral 1559

—:—

Agents for and Stockists of

the BEST

in Musical Instruments

REGULAR PAYMENTS ESSENTIAL

Date June 30th 1960

A/c. No. F235

Name Mr Paul McCartney

Address 20 Forthlin Rd. Liverpool, 18.

Total Amount £21 : – : –

Weekly Rent Monthly £ : 10 : –

Red Solid 7 Elec Gtr

IMPORTANT

Customers must notify their Change of Address : before Removal :

Always produce this book when making Instalments.

70951 66-68 WHITECHAPEL, LIVERPOOL. 1.

61797 66-68 WHITECHAPEL, LIVERPOOL. 1.

63533 66-68 WHITECHAPEL, LIVERPOOL. 1.

63222 66-68 WHITECHAPEL, LIVERPOOL. 1.

61241 66-68 WHITECHAPEL, LIVERPOOL. 1.

05524 62 STANLEY STREET, LIVERPOOL. 1.

31780 62 STANLEY STREET, LIVERPOOL. 1.

31977 62 STANLEY STREET, LIVERPOOL. 1.

Received from P McCartney

For FRANK HESSY LTD.

A/c No. F235

Ticket to Ride

WRITERS	Paul McCartney and John Lennon
ARTIST	The Beatles
RECORDED	Abbey Road Studios, London
RELEASED	Single, 1965 *Help!* 1965

I think I'm gonna be sad
I think it's today, yeah
The girl that's driving me mad
Is going away

She's got a ticket to ride
She's got a ticket to ride
She's got a ticket to ride
And she don't care

She said that living with me
Is bringing her down, yeah
For she would never be free
When I was around

She's got a ticket to ride
She's got a ticket to ride
She's got a ticket to ride
But she don't care

I don't know why she's ridin' so high
She oughta think twice
She oughta do right by me
Before she gets to sayin' goodbye
She oughta think twice
She oughta do right by me

I think I'm gonna be sad
I think it's today, yeah
The girl that's driving me mad
Is going away, yeah

She's got a ticket to ride
She's got a ticket to ride
She's got a ticket to ride
But she don't care

I don't know why she's ridin' so high
She oughta think twice
She oughta do right by me
Before she gets to sayin' goodbye
She oughta think twice
She oughta do right by me

She said that living with me
Is bringing her down, yeah
For she would never be free
When I was around

She's got a ticket to ride
She's got a ticket to ride
She's got a ticket to ride
But she don't care
My baby don't care
My baby don't care

JOHN AND I WENT HITCHHIKING. GEORGE AND I DID IT A COUple of times too. It was a way to get a holiday. Maybe our parents booked holidays, but we wouldn't have known how to. So we would head out, just the two of us, with our guitars. John was older, but I was in on the decision about where we might go. He'd got a hundred pounds from his uncle, who was a dentist in Edinburgh, for his twenty-first birthday, and we decided we'd hitchhike to Spain by way of Paris. We'd start over on the other side of a particular bridge because that's where all of the long-distance lorries started. We'd wear little bowler hats to get their attention!

When we got the lift, we sat together; we'd experience the lorry driver together. We knew what it was like to go on the cross-channel ferry; we knew what it was like to try and hang out in Paris. We would walk for miles around the city, sit in bars near Rue des Anglais, visit Montmartre and the Folies Bergère. We felt like we were fully paid-up existentialists and could write a novel from what we learnt in a week there, so we never did make it to Spain. We'd been together so much that if you had a question, we would both pretty much come up with the same answer.

Above: In Paris, 1961

It's a bit crude, but it's fair to say that, in general, I'd had a good life and John hadn't. His life had been tougher, and he had to develop a harder shell than I did. He was quite a cynical guy but, as they say, with a heart of gold. A big softy, but his shield was hard. So that was very good for the two of us. Opposites attract. I could calm him down, and he could fire me up. We could see things in each other that the other needed to be complete.

When it came to writing rock and roll, we were on the same page. You don't want to write, 'She said that living with me is upsetting.' It's just not rock and roll. It's too front parlour and lace curtains. That's why it has to be 'She said that living with me is *bringing her down*'.

John and I always liked wordplay. So, the phrase 'She's got a ticket to ride' of course referred to riding on a bus or train, but – if you really want to know – it also referred to Ryde on the Isle of Wight, where my cousin Betty and her husband Mike were running a pub. That's what they did; they ran pubs. He ended up as an entertainment manager at a Butlin's holiday resort. Betty and Mike were very showbiz. It was great fun to visit them, so John and I hitchhiked down to Ryde, and when we wrote the song we were referring to the memory of this trip. It's very cute now to think of me and John in a little single bed, top and tail, and Betty and Mike coming to tuck us in.

Above: John Lennon. Louvre Museum, Paris, 1961

Right: Paris diary and Beatles logo sketches, 1961

The singers have to go one better than the audience, so they lie on the floor, or jump on a passing drum, or kiss one of the guitars and then hit the man playing it. The crowd like this and many stand on chairs to see the fun, and soon the audience are all singing and shouting like one man, But he didnt mind. Vince ("Ron ~~[illegible]~~") Taylor finally appears and joins the fun, and in the end he has so much fun that he passes out, raising a cry of "Il cest unconscious" from the French people in the audience. But in spite of this it has been a wonderful show, lovely show, ... lovely.

featuring Danny et les Pirates, and many more, ~~even much more~~ groups for your evening's entertainment. Topping the bill was Vince ("Come back Ron") Taylor, star of English screen and "Two I's."

The atmosphere is like many a night club, but the teenagers stand round the dancing floor which you use as a stage. They jump on a woman who sings with golden trousers and a microphone and then hit the man when he says go away.

A group follows, and so do the rest of them—playing Apache worse than Joe Loss, or his brother—Geraldo Loss. When the singer joins the band—the leather jacket fiends who are the audience join in dancing and banging tables with the leg of a chair and joining in.

It was 10 o'clock, o'clock it was, when we are entering the "Olympia" in Paris, to see the Johnny Halliday rock show, cos we remember thinking at the time.

The cheapest seats in les theatre (French) were 7/6 (English) so we followed the woman with the torch.

When Johnny Halliday came, everybody went wild — and many was the stamping & cheering in the aisles; and dancing too. But the man said sit down, so we had to.

The excitement rose, and so did the audience and in the end there were many boys and girls dancing along the back rows. Also old men, which is even stranger, isnt it?

This was a real rock and roll riot — and we were ~~taking part~~ exciting to watch rock hitting the French town of Paris.

~~Later on~~ Meanwhile, later the same week we go to Les Rock Festival

Too Many People

WRITER	Paul McCartney
ARTIST	Paul and Linda McCartney
RECORDED	CBS Studios, New York
RELEASED	*RAM*, 1971
	B-side of 'Uncle Albert/Admiral Halsey' single, 1971

Too many people going underground
Too many reaching for a piece of cake
Too many people pulled and pushed around
Too many waiting for that lucky break

That was your first mistake
You took your lucky break and broke it in two
Now what can be done for you
You broke it in two

Too many people sharing party lines
Too many people never sleep in late
Too many people paying parking fines
Too many hungry people losing weight

That was your first mistake
You took your lucky break and broke it in two
Now what can be done for you
You broke it in two

Too many people preaching practices
Don't let them tell you what you want to be
Too many people holding back
This is crazy and baby, it's not like me

That was your last mistake
I find my love awake and waiting to be
Now what can be done for you
She's waiting for me

THIS SONG WAS WRITTEN A YEAR OR SO AFTER THE BEATLES breakup, at a time when John was firing missiles at me with his songs, and one or two of them were quite cruel. I don't know what he hoped to gain, other than punching me in the face. The whole thing really annoyed me.

I decided to turn my missiles on him too, but I'm not really that kind of a writer, so it was quite veiled. It was the 1970s equivalent of what we might today call a 'diss track'. Songs like this, where you're calling someone out on their behaviour, are quite commonplace now, but back then it was a fairly new 'genre'. The idea of too many people 'preaching practices' was definitely aimed at John telling everyone what they ought to do - telling me, for instance, that I ought to go into business with Allen Klein. I just got fed up with being told what to do, so I wrote this song. 'You took your lucky break and broke it in two' was me saying basically, 'You've made this break, so good luck with it.' But it was pretty mild. I didn't really come out with any savagery, and it's actually a fairly upbeat song; it doesn't really sound that vitriolic. If you didn't know the story, I don't know that you'd be able to guess at the anger behind its writing.

It was all a bit weird and a bit nasty, and I was basically saying, 'Let's be sensible. We had a lot going for us in The Beatles, and what actually split us up is the business stuff, and that's pretty pathetic really, so let's try and be peaceful. Let's maybe give peace a chance.'

The first verse and the chorus have pretty much all the anger I could muster, and when I did the vocal on the second line, 'Too many reaching for a piece of cake', I remember singing it as 'Piss off cake', which you can hear if you really listen to it. Again, I was getting back at John, but my heart wasn't really in it. This is me saying, 'Too many people are sharing the party line. Too many people are grabbing for a slice of the cake, a piece of the pie.' The 'sleep in late' thing - whether that was accurate, whether John and Yoko actually slept in late or not, I'm not sure (although John often was a late riser when I would drive out to Weybridge so that we could write together). They were all references to people thinking that their own truth was the only truth, which was certainly what was coming from John.

The thing is, so much of what they held to be truth was crap. War is over? Well no, it isn't. But I get what you're saying: war is over if you want it to be. So, if enough people want war to be over, it'll be over. I'm not sure that's entirely true, but it's a great sentiment; it's a nice thing to think and to say. I'd been able to accept Yoko in the studio, sitting on a blanket in front of my amp. I'd worked hard to come to terms with that. But then when we broke up and everyone was now flailing around, John turned nasty. I don't really understand why. Maybe because we grew up in Liverpool, where it was always good to get in the first punch of a fight.

The whole story in a nutshell is that we were having a meeting in 1969, and John showed up and said he'd met this guy Allen Klein, who had promised Yoko an exhibition in Syracuse, and then matter-of-factly John told us he was leaving the band. That's basically how it happened. It was three to one because the other two went with John, so it was looking like Allen Klein was going to own our entire Beatles empire. I was not too keen on that idea.

John actually had Allen Klein and Yoko in the room, suggesting lyrics during writing sessions. In his song 'How Do You Sleep?' the line 'The only thing you done was yesterday' was apparently Allen Klein's suggestion, and John said, 'Hey, great. Put that in.' I can see the laughs they had doing it, and I had to work very hard not to take it too seriously, but at the back of my mind I was thinking, 'Wait a minute, All I ever did was "Yesterday"? I suppose that's a funny pun, but all I ever did was "Yesterday", "Let It Be", "The Long and Winding Road", "Eleanor Rigby", "Lady Madonna", . . . - fuck you, John.'

I had to fight them for my bit of The Beatles and, in fact, for their bit of The Beatles, which many years later they realised and almost thanked me for. Nowadays people get it, but at the time I think the others felt they were the ones who were victims, who were being hurt by my actions. Allen Klein already had a history with The Rolling Stones. I just thought, 'Oy oy oy, no, this guy's got such a bad reputation.' And good old John says, 'Oh, if he's that badly talked about, he can't be all bad.' John had this kind of distorted thinking, which was amusing sometimes. But not when someone was going to take everything that John and George and Ringo and I owned and had worked really hard to get.

So, I stood up as the sensible one and said, 'This is not good.' Klein wanted twenty per cent, and I said, 'Tell him he can have ten, if you have to go with him.' 'Oh no, no, no,' they came back. 'No, he wants twenty.' It seemed to me they were just fucking out of it and making no attempt to do anything sensible. A lot of hurt went down during that period in the early 1970s - them feeling hurt, me feeling hurt - but John being John, he was the one who would write a hurtful song. That was his bag.

Right: John Lennon and Yoko Ono. Apple office, London, 1969

I had to fight them for my bit of The Beatles and, in fact, for their bit of The Beatles, which many years later they realised and almost thanked me for. Nowadays people get it, but at the time I think the others felt they were the ones who were victims, who were being hurt by my actions.

TOO MANY PEOPLE

Too many people going underground
Too many reaching for a piece of cake
Too many people pulling pushed around ...ed and
Too many waiting for that lucky break
That was your first mistake
You took your lucky break and broke it in two
Now what can be done for you
You broke it in two
That was your first mistake
You took your lucky break and broke it in two
Now what can be done for you
You broke it in two

Too may people sharing party lines
Too many people never sleeping late in
Too many people paying parking fines
Too many hungry people losing weight
Too many people preaching practices
Don't let them tell you what you want to be
Too many people holding back -this is crazy
And, baby, it's not like me.
That was your last mistake
I find my love awake and waiting to be
Now what can be done for you
She's waiting for me.

sleep in

6137
12

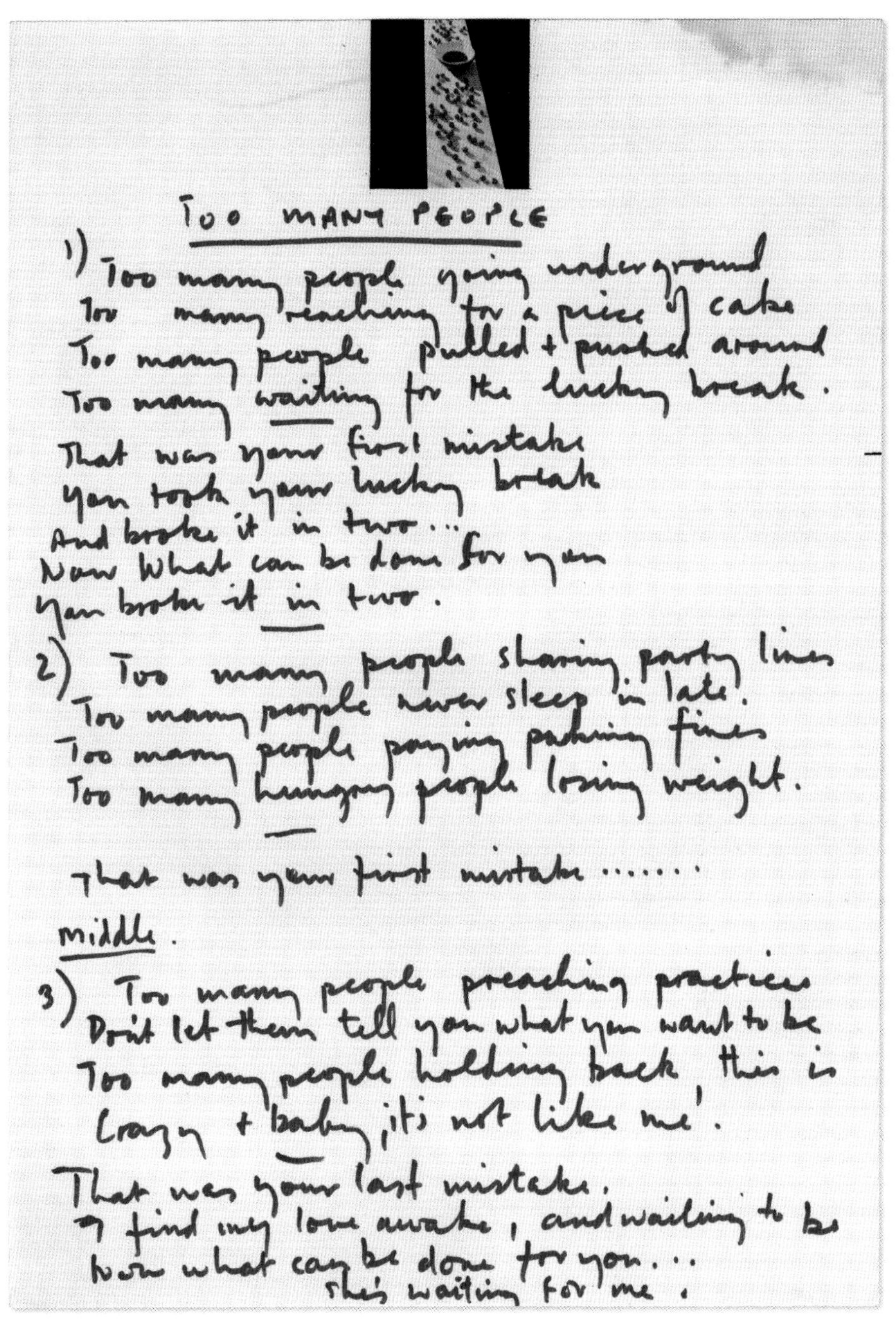

<u>TOO MANY PEOPLE</u>

1) Too many people going underground
Too many reaching for a piece of cake
Too many people pulled + pushed around
Too many <u>waiting</u> for the lucky break.

That was your first mistake
You took your lucky break
And broke it in two...
Now What can be done for you
You broke it <u>in</u> two.

2) Too many people sharing party lines
Too many people never sleep in late.
Too many people paying parking fines
Too many <u>hungry</u> people losing weight.

That was your first mistake.......

<u>middle</u>.

3) Too many people preaching practices
Don't let them tell you what you want to be
Too many people holding back, this is
Crazy + <u>baby</u>, it's not like me'.

That was your last mistake.
I find my love awake, and waiting to be
Now what can be done for you...
She's waiting for me.

I decided to turn my missiles on [John] too, but I'm not really that kind of a writer, so it was quite veiled. It was the 1970s equivalent of what we might today call a 'diss track'.

Too Much Rain

WRITER	Paul McCartney
ARTIST	Paul McCartney
RECORDED	AIR Studios, London
RELEASED	*Chaos and Creation in the Backyard*, 2005

Laugh when your eyes are burning
Smile when your heart is filled with pain
Sigh as you brush away your sorrow
Make a vow
That it's not going to happen again
It's not right, in one life
Too much rain

You know the wheels keep turning
Why do the tears run down your face?
We used to hide away our feelings
But for now
Tell yourself it won't happen again
It's not right, in one life
Too much rain

It's too much for anyone
Too hard for anyone
Who wants a happy and peaceful life
You've got to learn to laugh

Smile when you're spinning round and round
Sigh as you think about tomorrow
Make a vow
That you're going to be happy again
It's all right, in your life
No more rain

It's too much for anyone
Too hard for anyone
Who wants a happy and peaceful life
You've got to learn to laugh

GROWING UP IN 1950S LIVERPOOL AS A GUY, YOU MOST CERtainly had to hide away your feelings. Guys would never say 'I love you' to each other. We were just too busy trying to be macho, and we didn't realise it might make you a tad thoughtless sometimes. It was only later, as we matured, that we realised we were doing it because we were trying to be hard, young Liverpool guys. I think a lot of people still do hide away their feelings, but I'm lucky to have got out of that. Not totally, perhaps.

The beginnings of the song came from Charlie Chaplin. Not only was he the great comedian; he was also pretty good at penning a tune. He wrote 'Smile' for his film *Modern Times*, and it's always been a favourite of mine. That idea of smiling, even though your heart is breaking. Here we have simple encouragement: when you're down, you can get back up. 'Make a vow / That you're going to be happy again.' I sometimes refer to that idea as a 'get over it' song.

There's a pretty basic imagery in this song. We associate rain with things not going too well, and sunshine with things being great. There's really no more to it than that. I've used lines like 'meet you in the falling rain' or 'that was a glorious day with the rain' or 'it was great to stand out in the rain and be in love' once or twice in a song, but generally rain is bad news, so it's not right that in one life there should be too much rain.

Most of us can accept that some rain must fall into each life, because generally we don't have more than a little rain. But some human beings - say, refugees in flight, or some people in developing countries who've got absolutely nothing and are literally dying of hunger - have, in the most basic of terms, too much rain. It's not fair that some people should have so much to cope with when the rest of us have so much to be grateful for.

So, even though I might originally have been raised to be that Liverpool tough guy, I've learnt over the years to try to open myself up, to understand that so many people's hearts and lives have a lot of rain in them, a lot of pain. I'd like to think that some of my songs have done the same, have made people feel something they did not even know was there. People have told me they've had that experience. And plenty of songs have done the same for me. It's true that life can sometimes be 'too much for anyone', but that's why we have songs - to try and make the rain go away or, at least, hold an umbrella over you for a while.

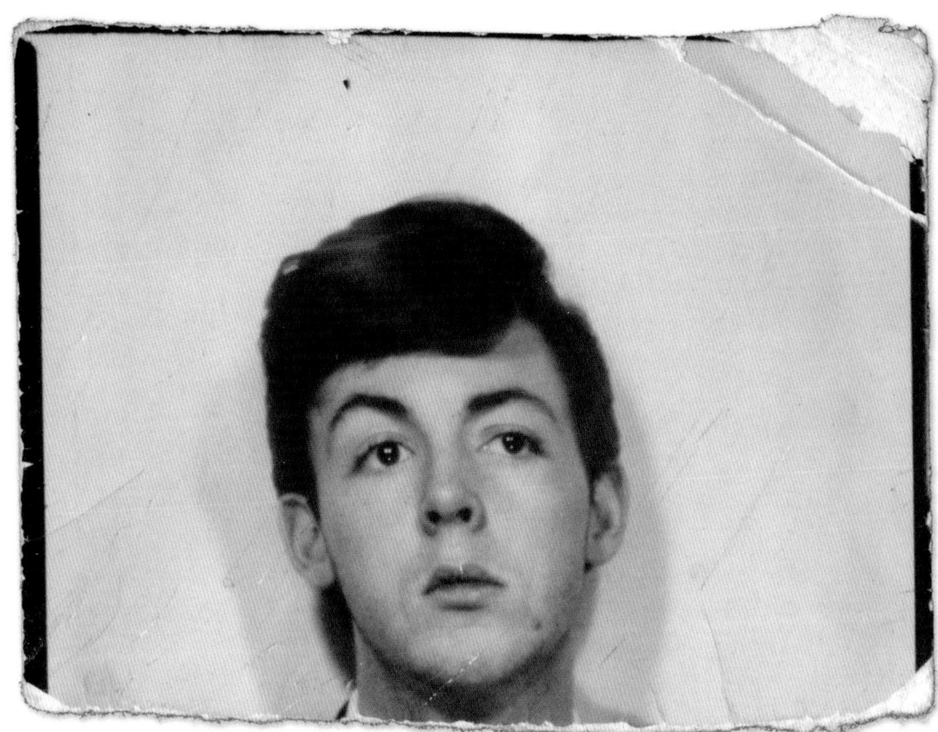

Left: Passport photo, late 1950s

Right: Photographed by brother Mike at home. Liverpool, early 1960s

Guys would never say 'I love you' to each other. We were just too busy trying to be macho, and we didn't realise it might make you a tad thoughtless sometimes. It was only later, as we matured, that we realised we were doing it because we were trying to be hard, young Liverpool guys.

GO AHEAD
YOUNG MAN

Tug of War

WRITER	Paul McCartney
ARTIST	Paul McCartney
RECORDED	Park Gate Studios, Sussex; and AIR Montserrat
RELEASED	*Tug of War*, 1982
	Single, 1982

It's a tug of war
What with one thing and another
It's a tug of war
We expected more
But with one thing and another
We were trying to outdo each other
In a tug of war

In another world
In another world we could stand on top of the
  mountain
With our flag unfurled
In a time to come
In a time to come we will be dancing to the beat
Played on a different drum

It's a tug of war
Though I know I mustn't grumble
It's a tug of war
But I can't let go
If I do you'll take a tumble
And the whole thing is going to crumble
It's a tug of war

Pushing and pushing
Pulling and pulling
Pushing and pulling

In years to come they may discover
What the air we breathe and life we lead
Are all about
But it won't be soon enough
Soon enough for me
No it won't be soon enough
Soon enough for me

In another world we could stand on top of the
  mountain
With our flag unfurled
In a time to come we will be dancing to the beat
Played on a different drum
We will be dancing to the beat
Played on a different drum
We will be dancing to the beat
Played on a different drum

It's a tug of war
What with one thing and another
It's a tug of war
We expected more
But with one thing and another
We were trying to outscore each other
In a tug of war

Pushing and pushing
Pulling and pulling
Pushing and pulling

THE TUG OF WAR WAS A VERY POPULAR EVENT WHEN I WAS growing up. In fact, it used to be an Olympic sport, and in 1908 a Liverpool police team won a medal in the Olympic Games. There were two teams of big rugby-playing types at either end of a great big rope, and they'd just keep tugging until one of them pulled the other team past a marker and won. That seemed like a nice metaphor.

When you're a kid you think things will be straightforward, but when you're older and you've experienced more, you realise it's an everlasting war between good and bad. I thought everyone had great families, but they don't. I thought the sun would always shine, but it won't. I thought that life would always be nice, but sadly, it isn't. So, what with one thing and another, it's a tug of war. You've got to try your hardest for other people because they may fall if you don't.

The song was written before John's death in December 1980, but when the album came out in April 1982, people thought it must be about him, that it was about our trying to outdo each other, that 'We were trying to outscore each other / In a tug of war'. Meanings are often attributed to something that creates a convenient narrative, though, of course, they aren't necessarily valid. But I don't mind. The song belongs to the listeners once I release it. It's theirs to do with whatever they want, and I don't normally go around saying, 'Well, no, that's not what it means.'

Of course I can see how it could fit that interpretation, because John and I did try to outscore each other – that was the nature of our competitiveness – and we were both very up front about it. But it's also important to realise that our work benefitted from this tug of war in so many ways. I always like the story that someone told me of how John's hearing 'Coming Up' prompted him to get back in the studio to record *Double Fantasy*. 'Beautiful Boy (Darling

Above: Stella at sports day. Sussex, 1984

Left: *Tug of War* recording sessions. AIR Studios, London, 1981

Right: With engineer Eddie Klein. Hog Hill Mill, Sussex, 1985

Page 734: Notes for the music video for 'Tug of War', 1982

Boy)' is a real favourite of mine. So, it's true that if he wrote a good song, I'd feel I had to write a better one, which is no less a form of inspiration than anything else.

There's a certain motivation when someone you respect comes up with something good. In the early twentieth century, Picasso and Braque were egging each other on. In the history of artists there have always been such tug of war collaborations - Shakespeare and Marlowe or Van Gogh and Gauguin, for example. Artists inspiring each other is a more positive way to think about it. You don't necessarily have to tell anyone, but in your own mind you just think, 'Well, I can do that, and I can do it better.'

But maybe this yin and yang and trying to see both sides comes from being a Gemini. I never really bother with astrological signs, but I do know that the conventional Gemini has two halves, pushing and pulling, and it fits with my character. Apparently, we're typically curious, intelligent, adaptable and sociable. It occurs to me that anyone who is a Gemini is going to think about the two-sidedness of things. I've noticed that tension does crop up a lot in my songs: 'Ebony and Ivory', say, or 'Hello, Goodbye' - 'You say yes, I say no / You say stop and I say go, go, go'.

I wanted to start 'Tug of War' with sound effects, to help set the scene. Then, by serendipity, I heard about a national indoor tug of war contest taking place nearby. I sent Eddie, my engineer, who always had a twinkling sense of humour, to record it, and the grunting you hear on the opening of the track - that sound collage - is the sound of a real tug of war. So the song segues wonderfully from the literal into the metaphorical.

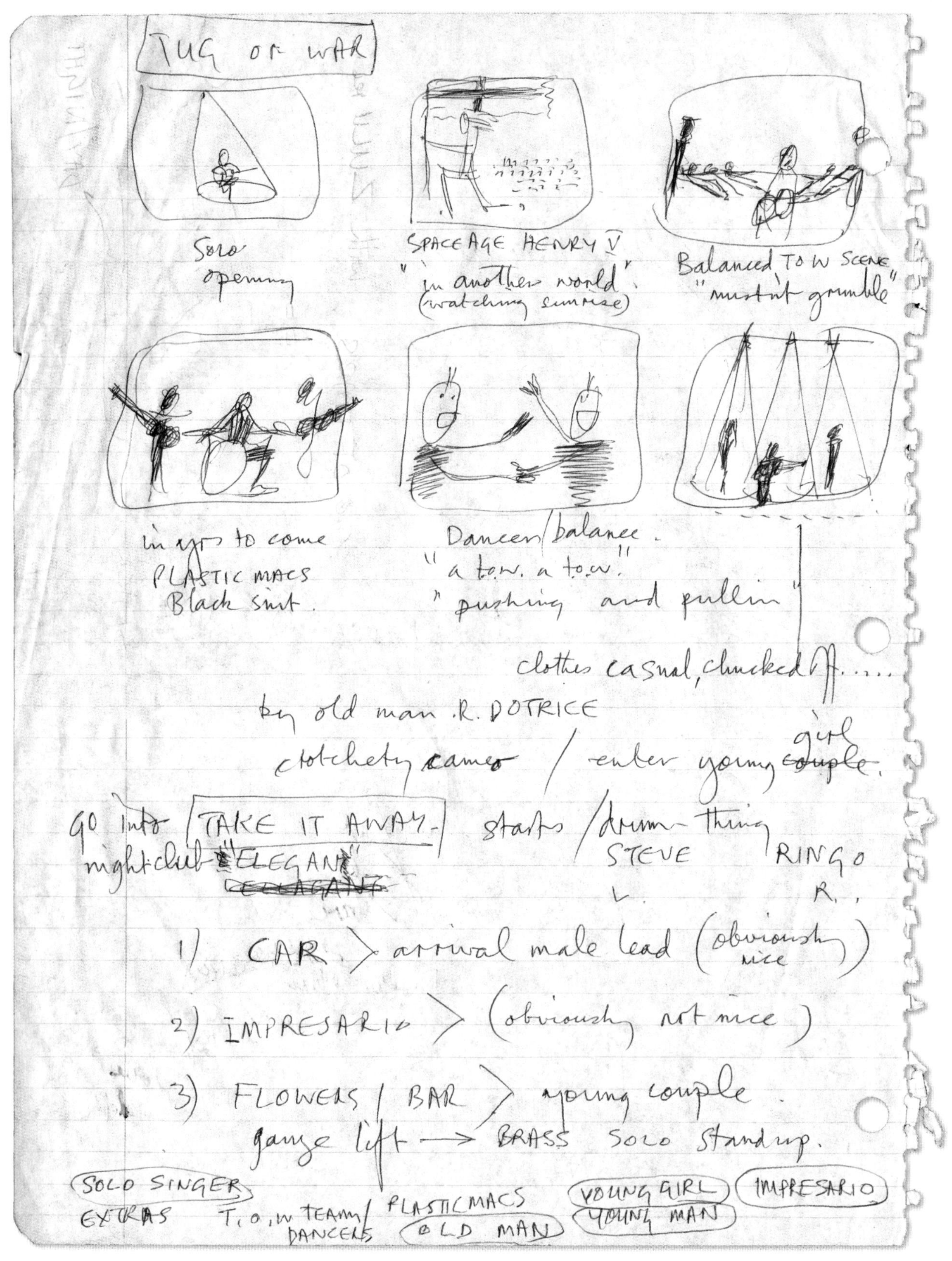
TUG OF WAR
Solo opening
SPACEAGE HENRY V "in another world" (watching sunrise)
Balanced TOW SCENE "mustn't grumble"
in yrs to come PLASTIC MACS Black suit.
Dancer/balance. "a tow. a tow." "pushing and pullin"
clothes casual, chucked off.....
by old man R. DOTRICE
crotchety cameo / enter young girl
GO into TAKE IT AWAY- starts / drum-thing
nightclub "ELEGANT"
STEVE RINGO
L. R.
1) CAR > arrival male lead (obviously nice)
2) IMPRESARIO > (obviously not nice)
3) FLOWERS / BAR > young couple.
garage lift → BRASS SOLO standup.
SOLO SINGER
IMPRESARIO
EXTRAS
T.O.W. TEAM/ DANCERS
PLASTIC MACS
YOUNG GIRL
YOUNG MAN
OLD MAN

TUG OF WAR.

1. It's a tug of war
what with one thing and another
its a tug of war
we expected more
but with one thing and another
we were trying to outdo each other
IN ~~its~~ a tug of war

In another world —
In another world we could stand on top of the mountain
with our flag unfurled —
In a time to come
In a time to come we will be dancing to the beat
played on a [STOP] different drum [STOP]

2. It's a tug of war
~~Though~~ ~~But~~ I know ~~we~~ I mustn't grumble
It's a tug of war
But ~~And~~ I can't let go
If I do you'll take a tumble
and the whole thing is going to crumble
IT'S a tug of war
(pulling and pushing) C, B, A (F)

In years to come they may discover [DAYLIGHT]
what the air we breathe & the life we lead
are all about
but it won't be soon enough — soon enough for me
(REPEAT) soon enough ~~soon enough~~ ~~soon enough~~ ~~for me~~
SOLO (another world) DANCING BEAT 3 TIMES. [STOP] different drum [STOP]

3. It's a tug of war
.... we were trying to outscore each other IN....
PULLING & pushing C, B, A. (C CHORD END.)

Two of Us

WRITERS	Paul McCartney and John Lennon
ARTIST	The Beatles
RECORDED	Apple Studio, London
RELEASED	*Let It Be*, 1970

Two of us riding nowhere
Spending someone's hard-earned pay
You and me Sunday driving
Not arriving on our way back home

We're on our way home
We're on our way home
We're going home

Two of us sending postcards
Writing letters on my wall
You and me burning matches
Lifting latches on our way back home

We're on our way home
We're on our way home
We're going home

You and I have memories
Longer than the road
That stretches out ahead

Two of us wearing raincoats
Standing solo in the sun
You and me chasing paper
Getting nowhere on our way back home

We're on our way home
We're on our way home
We're going home

LINDA AND I USED TO LOVE TO GO FOR A DRIVE, THE 'TWO of us riding nowhere'. It didn't matter which direction we took. Anywhere out of London where we would find a forest or a country field or a hillside. We had both been nature lovers when we were kids, and we would each go into the woods to search for a stream. Linda did that where she lived in Westchester County, New York, finding a stream at the back of a garden somewhere. I was living on a council estate in Liverpool, but I found my own stream and, being a boy, I would dam it up and then smash it down at the end of the day. Linda would find salamanders under rocks. We had this reservoir of childhood stories that we would tell each other.

One of the great things about Linda was that while I was driving and going, 'Oh my God, I think I'm lost,' she'd simply say, 'Great!' She loved getting lost. And she pointed out to me quite rightly that there would always be a sign somewhere saying 'London', so we'd just follow that.

One day we went out into the countryside and found a little wood that looked as if it might be a good place for a walk. I parked the car. There's a photograph of me in the Aston Martin, sitting with the driver's door open and my feet out. I've got my guitar. That's me writing 'Two of Us'.

There's a line that says, 'Spending someone's hard-earned pay'. I don't know where that came from or what it means. I don't necessarily want meaning. I don't root for meaning all the time. Sometimes it just feels right. I talked to Allen Ginsberg once about poetry and songs, and Allen told me about a conversation he'd had with Bob Dylan when he was trying to correct Dylan about the grammar of a lyric, and Dylan had said, 'This is a song; it's not a poem.' I know exactly what he means. Sometimes something just sings well. Take 'Spending someone's hard-earned pay'. It can't be 'spending someone's weekly pay packet'. You'd trip yourself up with those words.

Lying behind the phrase 'We're on our way home' is less the literal sense of going back to London, but more about trying to get in touch with the people we once were. The postcard sending does have a very literal feel, though. Whenever Linda and I went away, we would buy lots of postcards and send them to all our friends. John was also a great postcard sender, so you'd get some great stuff from him.

Then there's 'You and me burning matches'. I remember there was a point, much earlier on, when we would light matches just for the hell of it. My brother and I were firebugs when we were kids, and my dad worried that we would burn the house down, so he made us light a whole box of matches till we got totally fed up of it.

Lost in the Aston Martin
writing 'Two of Us'.
Somewhere in the UK, 1968

APPLE CORPS LIMITED
3 SAVILE ROW LONDON W1
TELEPHONE 01-734 8232
CABLES APCORE LONDON W1

TWO OF US (on our way home.)

① Two of us riding nowhere
Spending someone's hard earned pay
You and me Sunday driving
Not arriving on our way back home

CHORUS
We're on our way home
... ... we're going home.

② Two of us sending postcards,
Writing letters on my wall
You and me burning matches
Lifting latches on our way home.

CHORUS.

MIDDLE You and I have memories
Longer than the road
That stretches out ahead.

③ Two of us wearing raincoats
Standing solo in the sun
You and me chasing paper, getting nowhere,
On our way home

CHORUS and OUT.. A Quarrymen Original.

DIRECTORS N ASPINALL D O'DELL H PINSKER

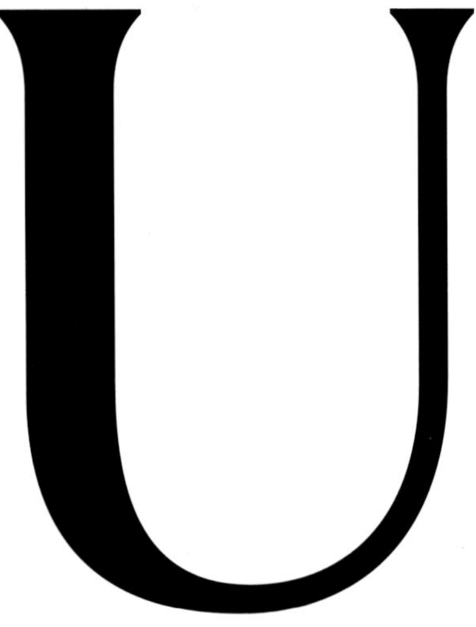

Uncle Albert/Admiral Halsey

WRITERS	Paul McCartney and Linda McCartney
ARTIST	Paul and Linda McCartney
RECORDED	CBS Studios, New York
RELEASED	*RAM*, 1971
	Single, 1971

We're so sorry, Uncle Albert
We're so sorry if we caused you any pain
We're so sorry, Uncle Albert
But there's no one left at home
And I believe I'm gonna rain

We're so sorry, but we haven't heard a thing all day
We're so sorry, Uncle Albert
But if anything should happen
We'll be sure to give a ring

We're so sorry, Uncle Albert
But we haven't done a bloody thing all day
We're so sorry, Uncle Albert
But the kettle's on the boil
And we're so easily called away

Hands across the water
Heads across the sky
Hands across the water
Heads across the sky

Admiral Halsey notified me
He had to have a berth or he couldn't get to sea
I had another look and I had a cup of tea
And a butter pie
A butter pie?
The butter wouldn't melt
So I put it in the pie, alright?

Hands across the water
Heads across the sky
Hands across the water
Heads across the sky

Live a little, be a gypsy, get around
Get your feet up off the ground
Live a little, get around
Live a little, be a gypsy, get around
Get your feet up off the ground
Live a little, get around

Hands across the water
Heads across the sky
Hands across the water
Heads across the sky

UNCLE ALBERT WORKED WITH MY DAD IN THE COTTON firm. Dad was a salesman, and Uncle Albert was something a little higher up. He certainly had more money, and he lived in Birkenhead, which was the posh bit of Liverpool.

Our family gatherings were very friendly, very humorous occasions. There may have been a bit of bitching behind the scenes, but I never saw it. Mind you, whenever they'd get together they would get pissed. A lot of the uncles were referred to as 'piss artists', meaning they drank a bit. Uncle Harry would get very drunk. Uncle Albert would too. Uncle Albert would stand on the table, roaring drunk, and recite the Bible. He also wanted to keep everyone on the straight and narrow.

I'm pretty sure this song reflects a new nostalgia for family at a time when I had moved away from Liverpool. I wouldn't see the family anywhere near as regularly. We might go back up for a New Year's Eve party, but in general, I'd moved away from all that. It had just gone. Of all The Beatles, I was the only one who did go back. The others hardly ever went back.

By this stage, I'm imagining Uncle Albert as a character in a playlet, and then I go into character – a very arrogant posh guy, instead of just a little kid from Liverpool. The shift of accent is enough. 'Hands across the water / Heads across the sky' refers to Linda and me being American and British.

Admiral William Halsey Jr. was an historically important person who was appointed commander of the US Third Fleet in 1944. I don't know exactly why he made his way into the song. I must have been reading about him somewhere. The song was included in our album *RAM*, and it was released as a single a few months later. It became my first post-Beatles number one in the US. I think I might also have been influenced by the title of the 1970

Above: With Linda. Scotland, 1971

Left: With mum Mary, Uncle Albert, Auntie Anne and brother Mike, late 1940s

Right: On the farm with Linda. Scotland, 1970

motorcycle drama *Little Fauss and Big Halsy*. It starred Robert Redford as Halsy, and featured a song written by Carl Perkins and sung by Johnny Cash. 'Uncle Albert' contains a lot of punning associated with Admiral Halsey, what with 'berth'/'birth' and 'sea'/'see': 'He had to have a berth or he couldn't get to sea'.

The 'butter pie' brings us back to Linda. We'd gone vegetarian and now had to figure out how to do Christmas turkey. We did a version of mac and cheese that we let cool and go solid, and then we'd slice it and we'd have that as our macaroni turkey. We were doing all sorts of things like that.

Our generation was doing things differently to our parents. For instance, my family were getting roaring drunk at get-togethers, whereas we were exploring other areas of recreation - such as smoking pot - which they would've found strange and weird. Our lifestyle was very free and easy, very hippy. I refer to it here as 'gypsy'. We were rebels with a sense of humour. Linda and I wanted our personal liberty.

16 TRACK IDENTIFICATION CHART
CBS RECORDS Paul McCartney

SESSION Studio

NO.	CC. NO.	TITLE Uncle Albert		
1	1 Bass Drum	2 Drums Left	3 Drums Right	4 Paul Guitar Acoustic
	1/27/71			
	9 Linda ~~Lead~~ Gr P. + Voc. Celeste Bounce	10 Bass	11 Rain	12 Vocal Tr Lead 1-2-3 Double

To Be phased

NO.	CO. NO.	TITLE Admiral Halse		
2	1 Bass Drum	2 Drums ~~Hi-Hat~~ Small Tom	3 Drums Floor Tom Snare-	4 "Water"-S Piano End
		1/28/7		
	9 Organ	10 Bass	11 Trumpets	12 Lead

NO.	CO. NO.	TITLE Too Many Peop		
3	1 Bass Drum	2 Drums Snare - Hi Hat Small Tom	3 Dru Floor Tom	4
			2/10/71	2/10/71
	9 2/18 B. G. / Perc.	10 Bass	11 2/18 B. G.	12 Paul Voc #2

CR 1721

JOB NO.	PRODUCER	ENGINEER	DATE
216827	Paul McCartney	TG/TB	11/6/70

5 Amp	6 Amp	7 (use)	8
Hugh Guitar O.D. Double ← use	Hugh Guitar ← use	Paul Guitar Acoustic	Rough Vocal Rain

1/27/71 1/27/71 1/27/71

violins	violas Harp	Basses + cellos	fr. Horn Bone

5	6	7	8
Hugh Amp	Hugh Acoustic	Piano	4/1 LEAD

1/28/71 1/28/71

13	14		16
Bone	WHISTLE OOH-END	fr. Horns	Cue T.B.E.

GUITS SOLOS 1/26/70

5	6	7	8
Guit Paul MX of TRK 9 + TRK 12	Hugh Acoustic	Paul Acoustic	Rough Vocal

2/10/71 2/10/71

13	14	15	16 Hugh
P+L voc DBL	Paul voc tripled	Guitar Double	Guitar O.D. Bongos + Shaker

Track sheet from *RAM* recording sessions, 1970

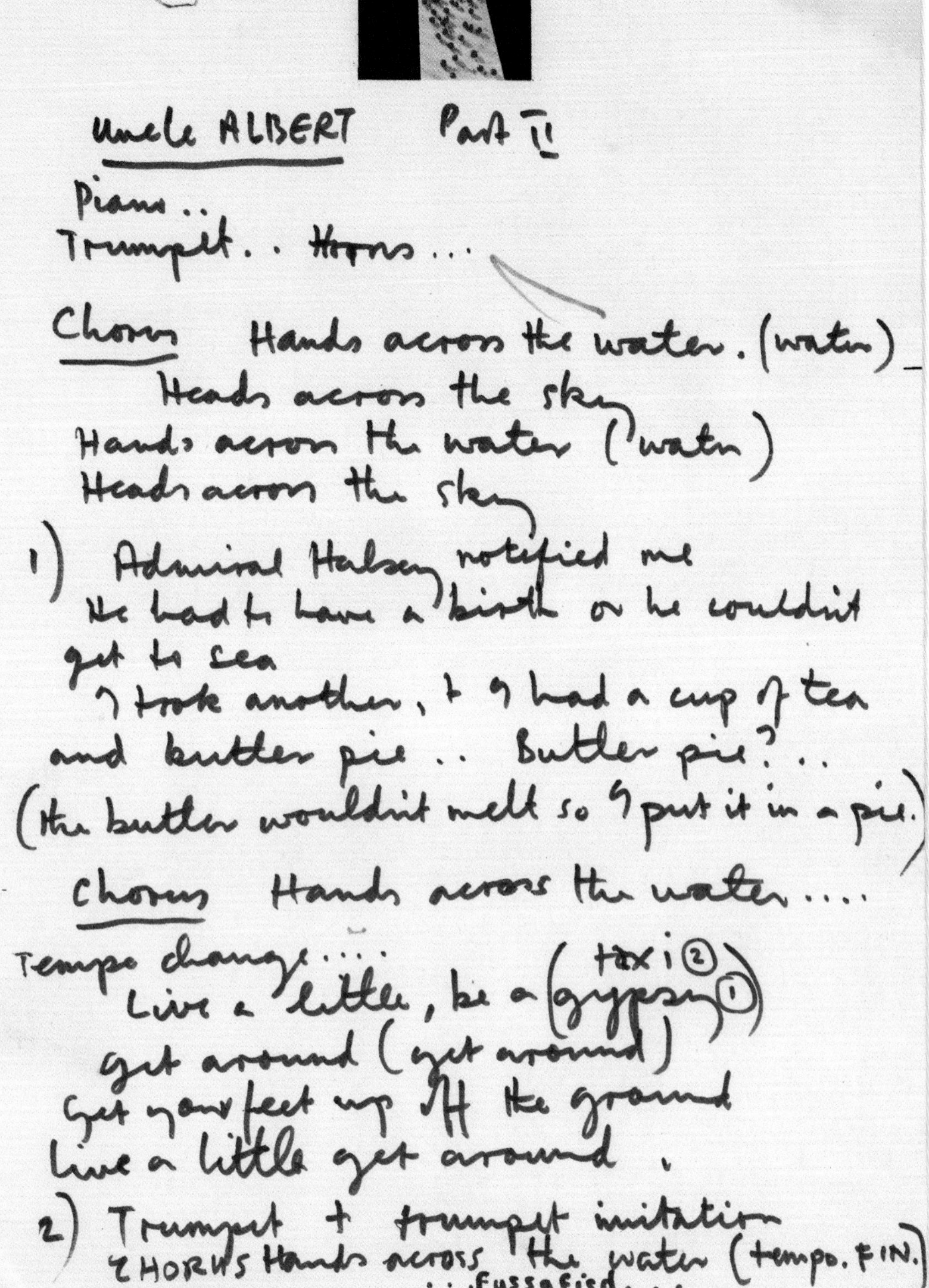

Uncle ALBERT   Part II

Piano..
Trumpet.. Horns...

Chorus Hands across the water. (water)
Heads across the sky
Hands across the water (water)
Heads across the sky

1) Admiral Halsey notified me
He had to have a berth or he couldn't get to sea
I took another, + I had a cup of tea
and butter pie.. Butter pie?..
(the butter wouldn't melt so I put it in a pie.)

Chorus Hands across the water....

Tempo change....
Live a little, be a (taxi ② / gypsy ①)
get around (get around)
Get your feet up off the ground
Live a little get around .

2) Trumpet + trumpet imitation
CHORUS Hands across the water (tempo. FIN.)
...Fussafied...

Admiral Halsey notified me
~~I hadn't~~ He had to have
~~He couldn't~~ ~~go~~ a birth (berth)
or ~~I~~ he couldn't get to see (sea)
I ~~had~~ took another look, & I had a cup of tea
and ~~a~~ butter pie (butter pie?)
(the butter wouldn't melt so I put ~~it~~ it in ~~the~~ a pie)
— trumpets.

(1) Hands across the water
Heads across the ~~sea~~ sky

(2) Hands across the table
Heads across the sea.

a fussafied person fussafied me,
~~I had to lie down on account of my knee,~~
~~I would have liked bonbon, I had to have tea,~~ drink
I'm fussafied — (fussafied?)

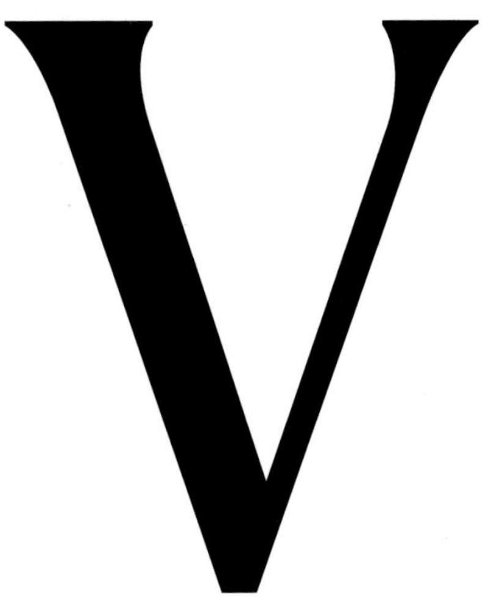

Venus and Mars/Rock Show/ Venus and Mars - Reprise

WRITERS	Paul McCartney and Linda McCartney
ARTIST	Wings
RECORDED	Sea-Saint Recording Studio, New Orleans
RELEASED	*Venus and Mars*, 1975
	'Venus and Mars'/'Rock Show' single, 1975

VENUS AND MARS

Sitting in the stand of the sports arena
Waiting for the show to begin
Red lights, green lights, strawberry wine
A good friend of mine follows the stars
Venus and Mars are alright tonight

ROCK SHOW

What's that man holding in his hand?
He looks a lot like a guy I knew way back when
It's silly willy with the Philly band
Could be, oo-ee
Tell me, what's that man movin' cross the stage?
It looks a lot like the one used by Jimmy Page
It's like a relic from a different age
Could be, oo-ee

If there's a ROCK SHOW
At the Concertgebouw
They've got long hair
At the Madison Square
You've got Rock and Roll
At the Hollywood Bowl
We'll be there
Oh yeah

The lights go down
They're back in town, okay
Behind the stacks
You glimpse an axe
The tension mounts
You score an ounce, olé
Temperatures rise as
You see the whites of their eyes

If there's a ROCK SHOW
At the Concertgebouw
You've got long hair
At the Madison Square
They've got Rock and Roll
At the Hollywood Bowl
We'll be there
Oh yeah

In my green metal suit
I'm preparing to shoot up the city
And the ring at the end of my nose
Makes me look rather pretty
It's a pity there's nobody here
To witness the end
Save for my dear old friend and confidante
Mademoiselle Kitty

What's that man movin' to and fro?
That decibel meter doesn't seem to be reading low
But they was louder at the Rainbow
Could be, oo-ee

If there's a ROCK SHOW
At the Concertgebouw
They've got long hair
At the Madison Square
You've got Rock and Roll
At the Hollywood Bowl
We'll be there
Oh yeah

Who's that there? Oh, it's you, babe
Come on now, we're going down to the rock show
Remember last week when I promised I was gonna
buy a good seat at the rock show?
Well I bought it
Come on now get your dress on, place your wig on
straight
We can't be late, come on, we've got a date
We're goin' down to the rock show

VENUS AND MARS – REPRISE

Standing in the hall
Of the great Cathedral
Waiting for the transport to come
Starship 21ZNA9

A good friend of mine
Studies the stars
Venus and Mars
Are alright tonight

Come away on a strange vacation
Holiday hardly begun
Run into a good friend of mine
Sold me her sign
Reach for the stars
Venus and Mars
Are alright tonight

SOMETIMES YOU WRITE A SONG TO BE A CONCERT OPENER because you wonder, 'What am I going to open with?' 'Magical Mystery Tour' is a good one because it's inviting people to a show – 'Roll up, roll up for the mystery tour'. We're inviting people to come in. 'A Hard Day's Night' we use nowadays because it's got that big-bang chord. Certain songs work just because they're welcoming, and I do like knowing I'm going to be doing them live. Sometimes I try and craft them with that in mind.

I've done this purposely a few times, and 'Venus and Mars' is definitely one of those songs – 'Sitting in the stand of the sports arena / Waiting for the show to begin'. It has a moody little opening and it's spirited, and the arrangement is slightly operatic. But I'm less keen on the rest of the song, when it segues into 'Rock Show'. I sort of get out of it quickly these days and segue to another song, like 'Jet'.

When you write something like 'Magical Mystery Tour' – 'Roll up, roll up' – you're the carnival barker, setting up the beginning of a show. 'Rock Show' is a song about the world of the band, and the lyrics describe the concerts and all festival stuff. Most of the places where we perform are sports arenas – Wembley Stadium, Madison Square Garden – but we've also played the Concertgebouw in Holland and the Hollywood Bowl. I'm thinking of that line "What's that man movin' to and fro?" We used to have decibel meters. Now people don't seem to mind it being loud, but back in the seventies they minded. Local governments would send around a guy and he'd stand in front of you, and if your meter went overboard he would report you. Still, there's a romance to being on the road. Not only people in bands, but the rest of us who grew up wanting to be in bands, are fascinated by that world. And I think probably that's one reason people like this song.

It was written in 1974, and in those days – and to some degree today – a lot of people who were into concerts were also into alternate thinking. They'd want to know what your sign was, and they'd place some relevance on that. I was never like that. As far as I was concerned, Venus and Mars were just two random planets. But when we released the record, I realised they're also characters – people as well as planets.

The guys in Wings at that time always wanted to do 'Rock Show', but I was a bit reluctant: 'Oh no, not axes and Jimmy Page and silly willy. I'm not sure I want to do all that.' To tell you the truth, I'm a little bit embarrassed by this song. I'm describing a rock show, but I would have never called it a 'rock show'. I would have called it a 'rock and roll show'. 'You're in a rock band?' 'No, I'm in a rock and roll band.' I don't call a guitar an 'axe'. 'Hey man, how's your axe?' One word we used to use a lot was 'gas'. 'It's a gas, man.' In Liverpool we used to say 'gear'. 'Gear' was the thing; it meant something was great. You'd pick up all these slang words, use them for a certain period, then move on to the next ones. But they don't always age well.

So. I was really throwing all of these ideas of the planets and 'the stars' and the live show – all of these period words – into this one song, which I don't perform a lot, because of the embarrassment factor. But I've also met people who love this song, so I've kind of learnt to shut up about it.

Top right: Pencil drawing of stage by Humphrey Ocean. *Wings Over America* tour, 1976

Bottom right: Pastel drawing of Cow Palace in San Francisco by Humphrey Ocean. *Wings Over America* tour, 1976

COW PALACE

1. VENUS AND MARS.

Sitting in the stand of the sports arena
Waiting for the show to begin
Red lights green lights
Strawberry wine,
A good friend of mine
Follows the stars —
Venus and Mars
are alright ~~tonight~~

ROCK SHOW.

Whats that man holding in his hand?
He looks a lot like a guy I knew way back when
Its silly willy with the Philly band
Could be, ... Oo - ee.....

Whats that man wheeling cross the stage
It look a lot like the one used by Jimmy Page
Looks like a relic from a different age
Could be,.... Oo — ee.....
If theres a ROCK SHOW
at the Concertgebow ——

2. ROCK SHOW

There'll be long hair
at the Madison Square,
They got, rock and roll
at the Hollywood Bowl.......

We'll be there....
Oh yeah...

The lights go down
They're back in town O.K.
Behind the stacks
You glimpse an axe
The tension mounts
You score an ounce, ole!
Temperatures rise as
you see the whites of their eyes...

In my green metal suit
I'm preparing to shoot up the city
And the ring at the end of my nose
Makes me look rather pretty
It's a pity, there's nobody here
To witness the end.....
Save for my dear old friend and confidante
mademoiselle KITTY...

3. ROCK SHOW.

What's that man movin' to and fro
His decibel meter doesn't seem to be reading Low
But they was louder at the Rainbow
Could be — oo ee.....

If there's a ROCK SHOW
at the Concertgebouw
They've got LONG HAIR
At the Madison Square
You got ROCK AND ROLL
at the Hollywood Bowl
We'll be there...
Oh yeah....

Repeat ROCK SHOW
Chorus

Chorus

Chorus

12. MEDECINE JAR.

Dead on your feet
You don't go far
If you keep on sticking your hand
In the Medicine Jar.

Dead on your feet
You don't go far
If you keep on sticking your hand
In the medecine jar.

What can I do?
I can't let go
You say time will heal
But very slow

13. VENUS AND MARS

Standing in the hall
Of the great cathedral
Waiting for the transport to come
Starship 21ZNA9.

A good friend of mine
Studies the stars,
Venus and Mars
are alright tonight

Come away on a strange vacation
Holiday hardly begun
Run into a good friend of mine
Sold me her sign
Reach for the stars
Venus and Mars
are alright tonight

Left and above: *Wings Over America* tour. Philadelphia and Denver, 1976

Right: Cibachrome print of *Venus and Mars* cover shot, 1975

Warm and Beautiful

WRITERS	Paul McCartney and Linda McCartney
ARTIST	Wings
RECORDED	Abbey Road Studios, London
RELEASED	*At the Speed of Sound*, 1976

A love so warm and beautiful
Stands when time itself is falling
A love so warm and beautiful
Never fades away

Love, faith and hope are beautiful
When your world is touched by sadness
To each his own is wonderful
Love will never die

Sunlight's morning glory
Tells the story of our love
Moonlight on the water
Brings me inspiration ever after

A love so warm and beautiful
Stands when time itself is falling
A love so warm and beautiful
Never fades away
Never fades away

THIS IS ONE OF MY FAVOURITE SONGS. IT'S A BALLAD WITH A brass section, but it's always felt Victorian in style to me. It's very heartfelt. 'A love so warm and beautiful / Stands when time itself is falling'. I like that idea, instead of just saying, 'It will go on forever.' I got a good feeling writing this song, and listening to it now, I still do. 'Love, faith and hope are beautiful'.

The brass solo is lovely for me because it harks back to the brass bands that were so common when I was a kid; there would often be brass bands in the park or in the streets. My dad played trumpet, as I never fail to mention, and he had his own little band - Jim Mac's Jazz Band. The first instrument he bought me was a trumpet, and he taught me the scale of C which, when you go on the piano, becomes B-flat. It's all very complicated. That's why we didn't even bother learning music. I realised that I wanted to swap the trumpet for a guitar, so I asked his permission, and he said, 'Yes, okay.'

'Warm and Beautiful' was written well after the demise of The Beatles, and at this time we knew sadness. I knew about delving into your mind to look for help and looking for some sort of solace in a song. I liked the idea of writing a song in a universal way that dispels the sadness. You write about the wonderful things you know in the world, and you try to write so that it will sing well and be well received by people dealing with grief - something that inevitably surrounds all of us at one time or another.

On a more personal level, the main inspiration for the song was Linda. There was no sadness associated with Linda, except when she later became ill. In that way, I think it's oddly prophetic. We had a very good relationship, but like all relationships, it wasn't perfect. We would sometimes disagree and get annoyed with each other, but that's how families function. She was a fun person to be with, very amusing and very witty. She had a great take on life, and of course she was very artistic. There really wasn't a lot of sadness about her at all. She was an upbeat lady.

Over twenty years later, I reworked the song to be played by a string quartet at her memorial concert.

Above: With the Black Dyke Mills Band. Bradford, 30 June 1968

WARM AND BEAUTIFUL
(Top notes)
(CHORDS) F - G6 - G7 C - E7 F - G6 G C - - -
Fm - G6 -
Cmaj7 - - C Fmaj7 - F6 C - E+ -
F - Fm - C Fm C Fm6 C

Left: Handwritten sheet music for 'Warm and Beautiful', 1976

Above: With Joe English and Denny Laine during *At the Speed of Sound* recording sessions. Abbey Road Studios, London, 1976

Linda. Scotland, 1970

She had a great take on life, and of course she was very artistic. There really wasn't a lot of sadness about [Linda] at all. She was an upbeat lady.

Waterfalls

WRITER	Paul McCartney
ARTIST	Paul McCartney
RECORDED	Lower Gate Farm, Sussex; and Spirit of Ranachan Studio, Scotland
RELEASED	*McCartney II*, 1980
	Single, 1980

Don't go jumping waterfalls
Please keep to the lake
People who jump waterfalls
Sometimes can make mistakes

And I need love
Yeah I need love
Like a second needs an hour
Like a raindrop needs a shower
Yeah I need love
Every minute of the day
And it wouldn't be the same
If you ever should decide to go away

And I need love
Yeah I need love
Like a castle needs a tower
Like a garden needs a flower
Yeah I need love
Every minute of the day
And it wouldn't be the same
If you ever should decide to go away

Don't go chasing polar bears
In the great unknown
Some big friendly polar bear
Might want to take you home

And I need love
Yeah I need love
Like a second needs an hour
Like a raindrop needs a shower
Yeah I need love
Every minute of the day
And it wouldn't be the same
If you ever should decide to go away

Don't run after motorcars
Please stay on the side
Someone's glossy motorcar
Might take you for a ride

And I need love
Yeah I need love
Like a castle needs a tower
Like a garden needs a flower
Yeah I need love
Said I need love
Like a raindrop needs a shower
Like a second needs an hour
Every minute of the day
And it wouldn't be the same
If you ever should decide to go away

Don't go jumping waterfalls
Please keep to the lake

‘DON’T GET INTO ANYONE’S CAR. DON’T TALK TO STRANGERS.’ This song was written when, as parents, Linda and I seemed to spend a lot of time doling out the kind of advice that parents are always giving children.

The protagonist of the song sounds very much like me talking to my kids, advising them to stay safe and not to get into any scrapes. You want them to grow up healthy and have their adventures, but you don’t want them doing dangerous stuff, because you don’t want to lose them. Heather would have been about seventeen when this was written, and that’s always an interesting time to be a parent. Mary would have been about ten, so not quite a teenager, but on the cusp and wanting more independence. Stella and James would still have been pretty young, about eight and two, so mostly doing as they were told. But then, like many of my songs, it just wanders where it fancies, and it becomes a bit more of a love song.

I think my favourite part is this:

Don’t go chasing polar bears
In the great unknown
Some big friendly polar bear
Might want to take you home

I think the waterfall idea came to me when I was on holiday in the US with my family. It was a song that I had started working on when I was still in Wings, but then it ended up on my solo record, *McCartney II*. In fact, it was the only song on that record that wasn’t made up during the recording sessions. I think I left it off the Wings album because I wasn’t happy with the lyrics; they had just spewed out, and I thought I would probably change them. But then, in time, I got to like them as they were. So I stripped it right

Above: With Stella, Linda, James, Mary and Heather. Barbados, 1981

down, kept it simple, and it became one of my favourite songs at the time. It could have been called 'I Need Love', but that's too ordinary for me.

There was another version, a completely different song, that was a big hit for someone else. I remember thinking, 'I wonder if they heard mine?' I think it had nearly the exact same line in the chorus, but then I also thought, 'Great. There must have been something right about it.' Either that or 'Sue the bastards.' But then, like I always say, songwriters are always stealing a bit from here and a bit from there.

Somebody in LA once claimed to have written all our Beatles songs, and we said, 'Well, they didn't, clearly!' But it was worth it to the guy making the false claim to bring a case because everyone would know about him. He'd say, 'I wrote The Beatles' songs,' and people might believe him or not, but they'd certainly hear about the guy who said it. *McCartney II* came out in 1980 and, as we know from what happened in December of that year, The Beatles had more than our fair share of obsessive fans. This song was obviously written before John's murder, but fame has its upsides and downsides, and some strange people do come out the woodwork. But the anxious parental advice at the start of the song is universal - all parents worry.

Around the time I put out *McCartney II*, I said that the album kind of happened by accident. I was getting a little tired of the formality of recording an album with a band and doing everything correctly. I just wanted to have some fun and experiment, so I borrowed some recording gear from Abbey Road for a couple of weeks and enjoyed it so much I kept it for six. I was just tinkering by myself like a mad professor locked up in his laboratory, and I accidentally finished about eighteen songs. I played them to a few people, who said, 'Take off this one and take off that one. Then there's your new record.' I wasn't so sure and was just thinking it would be some funky new music to play to friends in the car. So, the downside of doing that record so spontaneously was that a song like 'Waterfalls' didn't get the arrangement that perhaps it deserved. In the early days of synthesizers, you got fooled into thinking the synth strings always sounded good, which they didn't.

'Don't get into anyone's car. Don't talk to strangers.' This song was written when, as parents, Linda and I seemed to spend a lot of time doling out the kind of advice that parents are always giving children.

PAUL McCARTNEY

WATERFALLS

Don't go jumping waterfalls
Please keep to the lake
People who jump waterfalls
Sometimes can make mistakes

And I need love, yeah I need love
Like a second needs an hour
Like a raindrop needs a shower
Yeah I need love every minute of the day
And it wouldn't be the same
If you ever should decide to go away

And I need love, yeah I need love
Like a castle needs a tower
Like a garden needs a flower
Yeah I need love every minute of the day
And it wouldn't be the same
If you ever should decide to go away

Don't go chasing polar bears
In the great unknown
Some big friendly polar bear
Might want to take you home

And I need love, yeah I need love
Like a second needs an hour
Like a raindrop needs a shower
Yeah I need love every minute of the day
And it wouldn't be the same
If you ever should decide to go away

Don't run after motor cars
Please stay on the side
Someone's glossy motor car
Might take you for a ride

And I need love, yeah I need love
Like a castle needs a tower
Like a garden needs a flower
Yeah I need love, said I need love
Like a raindrop needs a shower
Like a second needs an hour
Every minute of the day
And it wouldn't be the same
If you ever should decide to go away

Don't go jumping waterfalls
Please keep to the lake

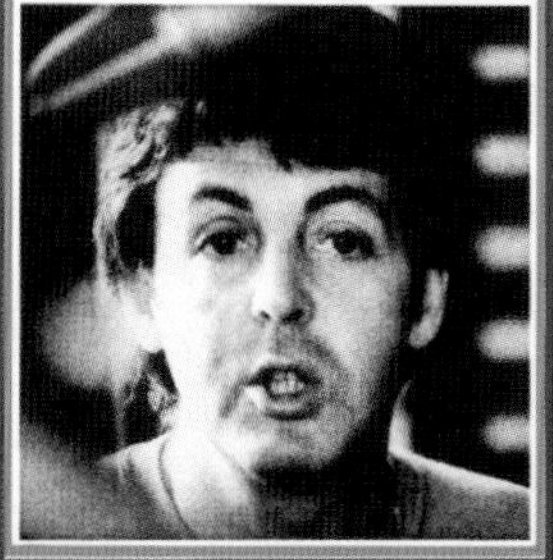

THE NEW SINGLE FROM HIS CURRENT ALBUM McCARTNEY II

SINGLE R6037 · ALBUM PCTC 258

Marketed by EMI Records (UK), 20 Manchester Square, London W1A 1ES. Sales and Distribution Centre, 1-3 Uxbridge Road, Hayes, Middlesex.

① Dont go jumping waterfalls
Please KEEP to the lakes
People who jump waterfalls
Sometimes can make mistakes

CHORUS and I need love
yes — I need love
like a second needs an HOUR
Ⓐ like a raindrop needs a shower
I need love every [illegible] of the day
and it would be the same if you ever should decide to go away.

② Dont go CHASING polar bears
SOLO In the great unknown
Some big friendly polar bear
Might want to take you home
— and I need love

③ VERSE
— I need love

④ Dont run after motor cars
Please stay on the side
Someone's GLOSSY motor car
might take you for a ride.

—

I need love

End... Dont go (chasing, jumping.)

Working lyrics for 'Waterfalls'

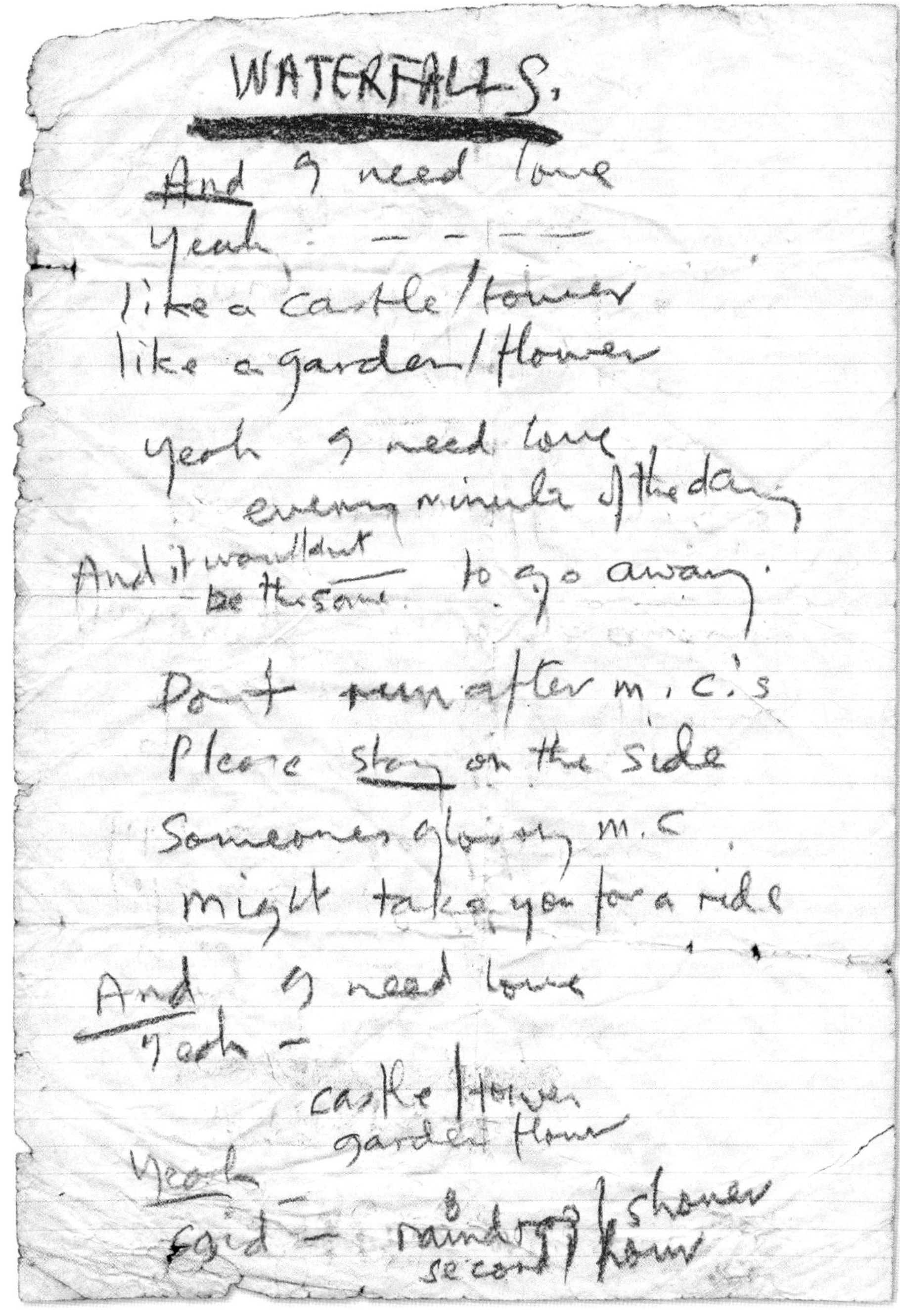
WATERFALLS.

And I need love
Yeah — — —
like a castle/tower
like a garden/flower

yeah I need love
every minute of the day
And it wouldn't be the same to go away

Don't run after m.c's
Please stay on the side
Someones glossy m.c
might take you for a ride

And I need love
Yeah —
castle/tower
garden/flower
Yeah —
Said — raindrops/shower
second/hour

The protagonist of the song sounds very much like me talking to my kids, advising them to stay safe and not to get into any scrapes.

We All Stand Together

WRITER	Paul McCartney
ARTIST	Paul McCartney and The Frog Chorus
RECORDED	AIR Studios, London
RELEASED	Single, 1984

Win or lose, sink or swim
One thing is certain we'll never give in
Side by side, hand in hand
We all stand together

Play the game, fight the fight
But what's the point on a beautiful night?
Arm in arm, hand in hand
We all stand together

La–
Keeping us warm in the night
La la la la
Walk in the light
You'll get it right

Win or lose, sink or swim
One thing is certain we'll never give in
Arm in arm, hand in hand
We all stand together

We all stand together

Above: Paul on the set of the 'We All Stand Together' music video

EVER SINCE I WAS A KID, I'VE LIKED RUPERT BEAR, A COMIC STRIP character in the *Daily Express*. He's a little white teddy bear dressed in very fruity, old-fashioned British clothes, and he's got a little yellow scarf with a black check on it.

I knew Rupert mainly from the comic strip, but every year they published an annual, and I would get it as a present at Christmas. There was something very comforting about it. My dad smoked a pipe and was always in the garden, and Rupert's dad smoked a pipe and was always in the garden. I imagined they were a bit posher than we were, but I didn't hold that against them. Whatever it was, Rupert could always get it done. He had a great post-war 'we can do this' attitude.

I was looking through one of these annuals, and I remember looking at the endpaper, the first page when you open the annual. It was a double-page spread in colour (unlike the rest, which was reprinted, black-and-white newspaper columns, and there were little pictures, with rhyming couplets underneath each one). I could almost hear the music. It showed a violinist frog with some singing frogs in a sort of choir. I got the idea that I wanted to

make a full-length feature film with Rupert, and I wrote some songs with that in mind, but I didn't realise what a daunting task it was going to be. I remember, when The Beatles were still together, I told John, 'I really fancy doing a full-length Rupert.' And he said, 'Great. Go on then.' That was good encouragement, but you need a little more than just 'go on then'.

It turned out I'd bitten off more than I could chew, but it was a good learning experience. All sorts of things were involved, like getting the rights from the newspaper, and it all became too difficult. So I decided to do a short with a friend of mine, Geoff Dunbar, who was an animator I admired. We basically took the inspiration for the song and its instrumentation from this one big drawing on the endpaper.

In 'We All Stand Together', I sang the lead vocal, but I also did various other voices in the frog chorus, because I like mimicry, and in animation it can be really difficult to get an actor in and teach them exactly what you want. We auditioned tons of stage kids from London. They all came streaming through the doors, and we gave them a little bit of dialogue to say, and the strange thing was that they nearly all said, 'Wupert, Wupert, Wupert'. And I kept going, 'No, it's *Rupert*. "Hello, my name's Rupert."' In the end Geoff said, 'You should do it.' So I ended up being Rupert's spoken voice too.

One memorable aspect was recording with The King's Singers and the choir of St Paul's Cathedral. The recording was supervised by George Martin, whom I hadn't worked with since 'Live and Let Die' in 1973, so that was a session I didn't want to miss. When someone like George Martin was involved, he was in charge, and you were there as a spectator, so if he ever said, 'Paul, what do you think?' he might value my opinion, but I didn't have the responsibility. The King's Singers sang the parts of the frogs - in harmony, so they had to sing it correctly. Which, being The King's Singers, they did.

It turned out to be a very enjoyable session, and the record was a huge success, reaching number three in the UK charts. Years later I heard that a very good comedienne in England was getting married, and she and her husband chose it as their marriage song: 'Win or lose, sink or swim / One thing is certain, we'll never give in / Side by side, hand in hand / We all stand together'. It was nice that she'd been amused enough to feature it at her wedding.

There's a longer version of the video with the frogs, where Rupert starts off at home with his mum, goes out and meets Edward Trunk the elephant and Bill Badger. June Whitfield played the mother. People will know her from things like *Absolutely Fabulous* and a 1980s sitcom called *Terry and June*, and she was just lovely. And I got to act with June Whitfield. Imagine that!

The song was recorded in 1980, as it took a little while to put the Rupert film together. But 'We All Stand Together' was the song I wanted to focus on. It keeps in that tradition of songs aimed at younger ears, like 'Yellow Submarine'. When I wrote it, Stella and James were still pretty young, so I probably had them in mind as the people I was singing to. It's a song of encouragement and about not giving up. The lyrics are quite communal and rousing, the sort of thing I can imagine being sung in the playground at school with youthful determination.

Top left: June Whitfield during the recording sessions for *Rupert and the Frog Song*. AIR Studios, London, 1982

Bottom left: Recording sessions for *Rupert and the Frog Song* featuring Roy Kinnear and director Geoff Dunbar. AIR Studios, London, 1982

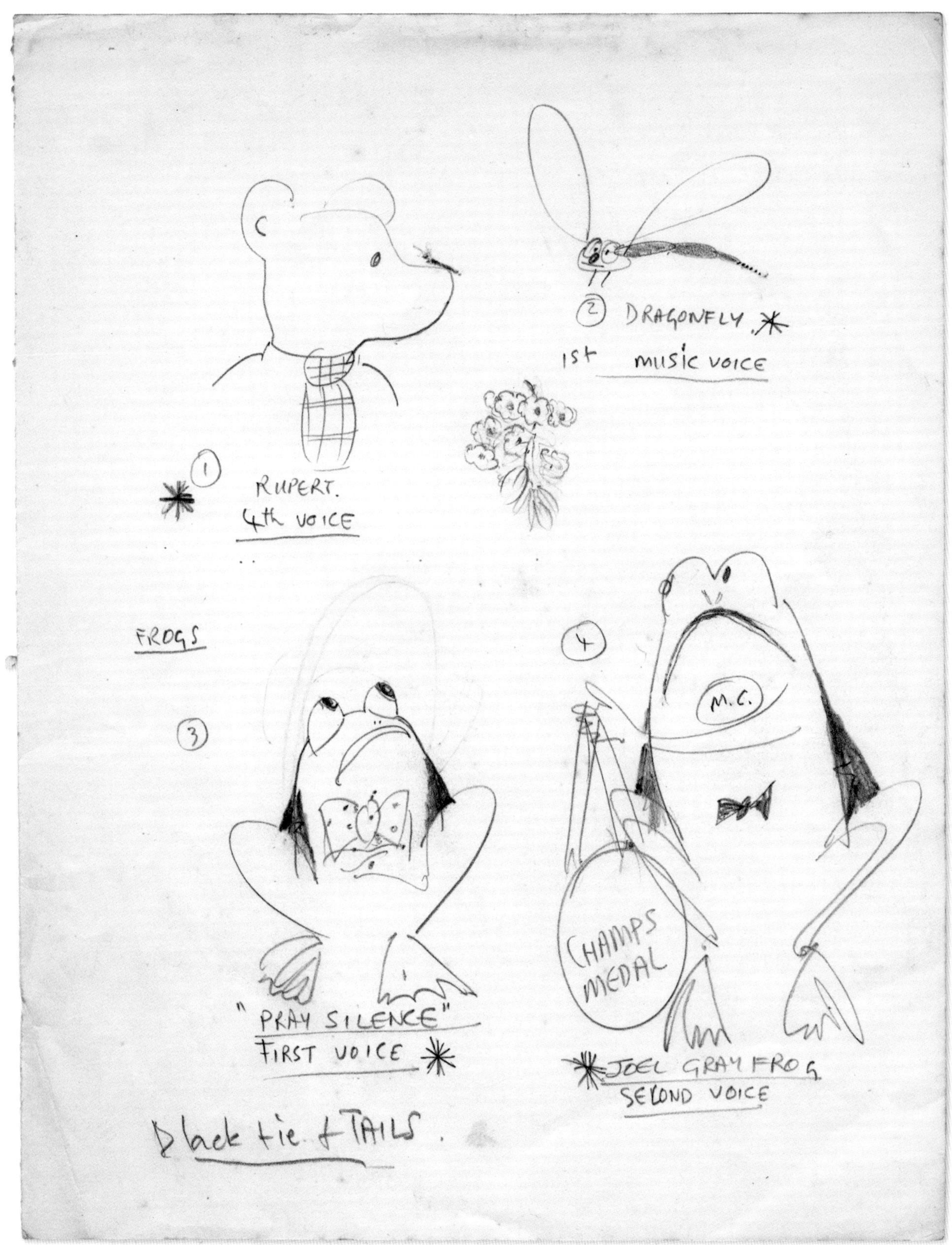
① RUPERT.
4th VOICE
② DRAGONFLY.
1st MUSIC VOICE
FROGS
③ "PRAY SILENCE"
FIRST VOICE
④ M.C.
CHAMPS MEDAL
JOEL GRAY FROG
SECOND VOICE
Black tie & TAILS.

ABCDEFGHIJKLMNOPQRSTUVWXYZ

... PULL TOGETHER .

(1) INTRO win or lose
sink or swim
one thing is certain
we'll never give in
side by side
hand in hand
we all (stand) together
intro ...

(2) Play the game
fight the fight
But what's the point on a beautiful night
arm in arm
hand in hand
we all stand together.

(3) Love ... keeping us warm in the night
la la la love ..... walk in the light
SLOW you'll get it right! .....

(4) SOLO — cats — owl — sh.....
Rupert "they're very good" aren't they?.

(5) love ... keeping us warm in the night
la la la love ... walk in the light .. you'll get it right.
REPEAT. (1) → pause on STAND TOGETHER!
all stand — DIVE. BALLET music

With Rupert Bear illustrator Alfred Bestall and George Martin. AIR Studios, London, 1982

I knew Rupert mainly from the comic strip, but every year they published an annual, and I would get it as a present at Christmas. There was something very comforting about it. My dad smoked a pipe and was always in the garden, and Rupert's dad smoked a pipe and was always in the garden.

We Can Work It Out

WRITERS	Paul McCartney and John Lennon
ARTIST	The Beatles
RECORDED	Abbey Road Studios, London
RELEASED	'We Can Work It Out'/'Day Tripper' double A-side single, 1965

Try to see it my way
Do I have to keep on talking til I can't go on?
While you see it your way
Run a risk of knowing that our love may soon be gone
We can work it out
We can work it out

Think of what you're saying
You can get it wrong and still you think that it's alright
Think of what I'm saying
We can work it out and get it straight or say goodnight
We can work it out
We can work it out

Life is very short and there's no time
For fussing and fighting, my friend
I have always thought that it's a crime
So I will ask you once again

Try to see it my way
Only time will tell if I am right or I am wrong
While you see it your way
There's a chance that we might fall apart before too long
We can work it out
We can work it out

Above: The Beatles. *Thank Your Lucky Stars*. London, 1964

IT WAS 1965. THINGS WERE NOT GOING SO SMOOTHLY BETWEEN JANE Asher and me. Everyone has mild arguments where you think, 'God, I wish they could understand where I'm coming from' or 'I wish they could get it.' They obviously don't; they think I'm some kind of idiot or tyrant or something. It was just normal boyfriend-girlfriend stuff where she'd want it one way, I'd want it another way and I would try to persuade her, or she would try to persuade me. Most of the time we got on really well, but there would be odd moments where one or other of us would get hurt.

Time has told me that millions of people go through these little squabbles all the time and will recognise just how common this is, but this particular song was not like that; it was, 'Try to see it my way.' When you're a songwriter, it's a good thing to just go off and get your point of view in a song, and with a Beatles song, if it's going to be heard by millions of people, you can spread a good message: 'We can work it out'. If you wanted to say it in one line, it would be, 'Let's not argue'. If you wanted to say it in two lines: 'Let's not argue / Listen to me'. Obviously, that is quite selfish, but then so is the song.

I started writing the song to try to figure my way out of feeling bad after an argument. It was really fresh in my mind. You can't write this kind of song two weeks later. You have to do it immediately. Writing a song is a good way to get your thoughts out and to allow yourself to say things that you might not say to the other person.

I wrote the first couple of verses, and then I wrote out the middle eight with John at his house. When we took it into the studio, George Harrison suggested we try the waltz pattern, with suspended triplets, that ended up giving the song a profound sense of friction and fracture.

But the fracture was real, and we did 'fall apart before too long'. Sadly, Jane and I did break up. And that meant breaking up with her mother too. Margaret Asher was a real mumsy type and, since I'd lost my mum, she had filled that role for me. Now I'd lost a mother for a second time.

WE CAN WORK IT OUT.

(1) Try to see it my way
do I have to keep on talking till I can't go on.
While you see it your way
you run the risk of knowing that our love may soon be gone.
we can work it out etc.

(2) Think of what you're saying
You can get it wrong and still you think that it's alright
Think of what I'm saying
We can work it out & get it straight or say goodnight
We can work it out

Left: With Jane Asher, 1965

We Got Married

WRITER	Paul McCartney
ARTIST	Paul McCartney
RECORDED	Hog Hill Mill, Sussex
RELEASED	*Flowers in the Dirt*, 1989

Going fast
Coming soon
We made love in the afternoon
Found a flat
After that
We got married

Working hard
For the dream
Scoring goals for the other team
Times were bad
We were glad
We got married

Like the way you open up your hearts to each other
When you find a meeting of the minds
It's just as well love was all we ever wanted
It was all we ever had

Further on
In the game
Waiting up til the children came
Place your bets
No regrets
We got married
We got married
We got married

Nowadays
Every night
Flashes by at the speed of light
Living life
Loving wife
We got married

I love the things that happen when we start to discover
Who we are and what we're living for
Just because love was all we ever wanted
It was all we ever had

It's not just a loving machine
It doesn't work out
If you don't work at it

Above: With Linda after getting married. Marylebone Registry Office, London, 12 March 1969

LINDA AND I GOT MARRIED IN MARYLEBONE TOWN HALL IN MARCH 1969. I suppose I could have written something like 'in the hall with the judge, we signed papers', and just used very literal memories and simple descriptions. But I wrote this song many years after our wedding, and I started to think more universally, imagining every man and every woman getting married. It's really the story of any marriage, not necessarily mine - though a lot of it could be mine.

'Going fast / Coming soon / We made love in the afternoon / Found a flat / After that / We got married'. That does sound like a shotgun wedding. John was the first in our group to get married, and it was indeed a shotgun wedding. In those days that was more embarrassing than it is now. Nowadays, people don't even bother getting married; there's no particular reason why they should. But John found a flat in London, and he got married to his first wife, Cynthia. I'm pretty sure I was channelling them a bit here too.

'Working hard / For the dream / Scoring goals for the other team'. I think no matter how hard you try, you don't get everything right, so even though you're working hard for the dream, you could end up scoring a goal for the other team. That's also known as an 'own goal'. This line could be a harking back to The Beatles' breakup - the idea that we all make mistakes. 'It's just as well love was all we ever wanted / It was all we ever had'. I like that line best of all. It has a very bluesy feel, a bit like Albert King's 'If it wasn't for bad luck / You know, I wouldn't have no luck at all'.

It's part of the magic about writing songs that things just fall in your lap. I didn't think hard about this song, but it came, and when it falls out sweetly like that you feel very lucky, very blessed. You often hear composers say, 'It just came to me.' It's not my way to sit down to analyse it, but you do learn

With Linda and Heather. Marylebone Registry Office, London, 12 March 1969

how to allow cadences and rhythms and rhymes to come to you. I think 'We Got Married' is one, then, that – as they say – 'just came to me', and one always feels very lucky when that happens. You think, 'Yeah, I'm gonna enjoy singing that.'

Early in the song we're talking about the other team; later we're talking about 'Further on / In the game'. I think this is so typical of young parents: 'Waiting up til the children came' – waiting till you have a child and, next thing you know, waiting up for the children to come home safely. You can take it either way, or both.

You learn a lot of tricks when you write as many songs as I do. I mean, to call them tricks might belittle them a bit. We could dress them up as 'skills', but they are tricks when you get down to it. You might not write them down and think, 'These are my tricks,' but they're stored in the back of your head, and when you're writing a song you use the ones you like best. One of my tricks is to have two short lines followed by one long line:

Going fast
Coming soon
We made love in the afternoon

I'm sure there are millions of echoes and parallels with things I've read, or even nursery rhymes like:

Rain, rain
Go away
Come again another day

Going fast coming soon
we made love in the afternoon
found a flat after that (2nd time simple as that!)
we got married.

(N.B. backing sounds "a" "oo" etc... "uh"...)

Working hard — for the dream
Scoring goals for the other team
(Things were) it was bad ~~[illegible]~~ we were glad
we got married.
Like the way you ~~[illegible]~~ open up your hearts,
to each other
— WHEN ~~[illegible]~~ YOU FIND ~~[illegible]~~ "A" meeting of the minds,

---

Early days, later on, children came to us one by one
Now we may — bless the day
we got married — — —.....) . .

When I'm Sixty-Four

WRITERS	Paul McCartney and John Lennon
ARTIST	The Beatles
RECORDED	Abbey Road Studios, London
RELEASED	*Sgt. Pepper's Lonely Hearts Club Band*, 1967

When I get older, losing my hair
Many years from now
Will you still be sending me a valentine
Birthday greetings, bottle of wine?
If I'd been out til quarter to three
Would you lock the door?
Will you still need me, will you still feed me
When I'm sixty-four?

You'll be older too
And if you say the word
I could stay with you

I could be handy, mending a fuse
When your lights have gone
You can knit a sweater by the fireside
Sunday mornings, go for a ride
Doing the garden, digging the weeds
Who could ask for more?
Will you still need me, will you still feed me
When I'm sixty-four?

Every summer we can rent a cottage
In the Isle of Wight
If it's not too dear
We shall scrimp and save
Grandchildren on your knee
Vera, Chuck and Dave

Send me a postcard, drop me a line
Stating point of view
Indicate precisely what you mean to say
Yours sincerely, wasting away
Give me your answer, fill in a form
Mine for evermore
Will you still need me, will you still feed me
When I'm sixty-four?

When it came to 'mending a fuse', I was something of a handyman. Certainly when stacked against John, who had no idea how to change a plug. In those days, back in the 1950s, most people could change a plug! And fuses blew all the time.

The melody of 'When I'm Sixty-Four' was fully worked out by the time I was about sixteen. It was one of my little party pieces, and when we were on the lookout for songs for The Beatles, I thought it would be quite good to put words to it. The melody itself has something of a music hall feel. I hit upon the idea that sixty-four would be more amusing than sixty-five. To be just shy of retirement age. I was always trying to put a little twist on things rather than, in this case, writing a straight-up music hall song.

I'm struck now by the relative sophistication of the songs from this era, perhaps partly because I was reading so much. One influence was the humour of Louis MacNeice's poem 'Bagpipe Music':

John MacDonald found a corpse, put it under the sofa,
Waited till it came to life and hit it with a poker,
Sold its eyes for souvenirs, sold its blood for whisky,
Kept its bones for dumb-bells to use when he was fifty.

MacNeice is great on the day-to-day. I think he would recognise 'You can knit a sweater by the fireside / Sunday mornings, go for a ride'. All comfortable things that retired people do. Then I would stick in 'Doing the garden, digging the weeds'. 'Digging the weed' is also a way of saying 'enjoying a little pot'. We would always slip in those little jokes because we knew our friends would get them.

If you look at the rhyme scheme here, you've got *abcc* ('hair / now / valentine / wine'). The more conventional thing would be *abab*. In many of the songs from this time I'm resisting the conventional structure of a verse. It's one of the things that gives this song, which is really quite simple, a little extra pizzazz.

Another of MacNeice's strengths is managing a cast of characters. Everyone down to the grandchildren: 'Vera, Chuck and Dave'. 'Chuck' is not a very common name in the UK, but there were a lot of 'Chucks' on television. Chuck Connors in *The Rifleman*, of course, which ran from 1958 till 1963. It's an amusing name at its heart - partly because 'chuck' means vomit in some quarters. Then there was Chuck Berry. When you say 'Chuck Berry', it doesn't sound the least bit amusing; it's all about context.

Then there's 'Send me a postcard, drop me a line / Stating point of view'. I used to think that the BBC got the title of *Points of View*, their television show based on viewers' letters, from 'When I'm Sixty-Four'. Somebody from the BBC even told me that. But the programme started in 1961, so it was probably the other way round.

I once ran into a lady who played piano at old people's homes. She said, 'Mr McCartney, I hope you don't mind, but I've had to update "When I'm Sixty-Four" to "When I'm Eighty-Four". Sometimes even "When I'm Ninety-Four".' Those people think sixty-four is rather young. I wrote 'When I'm Sixty-Four' when I was twenty-four-ish, so sixty-four seemed very old then. Now it looks quite sprightly.

when I get older losing my hair,
Many years from now
Will you still be sending me a Valentine
Birthdays Greetings bottle of wine,
If I'd been out till quarter to three
would you lock the door
Will you still need me, will you still feed me,
when I'm sixty four.

Middles. ....

You'll be older too,
And if you say the word, I could stay with you

I could be handy, mending a fuse
When your lights have gone.
You can knit a sweater by the fireside
Sunday mornings. go for a ride
Doing the garden, digging the weeds
Who could ask for more.
Will you still need me, etc.....

Mid. Every summer we can rent a cottage,
in the Isle of Wight, if its not too dear.
We shall scrimp and save
...Grandchildren on your knee
Vera, Chuck and Dave
....
Send me a postcard, drop me a line,
Stating point of view
Indicate precisely what you mean to say
~~waiting for you~~.
wasting away
Yours sincerely
Give me your answer fill in a form
mine for ever more...
etc...

Press event for the *Our World* TV live special broadcast. Abbey Road Studios, London, 25 June 1967

When Winter Comes

WRITER	Paul McCartney
ARTIST	Paul McCartney
RECORDED	Hog Hill Mill, Sussex
RELEASED	*McCartney III*, 2020

Must fix the fence by the acre plot
Two young foxes have been nosing around
The lambs and the chickens won't feel safe
until it's done

I must dig a drain by the carrot patch
The whole crop spoils if it gets too damp
And where will we be with an empty store
When winter comes

When winter comes
And food is scarce
We'll warn our toes
To stay indoors
When summer's gone
We'll fly away
And find the sun
When winter comes

I must find the time to plant some trees
In the meadow where the river flows
In time to come they'll make good shade
for some poor soul

When winter comes
And food is scarce
We'll warn our toes
To stay indoors
When summer's gone
We're gonna fly away
And find the sun
When winter comes

Must fix the fence by the acre plot
Two young foxes have been nosing around
And the lambs and the chickens won't feel safe
until it's done

When winter comes
And food is scarce
We'll warn our toes
To stay indoors
When summer's gone
We're gonna fly away
And find the sun
When winter comes

And find the sun
When winter comes

Above: On the farm. Scotland, 1973

AFTER THE BEATLES THING BECAME SO DEPRESSING, LINDA AND I decided we'd get out of London and start living full-time on our small holding in Scotland. It was quite a difficult period because of the band's breakup, but it allowed me to see another side of myself.

First and foremost, we did everything for ourselves, and at this point it was Linda, Heather, Mary - who was still a baby - and me. If we needed something to eat, we'd go into town in the little Land Rover, come back up, and cook it. We didn't have anyone helping us, except for one guy, the shepherd, because it was a little sheep farm. It was an experience that allowed me to be a man. If a picture needed hanging, I was your man. If something needed doing on the farm, I'd do it. If we needed a new table, I'd make it.

'When Winter Comes' is a series of memories of activities that had enriched me; each one makes up a nice little scene. I would fix fences, dig a drain, keep some chickens, somehow plant a vegetable garden. These are things I'd learnt. You've got to put a fence up or the fox will have your chickens. You've got to dig a drain because if the vegetable patch gets too wet, nothing will grow there. All these new experiences were feeding into the songs I was writing at the time, like 'Heart of the Country'.

I'd grown up in Liverpool and gone on the road with The Beatles around the world and then around again, and now here I was on a farm in the middle of nowhere, and it was sensational. There wasn't a bath in this little farmhouse, but there was a big steel tub in which they'd cleaned the milking equipment, so we would just start filling this thing and about two hours later it would be ready. It wasn't quick, but that was the joy of it. We'd get towels and just run - because the bath was in the barn next door, and it was bloody cold in the winter. We'd run in and jump in this bath, which was not easy to get into. But we were young and vigorous, and the kids were too

On the farm. Scotland, 1973

young to know to complain. We'd jump in the big tub and have this fantastic Japanese-style bath. This was the kind of thing I'd never done, ever, in my life, and it was amazingly liberating. I got to do all the things I think a lot of young people still dream about today – the famous 'gap year'. I sense a lot of people want that freedom, escaping the rat race.

'I must find the time to plant some trees'. That was something else I'd actually done, though I'd planted them very badly. But we were learning these new skills, and it was fun, and now I'm a dab hand at it. I just lifted a piece of sod, stuck the roots of a little one-foot seedling underneath it and plonked the sod back down. In Scotland the weather can be harsh, and this was a hill farm, so there weren't really many trees to speak of. On the hills where we were, the only things that could really survive were Douglas fir or Norway spruce and the like. By the time I wrote this song, around the early 1990s, those little one-foot things I'd planted in Scotland were bloody giants – thirty-foot giants.

I rediscovered this song in 2019 when I was listening to old demos for the *Flaming Pie* archive release. It felt special, so I pulled it out and worked on it for a short video of the song at my recording studio in the first pandemic-related UK lockdown of 2020. It actually ended up inspiring what became the *McCartney III* album.

WHEN WINTER COMES

(1) Must fix the fence by the acre plot
Two young foxes have been nosing around
The lambs and the chickens won't feel safe
Until it's done.

(2) Must dig a drain by the carrot patch
The whole crop spoils if it gets too damp,
And where will we be with an empty store
When winter comes

CH. When winter comes
And food is scarce
We'll warn our toes
To stay indoors
When summer's gone
We'll fly away
And find the sun
When winter comes

(3) I must find the time to plant some trees
In the meadow where the river flows
In time to come they'll make good shade
For some poor soul

When winter comes...

etc....

Repeat (1) ... & CH

On the farm. Scotland, 1969–73

Why Don't We Do It in the Road?

WRITERS	Paul McCartney and John Lennon
ARTIST	The Beatles
RECORDED	Abbey Road Studios, London
RELEASED	*The Beatles*, 1968

Why don't we do it in the road?
Why don't we do it in the road?
No one will be watching us
Why don't we do it in the road?

Why don't we do it in the road?
Why don't we do it in the road?
No one will be watching us
Why don't we do it in the road?

Why don't we do it in the road?
Why don't we do it in the road?
No one will be watching us
Why don't we do it in the road?

WE WERE MIXING IN STUDIO TWO, WHICH WAS REALLY THE dedicated Beatles studio at Abbey Road, and I was getting a bit fed up sitting around. Everyone had gone home, but we were still there at ten o'clock, eleven o'clock, midnight. There was no one else around except for a security sergeant, maybe somebody on the door. So I slipped into Studio Three with Ringo, just him and me. I wanted to do a let-it-all-hang-out song based on little more than a mantra.

The term 'mantra' is not entirely beside the point, because I got the idea for this song when I was in India with Maharishi Mahesh Yogi earlier in the year. I just happened to see a couple of monkeys copulating in the jungle in Rishikesh and was quite taken with the idea of how natural that seemed, the most natural thing in the world. They were totally free and uninhibited.

When Linda and I were having Mary, our first baby, I went along to the Family Planning Association to try and be a dutiful father and get some more dope on the experience we'd embarked on. It's not that I didn't know the facts of life, but I found myself saying, 'We're having a baby. Have you got any information?' They gave me a little booklet called 'From Conception to Birth'. That was a mind-blowing experience. It's when I discovered that the average ejaculation contains more than forty million sperm. Then there's the sheer determination of the sperm to find an egg, to make that new organism. And the fact that a foetus has genitalia so early in its development? You could have knocked me down with a feather.

Those details came later than this song, of course, but the booklet explained everything. It explained my obsession with girls in their summer clothing, and how I couldn't not look at them. How I had that primeval urge to lay everything in sight. Now I understood that one of the first impulses of this new organism is to replicate itself.

So, the feel of this song is a little more outspoken - a little more in your face - than I would normally be. But that's because of the primeval urge it's expressing. And that's one of the great strengths of rock and roll. It can be raw, raw, raw. It's very simple - crude even - and it connects to something deep inside us. Maybe even to the nervous system more broadly.

Above: Monkeys.
Rishikesh, 1968

Right: At the mixing desk with Ringo during *The Beatles* recording sessions. Abbey Road Studios, London, 1968

With a Little Help from My Friends

WRITERS	Paul McCartney and John Lennon
ARTIST	The Beatles
RECORDED	Abbey Road Studios, London
RELEASED	*Sgt. Pepper's Lonely Hearts Club Band*, 1967

What would you think if I sang out of tune?
Would you stand up and walk out on me?
Lend me your ears and I'll sing you a song
And I'll try not to sing out of key

Oh I get by with a little help from my friends
I get high with a little help from my friends
I'm gonna try with a little help from my friends

What do I do when my love is away?
Does it worry you to be alone?
How do I feel by the end of the day?
Are you sad because you're on your own?

No, I get by with a little help from my friends
Get high with a little help from my friends
I'm gonna try with a little help from my friends

Do you need anybody?
I need somebody to love
Could it be anybody?
I want somebody to love

Would you believe in a love at first sight?
Yes I'm certain that it happens all the time
What do you see when you turn out the light?
I can't tell you but I know it's mine

Oh I get by with a little help from my friends
Get high with a little help from my friends
I'm gonna try with a little help from my friends

Do you need anybody?
I just need someone to love
Could it be anybody?
I want somebody to love

Oh I get by with a little help from my friends
I'm gonna try with a little help from my friends
Oh I get high with a little help from my friends
Yes I get by with a little help from my friends
With a little help from my friends

POKING A LITTLE FUN AT RINGO WAS ACTUALLY A *LOT* OF FUN. 'What would you do if I sang out of tune?' Actually, John and I wrote this song within a vocal range that would cause no problems for Ringo, who had a style of singing different to ours. We tailored it especially for him, and I think that's one reason why it was such a great success for him on *Sgt. Pepper*.

The song was performed very much in the style of the *Sgt. Pepper* album as a whole – the style of a live show in which the song is sung by a certain 'Billy Shears'. For those old enough to remember, Billy Shears was the name of the person who supposedly replaced me in The Beatles when I'd 'died' after a road accident in 1966. That was a crazy rumour that had been doing the rounds. Now Billy Shears showed up, large as life, in the guise of Ringo Starr! So, this song is Ringo's intro as a character in this operetta.

'Lend me your ears' – well, you know where that's from. The Bard's four hundredth birthday had fallen in April 1964, and there'd been a production of *Julius Caesar* on television that year. It was still fresh in our minds.

John and I were able to include one or two little private jokes here: 'I get high with a little help from my friends'. Normally, we didn't write while we were actually high. There was only one song where that happened. It was called 'The Word', but I didn't think it was that good. I'm not even sure we wrote it while stoned. Though we probably got stoned after it.

And then when Joe Cocker did this song one year later, he took it to places nobody had imagined. I used to know a guy, Denny Cordell, who was a friend from late-night parties who would sit around and play records, and he'd heard the song. So he rang me up and said, 'I've done this song of yours, Ringo's song, with Joe Cocker, and I think it's really good. Can I play it to you?' I said, 'Yeah, sure,' so he came round. I think this was in the Apple Studio at 3 Savile Row. And wow, I mean I knew he was going to cover it, but I didn't know he would do this radical arrangement of slowing it down, because ours had been quite jaunty. Later it became something of a subversive song in the US because Spiro Agnew, vice president of the US at the time, tried to ban it, claiming it encouraged drug use. It was made even more famous by John Belushi as Joe Cocker. He did it slapstick and fell down. It was very funny.

The line I liked best in it was, 'What do you see when you turn out the light?' I was imagining turning out the light when you're in bed, under the covers. You're talking about your genitals; that's what it is. Everyone does that: touching themselves when the light goes out. But I couldn't say, 'What do you see when you turn out the light? Your dick.' It just doesn't scan.

With Ringo and John at the *Sgt. Pepper's Lonely Hearts Club Band* press launch. London, 19 May 1967

A LITTLE HELP FROM MY FRIENDS (BAD FINGER BOOGIE)

What would you think if I sang out of time
Would you ~~throw a tomato at me~~ stand up and walk out on me
Lend me your ears and I'll sing you a song,
+ I'll try not to ~~go~~ SING out of key

1 Oh I'll get by with a little help from my friends
high - - - - - - -
try . . . . . .

What do I do when my love is away
(does it worry you to be alone)
How do I feel by the end of the day
(are you sad because you're on your own)
No, I get by with a little help from my friends.
(etc. - - - - - - - -

Do you need anybody
+ I just need somebody to love
Could it be anybody
+ Yes, I just want somebody to love
— - —

H Would you believe in a love at first sight,
Yes I'm certain that it happens ~~every day~~ ALL THE TIME,
H What do you see when you turn out the light,
I can't tell you but I know it's mine,
Oh I get by - - . . . - -
+
H Do you need anybody
+ I just need somebody to love,
Could it be anybody - - etc. -
Oh I get by with a little help from my friends

End -

Left: Ringo at the *Sgt. Pepper's Lonely Hearts Club Band* press launch. London, 19 May 1967

Right: Joe Cocker. London, 1969

And then when Joe Cocker did this song one year later, he took it to places nobody had imagined.

Women and Wives

WRITER	Paul McCartney
ARTIST	Paul McCartney
RECORDED	Hog Hill Mill, Sussex
RELEASED	*McCartney III*, 2020

Hear me, women and wives
Hear me, husband and lovers
What we do with our lives
Seems to matter to others
Some of them may follow
Roads that we run down
Chasing tomorrow

Many choices to make
Many chains to unravel
Every path that we take
Makes it harder to travel
Laughter turned to sorrow
Doesn't get me down
Chasing tomorrow

When tomorrow comes around
You'll be looking at the future
So keep your feet upon the ground
And get ready to run

Now hear me, mothers and men
Hear me, sisters and brothers
Teach your children and then
They can pass it to others
Some of them may borrow
Tales you handed down
Chasing tomorrow

Hear me, women and wives
Hear me, husband and lovers
What we do with our lives
Seems to matter to others
Some of them may follow
Roads that we run down
Chasing tomorrow
Get ready to run

Chasing tomorrow
Get ready to run

HUDDIE LEDBETTER, OR LEAD BELLY, IS DEFINITELY ONE OF MY heroes. I'd been reading a very interesting book about his life, with a lot of photos. I was messing around on the piano – the book was sitting on the piano – and looking at it and casting around for ideas. I was just remembering his style, and they used to say his baritone voice was so big that you'd have to turn your record player down.

I started singing in a harder voice, a bit more bluesy, and this song popped out: 'Hear me, women and wives / Hear me, husband and lovers / What we do with our lives / Seems to matter to others'. It was a 'teach your children well' kind of thought, as in that song by Crosby, Stills, Nash & Young. It came out very easily, and I was happy with that.

When I brought the song into the studio, I tried to keep the inspiration of Lead Belly in my mind. It's a very simple little song, and I tried to keep that simplicity in the way we recorded it. I played the original bass that Bill Black had played on Elvis Presley's records, and it has a beautiful tone. I can't play it very well, so it had to be a simple line; most of the time it has to be open notes. I enjoy playing it, as long as I'm not having to do it all night in a jazz club. I would have to go and practise a bit first for that.

I'm lucky enough to have a nice memory associated with this song. While I was writing it, around the springtime of 2020, my daughter Mary came into the room. She said, 'Oh, I like that one,' and then started singing her own take on it. It adds so much if someone says, 'Oh, I like that one.' You can't buy that in a hardware store.

Above: Photographed by daughter Mary. Hog Hill Mill, Sussex, 2020

Right: With Bill Black's double bass. Sussex, 2020

I played the original bass that Bill Black had played on Elvis Presley's records, and it has a beautiful tone. I can't play it very well, so it had to be a simple line; most of the time it has to be open notes.

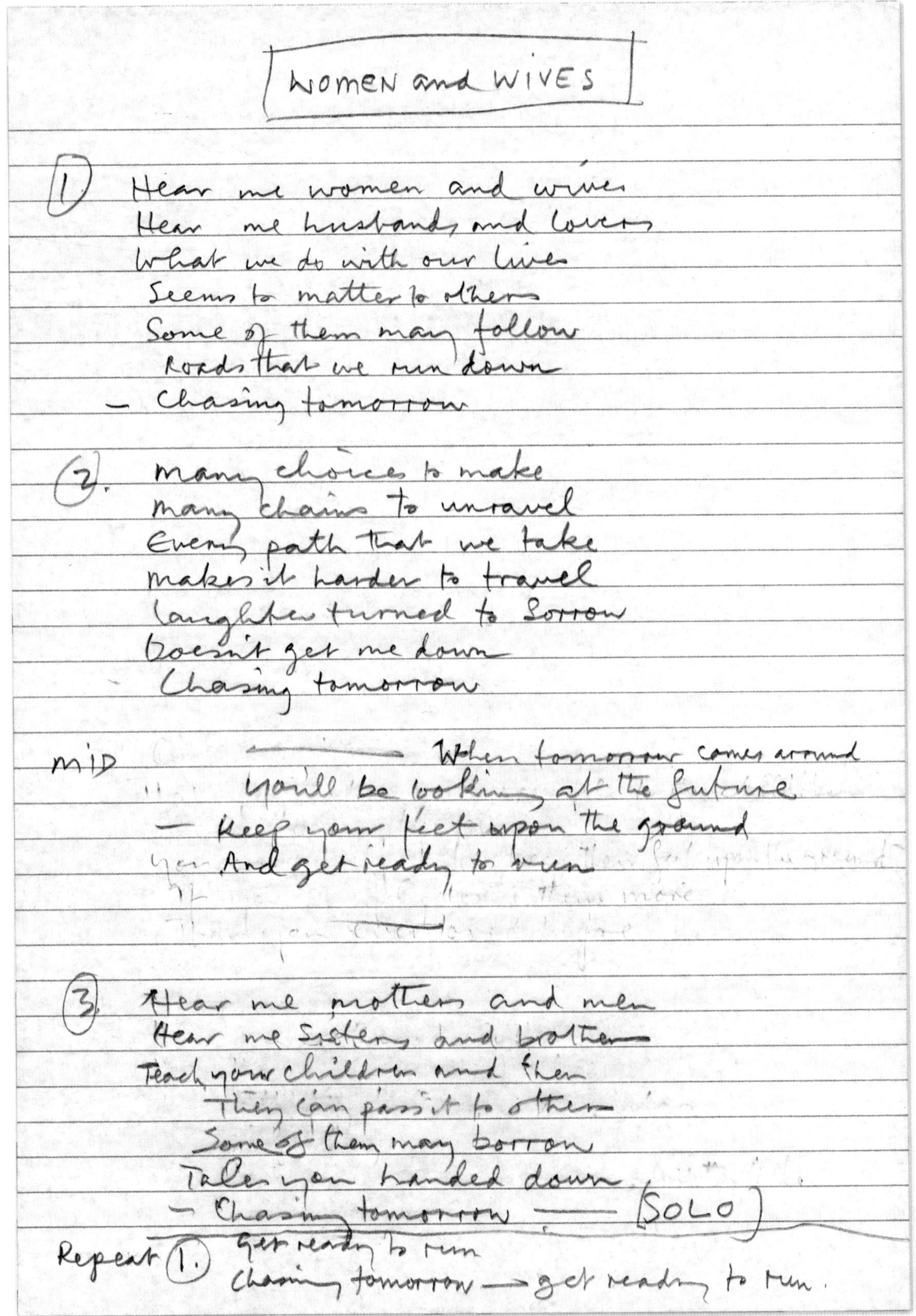
WOMEN and WIVES
(1) Hear me women and wives
Hear me husbands and lovers
What we do with our lives
Seems to matter to others
Some of them may follow
Roads that we run down
– Chasing tomorrow
(2). Many choices to make
Many chains to unravel
Every path that we take
makes it harder to travel
laughter turned to sorrow
Doesn't get me down
Chasing tomorrow
MID — When tomorrow comes around
You'll be looking at the future
– Keep your feet upon the ground
And get ready to run
(3) Hear me mothers and men
Hear me sisters and brothers
Teach your children and then
They can pass it to others
Some of them may borrow
Tales you handed down
– Chasing tomorrow — (SOLO)
Repeat (1.) Get ready to run
Chasing tomorrow → get ready to run.

Hear me (~~daughters~~ women) and wives
Hear me husbands and lovers
What we do with our lives
Seems to matter to others.
Some of them (~~will~~ may) follow
Roads that we run down
.. ~~making~~ CHASING tomorrow ...

Many choices to make
(~~Many~~ Heavy) chains to unravel
Every path that (~~you~~ WE 's) take
(~~getting~~ MAKES IT) harder to travel
Laughter turns to sorrow
Doesn't get me down
... ~~making~~ CHASING tomorrow ..

(~~Will~~ Can) you tell me
When tomorrow comes around
That you set a (~~good~~ cool) example
To the children (~~who were~~ who'll be) listening to you
(~~will you~~ you can) help them
Keep their feet upon the ground
If you simply love them more
Than you ever loved before.

Hear me mothers and men
Hear me brothers and sisters

The World Tonight

WRITER	Paul McCartney
ARTIST	Paul McCartney
RECORDED	Hog Hill Mill, Sussex
RELEASED	*Flaming Pie*, 1997
	Single, 1997

I saw you sitting at the centre of a circle
Everybody, everybody wanted
Something from you
I saw you sitting there

I saw you swaying to the rhythm of the music
Caught you playing, caught you praying to the
Voice inside you
I saw you swaying there

I don't care what you want to be
I go back so far I'm in front of me
It doesn't matter what they say
They're giving the game away

I can see the world tonight
Look into the future
See it in a different light
I can see the world tonight

I heard you listening to a secret conversation
You were crying, you were trying not to
Let them hear you
I heard you listening in

No never mind what they want to do
You've got a right to your point of view
It doesn't matter what they say
They're giving the game away

I can see the world tonight
Look into the future
See it in a different light
I can see the world tonight

I can see the world tonight

I saw you hiding from a flock of paparazzi
You were hoping, you were hoping that the
Ground would swallow you
I saw you hiding there

I don't care what you want to be
I go back so far I'm in front of me
It doesn't matter what they say
They're giving the game away

I can see the world tonight
Look into the future
See it in a different light
I can see the world tonight

A SONG ABOUT A PERSON SITTING AT THE CENTRE OF A CIRCLE, and everybody wants something from him? It could almost be me.

As young Beatles, once we got famous and our families and friends started seeing us on television, the first thing they said to us was, 'Oh, you've changed.' And we said, 'We haven't changed. Your perception of us has changed. We're just the same four guys, going round the world, having a laugh, but you see us differently.'

So that was the first thing, and then that bled into their wanting stuff. It would be simple things, small things, like help with a medical problem or help buying a house, you know – 'I haven't got the deposit', or 'I need a bridge loan', or whatever. At first this was something that you just went along with because it wasn't hugely painful and these were great people; these were family and friends. And having come from the family that I did, I knew that no one was well off, so it was good being able to help people, particularly with the medical things. I always say, one of the great advantages of having some money is that if someone's in dire straits because of an illness or a medical condition, you can send them to a good doctor, and then they don't have to wait six months to get the operation.

So that was quite gratifying. But then as time went by, there were other things, like 'Oh, just lend us this. I'll pay you back at the end of the year.' And you'd give out a loan, interest-free, no problem, and then when it didn't come in at the end of the year, you were now in a very embarrassing position, having to say, 'Er, what about that loan? Have you had any thoughts about it?' In other words, 'Pay up, you git!' But so often it went sour. I went into it quite innocently, and then I sort of grew up.

Above: Press photographers. *The New World Tour*, Santiago, 1993

I remember my dad saying to me that if ever he won the football pools, which is like the national lottery – in those days it would've been about

Right: Sussex, 1994

seventy-five thousand pounds, which would be like a million now – he would give a thousand pounds to each of his relatives and that's it. Obviously, he was older and more experienced with that kind of thing than I was. So I suddenly discovered, 'Ah, I see. That's what he was talking about.' Then I started to realise I wasn't required to help everybody. It goes on to this day.

'I saw you hiding from a flock of paparazzi'. That was truly becoming the way we lived, so I put it onto whoever this person is. 'You were hoping that the / Ground would swallow you' – that kind of sums it up. You just hope the ground will swallow you, or maybe swallow *them*. I like to use common phrases and put them in some kind of context where they sound uncommon. I think a lot of creative people do that.

With the paparazzi, it's just the unpleasantness of it, really. When I first got famous with The Beatles, I used to think of the press as loveable rogues. We knew a lot of them, and they owned up to being rogues. And they *were* loveable – at least some of them – so I thought that was the best spin I could put on it. I had a lot of friends who were journalists, and that was okay, but what started happening, and we're talking very early on, is that the photographers of the day would sneak shots of Jane and me. It was such an intrusion, like they'd caught you at hide-and-seek – only I wasn't playing some game of hide-and-seek. It really alters your entire way of being because you know that around any corner there might be a long lens.

It happens to this day, but now I've lived a life of it and I'm used to it. Just last week we were going for a walk on the beach, and I said to Nancy, 'There they are.' And sure enough, over the hood of a car, there were two guys. I just try not to get too distressed by it, but it will always be annoying. You'll be doing something where you think you're free; you think this is a moment you're having to yourself. In the old days, I would talk to them and say, 'God, don't you realise the terrible job you've got? You're like the school sneak.' I still don't like them, and I've revised my opinion about them being loveable rogues. Now they represent a part of the world I just don't want to know.

This song has a line that's one of my favourites of all the lines I've ever written: 'I go back so far I'm in front of me'. It's one of those lines where you don't know what it means but you do know what it means. I have no idea where it came from, though!

You just hope the ground will swallow you, or maybe swallow *them*. I like to use common phrases and put them in some kind of context where they sound uncommon. I think a lot of creative people do that.

SAW YOU SITTING.

(1) I saw you sitting
~~At~~ The centre of a circle
Everybody .... everybody
wanted something from you
I saw you sitting.

(2) I saw you swaying
To the rhythm of the music
caught you playing
caught you praying
(with) To the voice inside you
I saw you ~~swaying~~. (there).

(BR) I don't care how it used to be
I go back so ~~far~~ it's in front of me
I don't ~~care~~ what people say — YOU'RE GONNA
As long as the music goes hey hey hey
(people)

(CH) I can see the future
I can feel the world tonight
Love can make me happy
~~it's given me an appetite~~
LIVING IN THE MOONLIGHT.

(3) I heard you ~~talking~~ WHISPER
to a group of ~~[illegible]~~
They were hanging
They were hanging
On your every syllable
I heard a whisper

(BR) Never mind what they think of you
you be anything if you wanna do
~~LET them have~~ it all their way
As long as the music goes hey hey hey

I CAN SEE THE WORLD TONIGHT.

(1) I saw you sitting at the centre of a circle,
Everybody everybody
wanted something from you
I saw you sitting, there.

(2) Saw you swaying
To the rhythm of the music
Caught you playing
Caught you praying
To the voice inside you.
Saw you swaying, there.

[BR] I don't care what you wanna be
I go back so far, I'm in front of me
It doesn't matter what they say
They're ~~don't~~ giving the game away.

(CH.) I can see the world tonight
Look into the future
See it in a different light
I can see the world tonight.

(3) I heard you ~~talking to a secret conversation~~
listening to a secret conversation,
You were crying
you were ~~trying~~
NOT to let them hear you
I heard you listening in.

[BR] Never mind, what they want to do
You've got a right, to your point of view
It doesn't matter what they say
They're ~~don't~~ giving the game away

The World You're Coming Into

WRITERS	Paul McCartney and Carl Davis
ARTIST	Royal Liverpool Philharmonic Orchestra
RECORDED	Liverpool Cathedral
RELEASED	Single, 1991
	Paul McCartney's Liverpool Oratorio, 1991

MARY DEE
The world you're coming into
Is no easy place to enter
Every day is haunted
By the echoes of the past
Funny thoughts and wild, wild dreams
Will find their way into your mind

The clouds that hang above us
May be full of rain and thunder
But in time they slide away
To find the sun still there
Lazy days and wild, wild flowers
Will bring some joy into your heart
And I will always love you
I'll welcome you into this world

MARY DEE AND BOY SOLO
You're mine and I will love you

THIS SONG, ESSENTIALLY AN ARIA, IS FROM THE *LIVERPOOL ORAtorio*, but over time, it has come to mean more to me. I don't write too many songs in this classical form; the *Liverpool Oratorio* was really my first experience with it. But I was really moved that the philharmonic in the city where I grew up would come to me on such an important occasion – their 150th anniversary – and ask me to take part in their celebration. The song begins as a solo for the soprano, which is sung by Dame Kiri Te Kanawa on the record. She's singing to her baby. 'The world you're coming into / Is no easy place to enter'. Physically, for herself and for the baby, just the physical shock of birth is breathtaking. It's a mystery that any of us survive being born. It's a traumatic experience.

And that's not to mention the trauma of life, what we're thrown into. As almost all of us soon realise, and as we're finding out again and again with our current history, the world is not an easy place to enter. 'Every day is haunted / By the echoes of the past / Funny thoughts and wild, wild dreams / Will find their way into your mind'.

You'll hear that she's giving a little lesson to her unborn child. 'The clouds that hang above us / May be full of rain and thunder / But in time they slide away / To find the sun still there / Lazy days and wild, wild flowers / Will bring some joy into your heart'. And then: 'And I will always love you / I'll welcome you into this world'. Her child sings that last part with her. It's a beautiful duet between mother and child.

The song recalls, in a way, the Latin motto of my old school, the Liverpool Institute High School for Boys: *Non nobis solum, sed toti mundo nati* – 'Not for ourselves alone, but for the whole world were we born'. It's about the relationship between mother and child, but that child, when grown up, has to go out into the world. And that's where those lessons really start to come in handy. I still apply lessons from my parents, like Dad's saying 'Do it now'. The school's motto appears elsewhere in the oratorio too, in the words for 'Non Nobis Solum' in the opening 'War' section.

It struck me just the other day, when I was thinking about this piece, that in some ways it's a celebration of my mother Mary, who was a midwife. Maybe this is why the song keeps growing on me.

Above: Mum Mary with colleague

and the child... (1)

ACROSS TOWN

The working MEN (all male) concerned more about the rights and wrongs of adultery.

MR. DINGLE advises HIM to relax, and go for a drink, where they can forget their troubles.

SHE ... has a child inside

(7) CRISES. She comes through the traffic ... is home and sings a song to her unborn child as she sits in the bedroom.

He lurches home through traffic and enquires where his dinner is SHE regrets the passing of childhood HE too ...

THEY each have their (J)
own private worries and
an argument develops...
It is irrational but effective.
SHE reminds him she doesn't
need this.... she needs love
he isn't sure if she ever loved him.
CLIMAX.
As she leaves she breaks the news
that he is about to become a father.
SHE runs into street...
Dark, wind, rain umbrellas,
car headlights and is KNOCKED
down by a car. Slow motion
scene of her being taken to hospital!
The nurse sings to her
as she sleeps, and assures
her she will look after her but
says she is not sure if the
baby is in danger.. sleep.

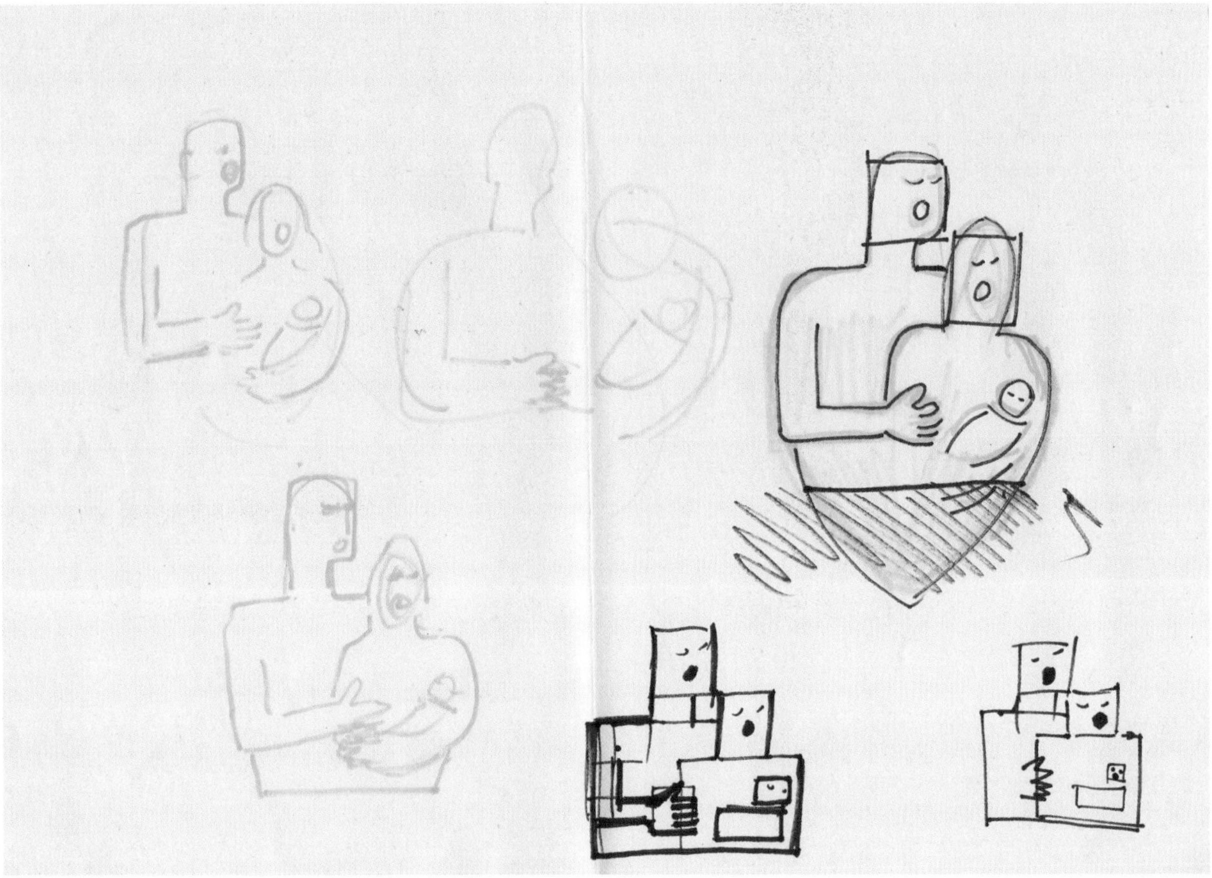

Above: Artwork sketches for the *Liverpool Oratorio* album cover, 1991

Left: With Carl Davis. Sussex, 1990

Right: Dame Kiri Te Kanawa. Liverpool Cathedral, 1991

Below: Set design sketch for *Liverpool Oratorio* performance, 1991

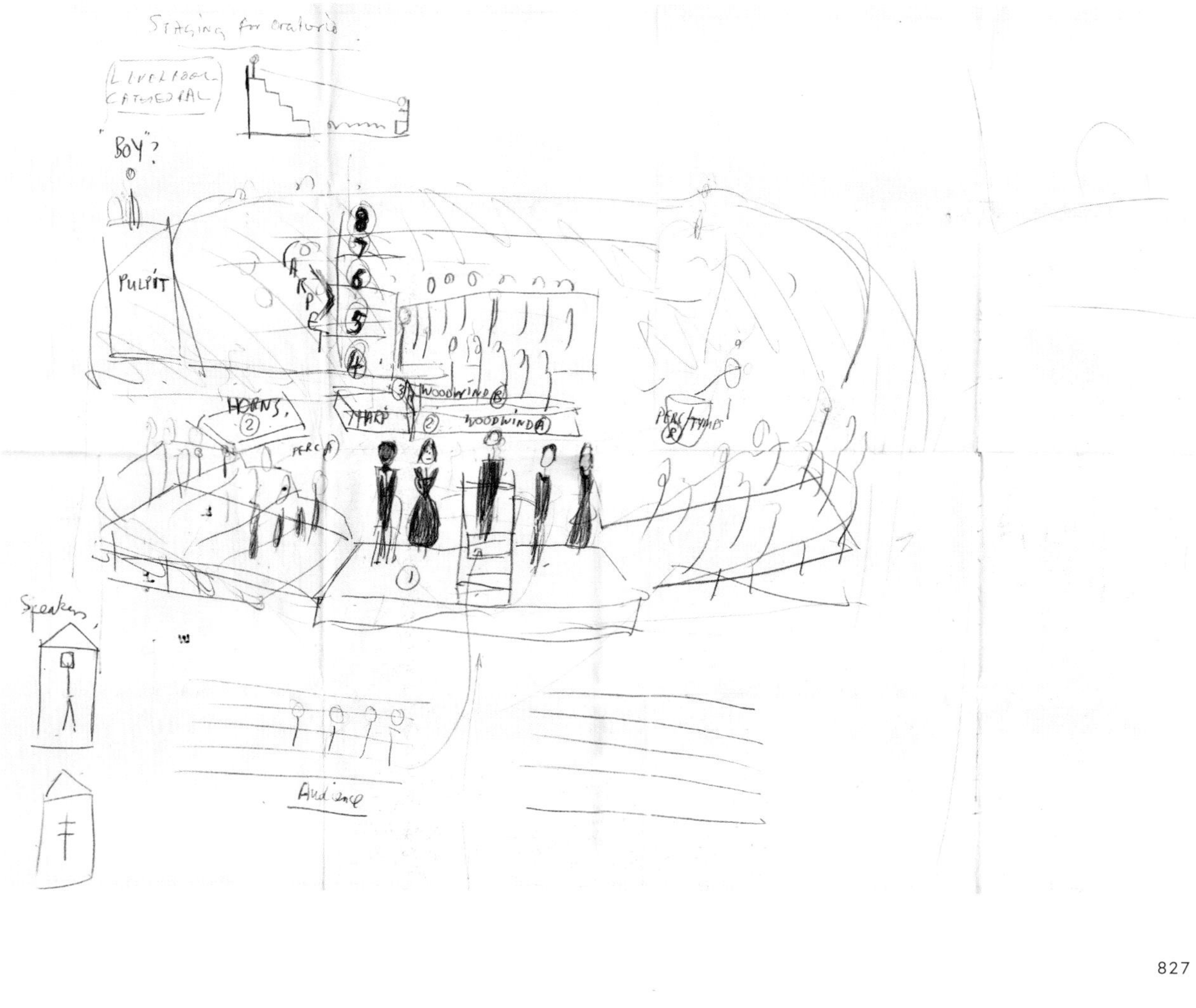

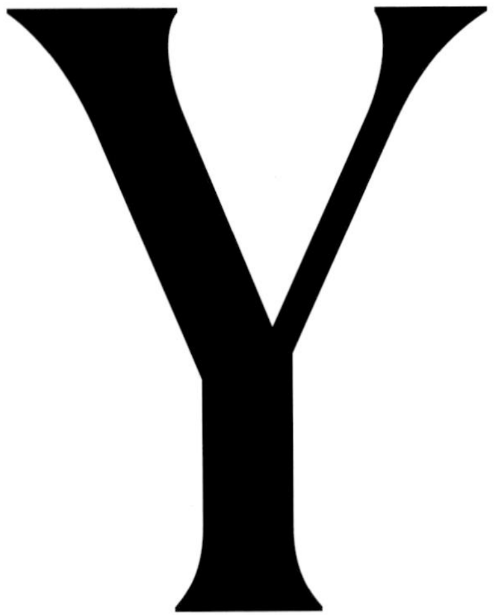
Y

Yellow Submarine

WRITERS	Paul McCartney and John Lennon
ARTIST	The Beatles
RECORDED	Abbey Road Studios, London
RELEASED	'Eleanor Rigby'/'Yellow Submarine' double A-side single, 1966 *Revolver*, 1966

In the town where I was born
Lived a man who sailed to sea
And he told us of his life
In the land of submarines

So we sailed on to the sun
Til we found the sea of green
And we lived beneath the waves
In our yellow submarine

We all live in a yellow submarine
Yellow submarine, yellow submarine
We all live in a yellow submarine
Yellow submarine, yellow submarine

And our friends are all aboard
Many more of them live next door
And the band begins to play

We all live in a yellow submarine
Yellow submarine, yellow submarine
We all live in a yellow submarine
Yellow submarine, yellow submarine

As we live a life of ease
Every one of us has all we need
Sky of blue and sea of green
In our yellow submarine

We all live in a yellow submarine
Yellow submarine, yellow submarine
We all live in a yellow submarine
Yellow submarine, yellow submarine

ALL THOSE BALLADS. 'SIR PATRICK SPENS'. *THE RIME OF THE Ancient Mariner*. All that stuff about a man going to sea. Not to mention Lewis Carroll:

'The time has come,' the Walrus said,
'To talk of many things:
Of shoes - and ships - and sealing-wax -
Of cabbages - and kings -
And why the sea is boiling hot -
And whether pigs have wings.'

The nonsense tradition was part of my sixth-form experience in English literature class with my teacher Alan Durband. He had studied at Cambridge under F. R. Leavis, probably the best-known English literary critic of the time. I know I've banged on about Alan Durband over the years, but I honestly can't overstate his influence on me. I hesitate to use such a hackneyed phrase, but he was genuinely inspirational.

A large part of the subtext of 'Yellow Submarine' was that, even then, The Beatles were living in our own capsule. Our own microclimate. Our own controlled environment. Mr Durband would have introduced me to a word like 'subtext'.

Another factor that can't be overstated was the incredible popularity of television programmes at the time that featured the underwater world. There were the Austrian underwater divers Hans and Lotte Hass. Lotte was a kind of pin-up. The series *Sea Hunt*, with Lloyd Bridges, was on the air at that time; and *Flipper*, the television show about a dolphin, ran between 1964 and 1967.

That underwater world was quite magical. And I think somehow the sense of possibility it opened up coincided with our post-war experiences. When we were kids in Liverpool - 'In the town where I was born' - it was all bombs and rationing and ruins. My dad was a fireman, so talk of incendiary bombs was an everyday thing. Our amusement was often homemade. The songs the old people sang were your entertainment. You learnt to make do with very little. So, when you got a bit more, it was like going from black and white to colour.

For The Beatles - though we didn't know it at the time - expressing our joy at coming out of the black-and-white world actually contributed to that new burst of colour. It's hard to believe, but we played an active role in it. We helped to make the 'Sky of blue and sea of green' so vibrant.

A large part of the subtext of 'Yellow Submarine' was that, even then, The Beatles were living in our own capsule. Our own microclimate. Our own controlled environment. Alan Durband would have introduced me to a word like 'subtext'.

Left: Original cel from *Yellow Submarine*, 1968

Above: With Ringo Starr and George Harrison attending a press screening for *Yellow Submarine*. London, 8 July 1968

J P McCARTNEY ESQ.
6AM2.

English
Literature.

a rather grand effect and possibly to explain more clearly to other scholars the position Eve was in. Besides the classical references being used to acheive a feeling of greatness, they are used earlier in the book to give an impression of vast distances. In his search for Adam and Eve, Satan travels the length of the world. To show the extent of this paradise, Milton mentioned such distant-sounding names as "... Pontus, the pool Maeotis, the river Ob, Orontes, Darien, the Ganges, and the Indus."

Milton's ability to delve into the minds of his characters and give a clear representation of what he sees there, gives an indication of an imaginative mind. Satan's

first impression of Eve is one of a deep infatuation for her, so much so that "her heavenly form angelic ... her graceful innocence, her every air of gesture or least action, overawed his malice" and left him feeling "stupidly good, of enmity disarmed, of guile, of hate, of envy, of revenge."

Milton often allows his imagination to run away with him, and he inserts opinions, which are obviously his own, into the minds of his characters. Adam says that "nothing lovelier can be found in woman than to study household good, and good works in her husband to promote."

In spite of this insertion of his own opinions, he makes his

ABOVE: (TOP TO BOTTOM)
Nichols, Me, Gill, Hooper.

Above: Extract of essay on John Milton's *Paradise Lost* in Paul's English Literature schoolbook with comments by Alan Durband

Yesterday

WRITERS	Paul McCartney and John Lennon
ARTIST	The Beatles
RECORDED	Abbey Road Studios, London
RELEASED	*Help!* 1965
	US single, 1965
	"Yesterday"... and Today, 1966

Yesterday
All my troubles seemed so far away
Now it looks as though they're here to stay
Oh, I believe in yesterday

Suddenly
I'm not half the man I used to be
There's a shadow hanging over me
Oh yesterday came suddenly

Why she had to go I don't know, she wouldn't say
I said something wrong, now I long for yesterday

Yesterday
Love was such an easy game to play
Now I need a place to hide away
Oh I believe in yesterday

Why she had to go I don't know, she wouldn't say
I said something wrong, now I long for yesterday

Yesterday
Love was such an easy game to play
Now I need a place to hide away
Oh I believe in yesterday

Above: View from 'the garret' on Wimpole Street. London, 1964

THE ASHERS' HOUSE IN WIMPOLE STREET. A VERY SMALL attic room with one window. A garret. Perfect for an artist. There wasn't any room for me to keep my records - many of which had been mailed to me from the US before they were available in the UK - in there. They had to be kept outside on the landing. But somehow I had a piano in there - a small, sawn-off piano that stood by my bed. Somewhere in a dream, I heard this tune. When I woke up, I thought, 'I love that tune. What is it? Is it Fred Astaire? Is it Cole Porter? What is it?'

I fell out of bed and the piano was right there, just to the side. I thought I'd try and work out how the song went. I thought it had to be some old standard I'd heard years earlier and had forgotten. I just had this tune, and I now had some chords. And to solidify it in my memory I blocked it out with some dummy words: 'scrambled eggs, oh my baby, how I love your legs, scrambled eggs'. Using dummy lyrics wasn't something I did a lot. It was a rare thing.

So, I had this tune, and I think the first person I saw that morning outside the house was John. I said, 'What's this song?' He said, 'I don't know. I've never heard it.' I got the same response from George Martin and my friend, the singer Alma Cogan, who had pretty comprehensive knowledge of popular songs. After a couple of weeks, it became clear that no one knew the song and it didn't exist, except in my head. So I claimed it and spent time playing around with it, adding to it and perfecting it. It was like finding a £10 note on the street.

Not long after the song came to me, we were working on the film *Help!* - although at the time it was called *Eight Arms to Hold You*, but we weren't keen on that title. *A Hard Day's Night* had been such a success the year before that there was pressure on us to make a follow-up, but the scripts just weren't right. I think we had rejected so many versions that by the time we

With Ringo Starr and George Harrison on the set of *Help!* Bahamas, 1965

came to say yes to one, we had only really just browsed it, rather than taking it very seriously. It made us appreciate actors whom you hear saying, 'I'd love to work, darling, but I just can't find a decent script.'

The script we eventually agreed to had a plot about getting back Ringo's ring. It was all just a bit higgledy-piggledy, and we weren't really that interested. I suppose we were more interested in smoking pot at that time. We weren't very good at learning our lines, sometimes reading them properly for the first time in the car on the way to film the scene. To be honest, we were starting to outgrow these 'mop top' caricatures that we were being typecast as. One thing the film had going for it, though, was that if we said something like, 'Can we go somewhere nice to film this bit?' they'd say yes. Jumping from one place to the next might not have helped the film much, but that bit was fun. We'd say things like, 'I've never been to the Caribbean. Can you work that into the story, please?' So they did. 'Have you been skiing before?' 'No!' 'Okay, let's get that in the film too!'

All this was going on during the incubation of 'Yesterday', and when there was a chance, I would ask for a piano to be nearby so I could work on the song. I think the middle eight was written on set. And it got to the point where the film's director, Richard Lester, started to get annoyed at always hearing the song. One day he shouted, 'If I hear that once more, I'll have the bloody piano taken away!' I don't think it helped matters that when he would ask what the song was called, I'd reply, 'Scrambled Eggs'.

Putting the music together went well, but for lyrics I still only had the line 'scrambled eggs, oh my baby, how I love your legs, scrambled eggs'. So, during a break in the filming, Jane and I went to Portugal for a little holiday and we landed in Lisbon and took a car ride. Three or so hours - about 180 miles - down to Albufeira, near Faro. We were going to stay at Bruce Welch's house. He was a very generous guy from The Shadows, Cliff Richard's band, and we were meeting him there so that he could let us in and show us around the apartment he was lending us. We were heading down to Albufeira, and I was in the back of the car, doing nothing. It was very hot and very dusty, and I was sort of half asleep. One of the things I like to do when I'm like that is try to think. '"Scrambled eggs, bah, bah, bah . . ." What can that be?' I started working through some options. I wanted to keep the melody, so I knew I'd have to fit the syllables of the words around that. 'Scrambled eggs' - 'da-da-da'. You have possibilities like 'yes-ter-day' and 'sud-den-ly'. And I also remember thinking, 'People like sad songs.' I remember thinking that even I like sad songs. By the time I got to Albufeira, I'd completed the lyrics.

When we got back home, I took the song to the band, and although we did sometimes play it as a four-piece in concert, for the recording Ringo said, 'I don't think I can really drum on that.' George added, 'Well, I'm not sure I can put much guitar on it either.' And then John said, 'I can't think of anything. I think you should just do it by yourself. It's really a solo song.' Now, this was kind of a big deal at the time, because we'd never recorded like that before. It had always been the band.

After some hesitation I decided to give it a go, and George Martin - who had now been our producer for a few years and, even though he wasn't yet forty at this point, was someone we trusted and looked up to - had the idea to put a string quartet on it. I was worried about that; I thought it would sound too classical. But he did his fatherly thing of saying, 'Let's just try it. If you don't like it, we can take it off.' So I went to his house, we had a cup of tea and then we worked out how the strings should sound. George thought that Bach would be a good reference. Trying to keep things modern, I wanted to add in a few notes that Bach wouldn't have thought to use, so we added in the flattened seventh, which is also known as a 'blue note'. So it has a quite distinctive arrangement.

Another thing that happened around this time is that we realised the song would sound better in the key of F. But I'd written it in G. You can get used to playing a song with certain chords, and if you try to play them differently on a guitar, you have to relearn the song, which can alter the way the song sounds. If you want to go higher, you can use a little device called a capo. But if you want to go lower, it's not always so easy; you can run out of room. So, what we did here was to detune the guitar by a whole tone. This means that when you're playing the note G, what actually sounds is the

YESTERDAY.

Yesterday, all my troubles seemed so far away.
now it looks as though they're here to stay
oh I believe in yesterday.

Suddenly, I'm not half the man I used to be
There's a shadow hanging over me
Yesterday came suddenly.

middle 8.
Why she had to go, I don't know
she wouldn't say,
I said something wrong. now I long
for yesterday.....

Yesterday, love was such an easy game to
play
Now I need a place to hide away
oh I believe in yesterday.

note F. These kinds of different tunings are quite common now, but tuning all six strings down a whole tone was a new trick back then, and it meant I could play the guitar the way I'd written the song, but in the key that we thought sounded best.

Another interesting thing about 'Yesterday' is that it was almost recorded as an electronic avant-garde song. When we were trying to work out how to record it, I was very intrigued by the work of Delia Derbyshire. She was a pioneer of electronic music who worked for the BBC Radiophonic Workshop and is probably best known for her work on the *Doctor Who* theme music. George Martin had done some work with the Radiophonic Workshop a few years before and actually put out their first commercial release with a song called 'Time Beat' under the pseudonym Ray Cathode. I went to see Delia, and she took me to a hut she had in the garden, a sort of laboratory. And we talked about how she worked, but in the end we went with George's arrangement.

When the *Help!* album was released, Dick Lester was away on holiday, so I sent him a copy of it with a note saying, 'I hope you like "Scrambled Eggs"!' And then the song did phenomenally well. The record label wanted to release it as a single. We wouldn't let them do it in the UK, since we were a rock and roll band, but we let them get away with it in the US because we didn't live there. And some great people did covers of it too; Marvin Gaye's version is a particular favourite of mine. Margaret Asher also used the song as a test piece for her students at Guildhall School of Music.

It's still strange to me when people tell me things like 'Yesterday' is the number one pop song of all time. Apparently, *Rolling Stone* described it as the best song of the twentieth century. It all seems quite grand for something that came into the world so mysteriously.

Some people find it hard to believe that I was twenty-two when I wrote 'Yesterday'. Every time I come to the line 'I'm not half the man I used to be', I remember I'd lost my mother about eight years before that. It's been suggested to me that this is a 'losing my mother' song, to which I've always said, 'No, I don't believe so.' But, you know, the more I think about it – 'Why she had to go I don't know, she wouldn't say' – I can see that that might have been part of the background, the unconsciousness behind this song after all. It was so strange that the loss of our mother to cancer was simply not discussed. We barely knew what cancer was, but I'm now not surprised that the whole experience surfaced in this song where sweetness competes with a pain you can't quite describe.

A while back, someone asked me whether I relate differently to my songs as I grow older. A recording doesn't change, but of course we continue to age and grow, and as you get older, your relationship to a song can grow too. When I wrote 'Yesterday', I had just moved to London from Liverpool, and I was starting to see a whole new world of possibilities open up before me. But all my yesterdays covered a pretty small period at that point. Now the song seems even more significant – yes, more poignant – because of the time that has passed since I wrote it. I must admit, that's an aspect of writing songs and playing music that I really like.

YESTERDAY ÷ By Paul McCartney John Lennon
& George Martin Esq.
and Mozart
Violin 1
Violin 2
Viola
Cello
A
B
C
A1
A2
A3

George Martin's handwritten score for 'Yesterday' signed by Paul, John Lennon and 'Mozart', 1965

Left: Richard Lester. London, 1989

Right: Filming *Help!* Austrian Alps, 1965

And it got to the point where the film's director, Richard Lester, started to get annoyed at always hearing the song. One day he shouted,'If I hear that once more, I'll have the bloody piano taken away!'

You Never Give Me Your Money

WRITERS	Paul McCartney and John Lennon
ARTIST	The Beatles
RECORDED	Olympic Sound Studios, London; and Abbey Road Studios, London
RELEASED	*Abbey Road*, 1969

You never give me your money
You only give me your funny paper
And in the middle of negotiations
You break down

I never give you my number
I only give you my situation
And in the middle of investigation
I break down

Out of college, money spent
See no future, pay no rent
All the money's gone
Nowhere to go

Any jobber got the sack
Monday morning turning back
Yellow lorry slow
Nowhere to go

But oh, that magic feeling
Nowhere to go
Oh that magic feeling
Nowhere to go, nowhere to go

One sweet dream
Pick up the bags and get in the limousine
Soon we'll be away from here
Step on the gas and wipe that tear away
One sweet dream
Came true today

One, two, three, four, five, six, seven
All good children go to heaven

THE BEATLES STUFF ALL GOT TOO HEAVY, AND 'HEAVY' AT THAT time had a very particular meaning for me. It meant more than oppressive. It meant having to go into meetings and sit in the boardroom with all the other Beatles and with the accountants and with this guy Allen Klein. He was a New York spiv who had come over to London and talked to The Rolling Stones and persuaded them he was the man for them. Prior to that, he had persuaded Sam Cooke he was the man for him. I smelled a rat but the other chaps didn't, so we had a fight over it and I got voted down. I was trying to be Mr Rational and Mr Sensible, and it all went haywire.

It was early 1969, and The Beatles were already beginning to break up. John had said he was leaving, and Allen Klein told us not to tell anyone, as he was in the middle of doing deals with Capitol Records. So, for a few months we had to keep mum. We were living a lie, knowing that John had left the group.

Allen Klein and Dick James, who sold our publishing in Northern Songs without giving us a chance to buy the company, were both hanging around in the background of this song. All the people who had screwed us or were still trying to screw us. It's fascinating how directly we acknowledged this in the song. We'd cottoned on to them, and they must have cottoned on to the fact that we'd cottoned on. We couldn't have been more direct about it.

The thing is that we'd grown up as kids with pocket money. Someone gave you a little money at the end of the week, and that's how life worked. We were still a bit like that. When we first got some real money, we were talking to accountants, and they asked us what we were going to do with it. We said we'd put it in the bank. Those were still the days when you could actually make money on the interest on a savings account. But they said, 'No, no, no. That's not what you do. You've got to invest it.'

I didn't want to do that, because I considered investment too risky. We knew that property would throw off some money one day, but we didn't really get it. So, this whole idea of 'funny money' was very much on our minds. Contracts were written on funny paper. Lying behind the song is the idea of the contract as a relationship between two people. The negotiations are at once business negotiations and romantic negotiations; I'm thinking of the lines 'And in the middle of negotiations / You break down'. The breakdown in negotiations is also a kind of nervous breakdown.

The problem was that, by this stage, everything was up for negotiation, and miscommunication was the order of the day. We weren't really writing together anymore. Each person was bringing in little bits of this and little bits of that. And we all knew that phase of our lives, of being The Beatles, was coming to an end. We were working towards an album, knowing it was probably going to be our final fling. Though *Let It Be* was released later, *Abbey Road* was indeed the last album we recorded in the studio.

There was an upside, however. I'd got married to Linda, and our relationship offered some respite from the dreary infighting and the financial stuff. The lines 'One sweet dream / Pick up the bags and get in the limousine' were a reference to how Linda and I were still able to disappear for a weekend in the country. That saved me.

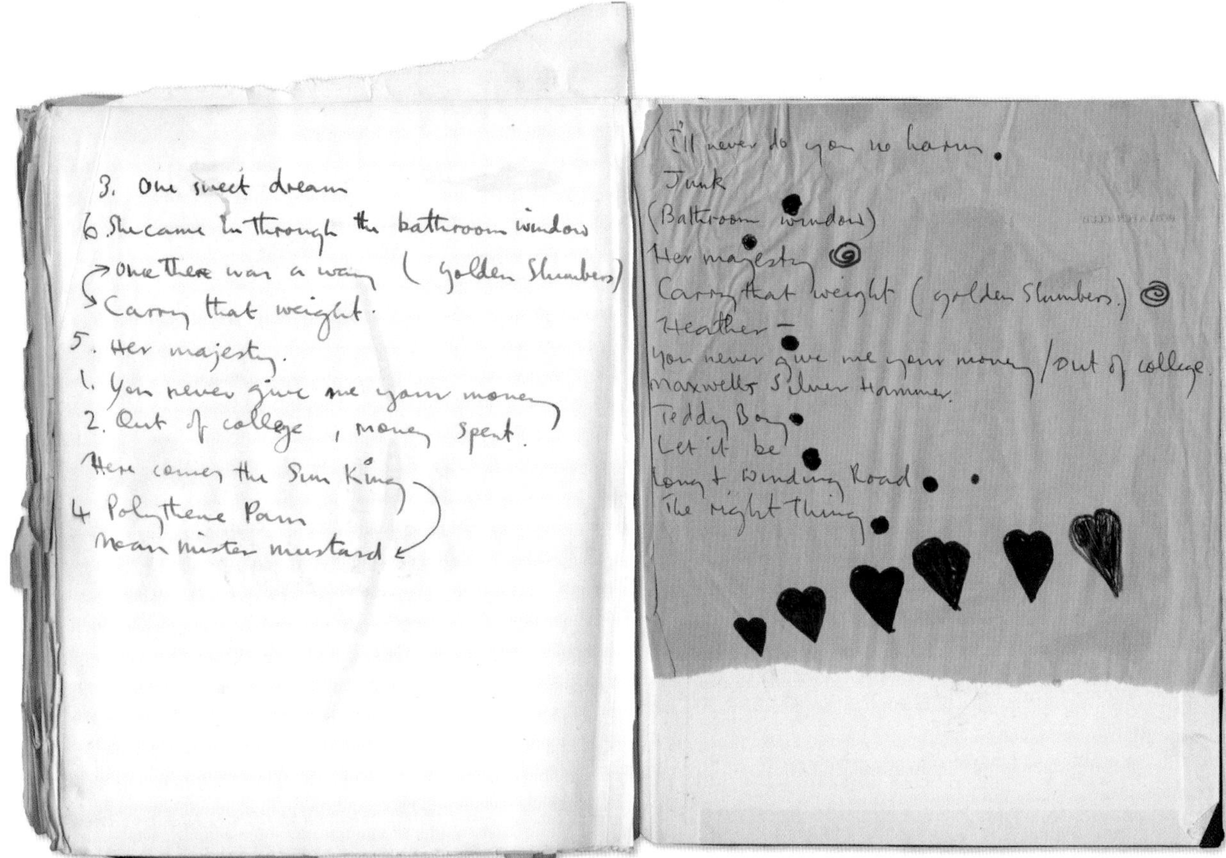
3. One sweet dream
6. She came in through the bathroom window
Once there was a way (Golden Slumbers)
Carry that weight.
5. Her majesty.
1. You never give me your money
2. Out of college, money spent.
Here comes the Sun King
4 Polythene Pam
Mean mister mustard

I'll never do you no harm.
Junk
(Bathroom window)
Her majesty
Carry that weight (Golden Slumbers.)
Heather –
You never give me your money / Out of college.
Maxwells Silver Hammer.
Teddy Boy
Let it be
Long + winding Road
The right thing

Right: Wedding Day, 1969

The problem was that, by this stage, everything was up for negotiation, and miscommunication was the order of the day. We weren't really writing together anymore. Each person was bringing in little bits of this and little bits of that. And we all knew that phase of our lives, of being The Beatles, was coming to an end.

Above left: Linda photographed by Maureen Starkey. Apple office, London, 1969

Above right: With John Eastman, John Lennon, Yoko Ono, Allen Klein, Maureen Starkey, Ringo Starr and Peter Howard. Apple office, London, 1969

You Tell Me

WRITER	Paul McCartney
ARTIST	Paul McCartney
RECORDED	Abbey Road Studios, London; and Hog Hill Mill, Sussex
RELEASED	*Memory Almost Full*, 2007

When was that summer when the skies were blue?
The bright red cardinal flew down from his tree
You tell me

When was that summer when it never rained?
The air was buzzing with the sweet old honeybee
Let's see
You tell me

Were we there, was it real?
Is it truly how I feel?
Maybe
You tell me

Were we there, is it true?
Was I really there with you?
Let's see
You tell me

When was that summer of a dozen words?
The butterflies and hummingbirds flew free
Let's see
You tell me
Let's see
You tell me

THERE'S THAT OLD MAURICE CHEVALIER SONG FROM *GIGI* CALLED 'I Remember It Well', which goes, 'We met at nine, we met at eight, I was on time, no, you were late / Ah, yes, I remember it well'. I love that. A great little routine. The man in the song doesn't quite remember, but the woman does, and 'You Tell Me' is a little bit like that.

This is just memory. Often I think, 'Oh my God, I really met Elvis Presley. I was really in his house, and it was a moment in time that really happened.' That's all there is to it. It just happened. Sometimes I pinch myself and think, 'Was I really on the same couch as Elvis, talking about this stuff?' I want to remember it three hundred per cent more; I want to bring it back: 'Were we there, was it real? / Is it truly how I feel? / Maybe / You tell me'.

The song is from the album *Memory Almost Full*. Shortly after its release, it was pointed out to me that the title is a perfect anagram of 'For my soulmate LLM' - and Linda's middle name was Louise. That wasn't at all deliberate, but I like the mystery of it. The album title actually came from a prompt on my phone saying I had too much stuff on there. But I thought, 'Our memories are almost always full these days; there's just so much going on.' I thought it was a poetic way to sum up modern life.

Because Linda's father had a place in the Hamptons, I started going out there with her. That's way over forty years ago - could be over fifty. I think that's also where I wrote this, sometime in the early 2000s, and perhaps where the line about the red cardinal came from too, since you see them out there. 'When was that summer of a dozen words?' When everything's going really well, nobody needs to talk, so you may just be sitting around with someone and reading books, or reading a newspaper, and you hardly even speak because there's no need to; you're in such a comfortable situation. 'When was that summer when it never rained?' I like that I'm not even going to try and remember what year it was.

I remember hearing a story in the 1960s, when everyone was looking towards India and Indian mysticism, of some guy who was visiting a friend, and he came into the room and just sat down in a corner, and they didn't speak. The idea was they were such good friends that they wouldn't speak until someone had something to say. It wouldn't just be, 'What did you think of the football the other day?' They were absolutely in each other's presence, not needing to say anything. When they spoke it had to be meaningful. I liked the image of the peacefulness in that room.

David Gilmour and Paul Weller, a couple of musicians whose opinion I value, independently sent me messages to say, 'Wow, I like that one' - to say that this song was one of their favourites of mine. Your main feedback is generally from critics, so it's nice to get responses from people who've heard the song, especially real musicians, and were affected enough that they can be bothered to actually write to you. These days, it's a message on your phone; there aren't many people now who would sit down with beautiful old Basildon Bond stationery and expand it a bit.

I don't do too much letter writing myself anymore, but I have to admit I do like handwriting. I enjoyed being taught it at school, and I had a 'proper' way

Left: With Paul Weller. AIR Studios, London, 1982

Top right: Geography essay from school, 1956

Bottom right: Family photograph of the McCartneys and Eastmans. East Hampton, 1975

of handwriting. I miss the old stationery. I love the civility of letter writing. George Martin always wrote a letter to thank me for his birthday gift. We'd done 'When I'm Sixty-Four' together, so I would always send a birthday bottle of wine, and he would handwrite me a very elegant note. It was always a delight. In fact, I've kept most of them. George's widow, Lady Judy Martin, has the same sensibility. It was very much what you did when I was growing up, but also, a certain class did it. I don't know of many of my working-class friends in the street who did it, but my family did, and I had friends later, who lived in places like Hampstead, who would open their mail in the morning and answer it. They had one of those little envelope slitters, and they would be quite organised: 'Dear Henry, What a surprise to hear from you. I was thinking of you only the other day . . .' I like the civility of that.

You know, the working-class equivalent of letters was the postcard. You used to write and try to be amusing. That's when you could say things like, 'The air was buzzing with the sweet old honeybee'. Now we have Instagram, but the postcard was the Instagram of its day.

Peru:

Mainly mestizo & indian. Boundaries indeterminate. Until 1940's boundaries in dispute. Home of the Incas. An Andean country, including part of Pacific coast + pt. of Amazon Basin. ∴ varied features + climate.

<u>Coastal Region</u>. mostly no coast range.

From 3°s to 18°s lat. Hot desert climate. mechanism is same as N. Chile (Cold Offshore current etc.....) Condensation – fog: the "garua". Sufficient moisture for some drought resisting plants. Series of sea-birdinhabited islands – guano (droppings) for fertilizer. Deposits depleted by ruthless collectors. In 1919 the president of ~~Chile~~ Peru reorganised trade. Limited diggings etc... Important crops –

YOU TELL ME.

B min

(1) When was that summer when the skies were blue
the bright red cardinal flew down FROM HIS tree
- you tell me.

(2) When was that summer when it never rained
The air was (BUZZING) with the sweet old honey bee
- you tell me.
lets see

M I D
Were we there, was it real
Is it (TRULY), (HOW) I feel,
maybe - you tell me. / chord / repeat line.

(3) When was that summer when the air was still
A fragrant ocean breeze filtered from the sea.
SOLO - you tell me

M I D
Were we there, is it true
was I really there with you
Lets see - you tell me.

When was that summer of the blazing heat
The air was buzzing with the sweet old honey bee
maybe - you tell me. ?

(4) When was that summer of a dozen words
The butterflies & humming birds (FLEW) free
lets see - you tell me
(REPEAT) END.

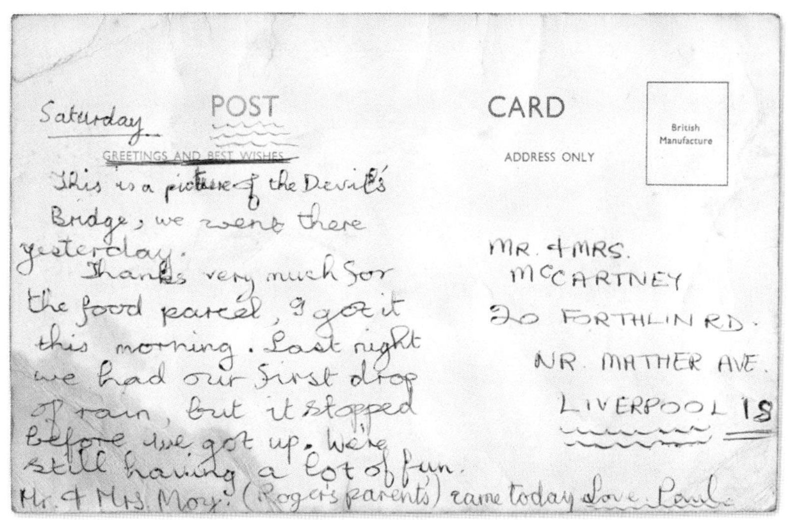

Saturday POST CARD

GREETINGS AND BEST WISHES

This is a picture of the Devil's Bridge, we went there yesterday.
Thanks very much for the food parcel, I got it this morning. Last night we had our first drop of rain, but it stopped before we got up. We're still having a lot of fun.
Mr. & Mrs. Moy: (Roger's parents) came today Love Paul

British Manufacture

ADDRESS ONLY

MR. & MRS.
McCARTNEY
20 FORTHLIN RD.
NR. MATHER AVE.
LIVERPOOL 18

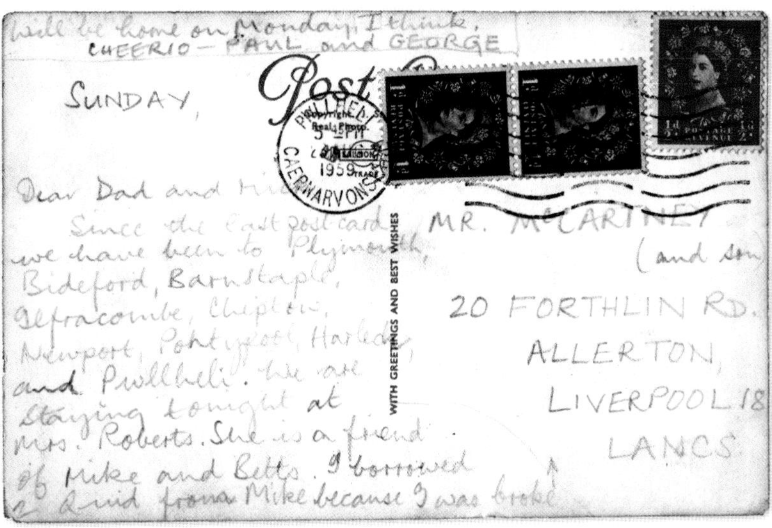

will be home on Monday, I think.
CHEERIO — PAUL and GEORGE

SUNDAY,

Post Card

PWLLHELI 1959 CAERNARVONSHIRE

Dear Dad and Mike
Since the last post card we have been to Plymouth, Bideford, Barnstaple, Ilfracombe, Chepstow, Newport, Pontypool, Harlech, and Pwllheli. We are staying tonight at Mrs. Roberts. She is a friend of Mike and Betts. I borrowed a quid from Mike because I was broke

WITH GREETINGS AND BEST WISHES

MR. McCARTNEY
(and son)
20 FORTHLIN RD.
ALLERTON,
LIVERPOOL 18
LANCS.

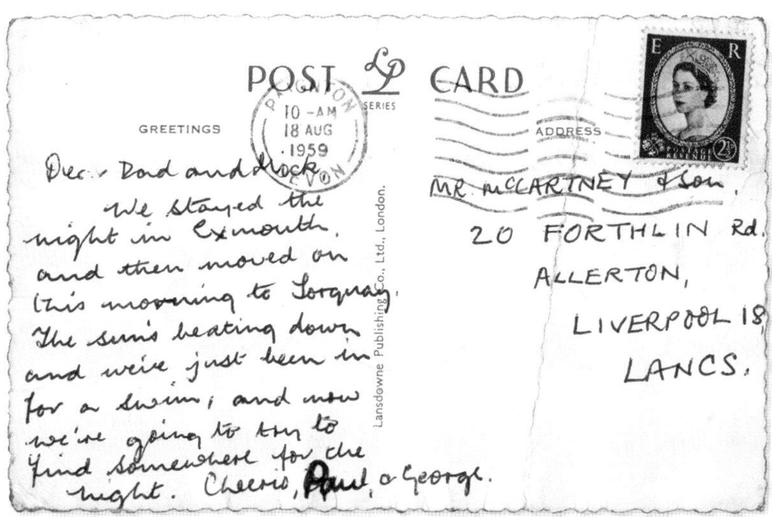

POST LP CARD
SERIES

GREETINGS

PAIGNTON 10 -AM 18 AUG 1959 DEVON

ADDRESS

Dear Dad and Mick,
We stayed the night in Exmouth, and then moved on this morning to Torquay. The sun's beating down and we've just been in for a swim, and now we're going to try to find somewhere for the night. Cheerio, Paul & George.

Lansdowne Publishing Co., Ltd., London.

MR. McCARTNEY & Son,
20 FORTHLIN Rd.
ALLERTON,
LIVERPOOL 18,
LANCS.

Family postcards from the 1950s

Your Mother Should Know

WRITERS	Paul McCartney and John Lennon
ARTIST	The Beatles
RECORDED	Chappell Recording Studios, London; and Abbey Road Studios, London
RELEASED	*Magical Mystery Tour*, 1967

Let's all get up and dance to a song
That was a hit before your mother was born
Though she was born a long, long time ago
Your mother should know
Your mother should know
Sing it again

Let's all get up and dance to a song
That was a hit before your mother was born
Though she was born a long, long time ago
Your mother should know
Your mother should know

Lift up your hearts and sing me a song
That was a hit before your mother was born
Though she was born a long, long time ago
Your mother should know
Your mother should know

Sing it again
Da, da, da, da, da, da, da, da, da
Da, da, da, da, da, da, da, da, da, da, da
Though she was born a long, long time ago
Your mother should know
Your mother should know

ONE OF THE REASONS AUNTIE JIN CAME DOWN TO VISIT ME IN London when I was about twenty-four or twenty-five was to talk to me about the sin of smoking pot. Her nickname was 'Control', and she had been sent down by the family as an emissary. I suppose the word had got back that 'our Paul' was going a bit wild in London, so someone needed to go and check in on him. Anyway, she came down to visit me in Cavendish Avenue, where I'd been living for a while. When your auntie comes to visit, you do some of the old things you did when you were younger. So I was sitting around, playing a bit of piano, having a drink, playing cards, and having a good old chat. It was a very warm atmosphere, and the song arose out of that sense of family.

The well-known phrase that ghosts the song is 'mother knows best', and many of our fans would have been beginning to think that their parents were just a bunch of old fuddy-duddies who had no idea about anything. In fact, however, some of those parents might have harboured quite a strong feeling that The Beatles were dangerous. That didn't really bother us much, because we knew we weren't and the bulk of our work is very optimistic and very well-intentioned.

'Your Mother Should Know' definitely falls into that category. It's a very simple thought, really, that could have translated easily into the sort of ragtime song that was popular in my parents' era. No one thought it at the time, but we really were big fans of the music that came out of our parents' generation. We recognised the impact of the memorable melodies and the structure of so many of the songs. Something about the structure - verse, chorus, verse, chorus, middle eight, verse, chorus - allowed those songs to last.

Nowadays, I joke with folks when we're in a club or a restaurant or a gym and we're listening to a monotonous thud that goes on for four or five minutes. I always imagine a classic songwriter like Cole Porter - who often wrote in that verse-chorus-middle eight structure - coming back and listening to this 'music'. He likely wouldn't recognise it as anything other than a beat to set some real music to.

I know I'm running the risk of sounding like the very people who described The Beatles as rubbish and said that our stuff would never last. I remember hearing my dad say that *his* dad had complained that his music, which was Chicago jazz - Jelly Roll Morton and Louis Armstrong - was 'tin can' music.

But it all comes back to what was popular at the time, and I suppose the word 'hit' resonates. We were, after all, in the business of writing hits for The Beatles. Actually, I'm in the same business today. I don't see any problem with trying to write hits. You can look at the word 'hit' in two ways - as either crass commercialism or trying to reach people. We knew that what made a song a hit 'before your mother was born' was precisely what would make a hit now and in the future. I say 'precisely', but it's actually an intangible quality that pulls us all together. It's what makes us a worldwide community of listeners.

Below: With Auntie Jin and cousin Cath. Liverpool, 1967

Right: With John Lennon on the set of *Magical Mystery Tour*. RAF West Malling, Kent, 1967

Acknowledgements

Special thanks to Nancy, my kids and my loving family, also John Eastman, Lee Eastman, Robert Weil and Stuart Proffitt.

MPL
Alex Parker
Aoife Corbett
Ben Humphreys
Issy Bingham
Mark Levy
Nancy Jeffries
Nansong Lue
Patricia O'Hearn
Richard Miller
Sarah Brown
Steve Ithell
And everyone at MPL London

LIVERIGHT/W.W. NORTON
Anna Oler
Cordelia Calvert
Don Rifkin
Drake McFeely
Elisabeth Kerr
Elizabeth Clementson
Gabriel Kachuck
Haley Bracken
Joe Lops
Julia Reidhead
Nick Curley
Peter Miller
Rebecca Homiski
Stephanie Hiebert
Steve Attardo
Steven Pace
William Rusin

ALLEN LANE/PENGUIN PRESS
Alice Skinner
Isabel Blake
Jim Stoddart
Katy Banyard
Liz Parsons
Rebecca Lee
Sam Voulters
Thi Dinh

DESIGN
Triboro

Credits

VOLUME 1

Case: Handwritten lyrics for 'Average Person' and 'Band on the Run' courtesy of MPL Communications Inc/Ltd

Front endpaper: Photograph by Linda McCartney. © 1982 Paul McCartney

Back endpaper: Photograph by Linda McCartney. © 1969 Paul McCartney

VOLUME 2

Case: Handwritten lyrics for 'When I'm Sixty-Four' and 'Penny Lane' courtesy of MPL Communications Inc/Ltd

Front endpaper: Photograph by Linda McCartney. © 1979 Paul McCartney

Back endpaper: Photograph by Linda McCartney. © 1978 Paul McCartney

PHOTOGRAPHY

All photography by Linda McCartney © Paul McCartney or from the MPL archive © MPL Communications Inc/Ltd with the exception of the following:

Page 6 (top) © Getty Images / Bettmann Archive

Page 6 (bottom) © Getty Images / Mirrorpix

Pages 8 (top), 311, 356-357, 443, 586 (top) © Apple Corps Ltd.

Pages 9, 11, 66 (bottom left), 67, 213 (bottom), 284, 435, 506, 509, 605, 619, 679 (bottom), 718, 837 © Paul McCartney / Photographer: Paul McCartney

Page 13 © Trinity Mirror / Mirrorpix / Alamy Stock Photo

Page 27 © Keystone Press / Alamy Stock Photo

Pages 36 (bottom left), 251, 261, 290-291, 482-483, 607, 811, 813 © Mary McCartney

Page 69 Courtesy of STUDIOCANAL / James Gillham

Pages 106-107 © Getty Images / Larry Ellis

Page 136 © Pictorial Press Ltd / Alamy Stock Photo

Pages 162 (top), 328, 329, 344-345, 349 (top), 349 (bottom), 477 (top left and top right), 595, 652 (top), 653, 729 © Mike McCartney

Page 186 © Getty Images / V&A Images

Page 211 © Getty Images / Don Cravens

Page 213 (top) © Getty Images / Mirrorpix

Page 270 (right) © Getty Images / Express

Page 271 © 2018 PA Images / Alamy Stock Photo

Page 287 René Magritte painting and poster in the background. Used with permission. René Magritte © 2021 C. Herscovici / Artists Rights Society (ARS), New York

Page 389 © AHDN, LLC, courtesy of Bruce and Martha Karsh

Page 555 © Getty Images / Manchester Daily Express

Page 556 (top) © Geoff Rhind

Pages 556 (bottom), 587 (bottom) © Subafilms Ltd

Page 569 - The Quarry Men © Getty Images / Michael Ochs Archives

Page 775 Rupert Bear Courtesy of Universal Studios Licensing LLC

Page 784 (bottom) © Trinity Mirror / Mirrorpix / Alamy Stock Photo

Page 787 © Trinity Mirror / Mirrorpix / Alamy Stock Photo

MEMORABILIA

All memorabilia from the MPL archive © Paul McCartney / MPL Communications Inc/Ltd with the exception of the following:

Pages 8 (bottom), 107 (bottom), 110 (bottom left), 241(bottom), 273, 287 (top right and bottom right), 289 (bottom), 319, 428 © Apple Corps Ltd.

Page 68 - 'A World Without Love' record, Peter and Gordon © unknown

Pages 128 (top and bottom), 270 (bottom left), 532, 563 paintings © Paul McCartney

Page 187 © William Harry / Mersey Beat

Page 471 (top) Donald Duck © Disney
Page 832 © Subafilms Ltd.
Pages 842–843 'Yesterday' arranged by George Martin, courtesy of George Martin / Airborn Productions Ltd.

HANDWRITTEN LYRICS

Page 159 'Eleanor Rigby' and page 235 'Good Day Sunshine' courtesy of John Cage Notations Project Manuscript Scores, Northwestern University Music Library, Evanston, IL USA
Page 477 'Michelle' courtesy of Hunter Davies and The British Library, Loan MS 86/9
Page 840 'Yesterday' courtesy of Hunter Davies and the British Library, Loan MS 86/7
All other handwritten lyrics courtesy of MPL Communications Inc/Ltd

SONG AND POETRY CREDITS

'All My Loving', 'And I Love Her', 'Can't Buy Me Love', 'Eight Days a Week', 'A Hard Day's Night', 'I'll Follow the Sun', 'I'll Get You', 'She's a Woman', 'Things We Said Today':

'Another Day', 'Average Person', 'Band on the Run', 'Café on the Left Bank', 'Country Dreamer', 'Dear Friend', 'Despite Repeated Warnings', 'Do It Now', 'Dress Me Up as a Robber', 'Eat at Home', 'Ebony and Ivory', 'Give Ireland Back to the Irish', 'Helen Wheels', 'Hi, Hi, Hi', 'I Don't Know', 'I'm Carrying', 'Jet', 'Junior's Farm', 'Let Me Roll It', 'Magneto and Titanium Man', 'Mrs. Vandebilt', 'My Love', 'Nineteen Hundred and Eighty Five', 'No More Lonely Nights', 'Picasso's Last Words (Drink to Me)', 'Single Pigeon', 'Spirits of Ancient Egypt', 'Uncle Albert/Admiral Halsey', 'Venus and Mars'/'Rock Show'/'Venus and Mars – Reprise':

'Anything Goes':
Words and music by Cole Porter.

'Arrow Through Me', 'Calico Skies', 'Check My Machine', 'Coming Up', 'Confidante', 'Cook of the House', 'Distractions', 'Getting Closer', 'Ghosts of the Past Left Behind', 'Girls' School', 'Golden Earth Girl', 'Great Day', 'Here Today', 'Hope of Deliverance', 'House of Wax', 'I Lost My Little Girl', 'In Spite of All the Danger', 'Jenny Wren', 'The Kiss of Venus', 'Let 'Em In', 'London Town', 'Mull of Kintyre', 'My Valentine', 'The Note You Never Wrote', 'Nothing Too Much Just Out of Sight', 'Old Siam, Sir', 'Once Upon a Long Ago', 'Only Mama Knows', 'The Other Me', 'Pipes of Peace', 'Pretty Boys', 'Pretty Little Head', 'Put It There', 'San Ferry Anne', 'She's Given Up Talking', 'Silly Love Songs', 'Simple as That', 'Somedays', 'Temporary Secretary', 'Too Much Rain', 'Tug of War', 'Warm and Beautiful', 'Waterfalls', 'We All Stand Together', 'We Got Married', 'When Winter Comes', 'Women and Wives', 'The World Tonight', 'The World You're Coming Into', 'You Tell Me':

'Back in the U.S.S.R.', 'Birthday', 'Blackbird', 'Carry That Weight', 'Come and Get It', 'A Day in the Life', 'Drive My Car', 'Eleanor Rigby', 'The End', 'Fixing a Hole', 'The Fool on the Hill', 'For No One', 'Get Back', 'Golden Slumbers', 'Good Day Sunshine', 'Goodbye', 'Got to Get You into My Life', 'Helter Skelter', 'Her Majesty', 'Here, There and Everywhere', 'Hey Jude', 'Honey Pie', 'I Will', 'I'm Down', 'I've Got a Feeling', 'Junk',

'Lady Madonna', 'Let It Be', 'The Long and Winding Road', 'Lovely Rita', 'Martha My Dear', 'Maxwell's Silver Hammer', 'Maybe I'm Amazed', 'Michelle', 'Mother Nature's Son', 'Ob-La-Di, Ob-La-Da', 'Oh Woman, Oh Why', 'Paperback Writer', 'Penny Lane', 'Rocky Raccoon', 'Sgt. Pepper's Lonely Hearts Club Band', 'She Came in Through the Bathroom Window', 'She's Leaving Home', 'Teddy Boy', 'Ticket to Ride', 'Too Many People', 'Two of Us', 'We Can Work It Out', 'When I'm Sixty-Four', 'Why Don't We Do It in the Road?', 'With a Little Help from My Friends', 'Yellow Submarine', 'Yesterday', 'You Never Give Me Your Money', 'Your Mother Should Know':
© 1965 to 1971 Sony Music Publishing LLC.
All rights administered by Sony Music Publishing LLC, 424 Church Street, Suite 1200, Nashville, TN 37219.
All rights reserved. Used by permission.

'Bagpipe Music' from *Collected Poems* by Louis MacNeice (Faber & Faber):
© 1938 Reproduced by permission of David Higham Associates Ltd.
All rights reserved. Used by permission.

'Cheek to Cheek':
From the RKO Radio Motion Picture *Top Hat*.
Words and music by Irving Berlin.
© Copyright 1935 by Irving Berlin.
Copyright renewed.
International copyright secured. All rights reserved.
Reprinted by permission of Hal Leonard LLC.

'Every Night':
Written and composed by Paul McCartney.
© 1970 Sony Music Publishing LLC.
All rights administered by Sony Music Publishing LLC, 424 Church Street, Suite 1200, Nashville, TN 37219.
All rights reserved. Used by permission.

'Frankie and Albert':
Words and music by Huddie Ledbetter.
Collected and adapted by John A. Lomax and Alan Lomax.
TRO-© Copyright 1936 (Renewed) 1959 (Renewed) Folkways Music Publishers, Inc., New York, NY and Global Jukebox Publishing, Marshall, TX.
TRO-Folkways Music Publishers, Inc., controls all rights for the World outside the U.S.A.
All rights reserved. Used by permission.

'From Me to You', 'I Saw Her Standing There', 'I Wanna Be Your Man', 'She Loves You':
© 1963 to 1964 MPL Communications Inc, and Gil Music Corp.
Administered in the U.S. by MPL Communications Inc and Round Hill Works on behalf of Gil Music Corp.
Administered outside the U.S. by Round Hill Works on behalf of Gil Music Corp.
All rights reserved. Used by permission.

'How Do You Sleep?':
Written by John Lennon.
© 1971 Lenono Music.
All rights reserved. Used by permission.

'I Want to Hold Your Hand':
© 1963 MPL Communications Inc, Sony Music Publishing LLC and Songs of Universal Inc.
Administered in the U.S. by MPL Communications Inc and in the U.S. and Canada by Songs of Universal Inc.
Administered outside the U.S. and Canada by Sony Music Publishing LLC., 424 Church Street, Suite 1200, Nashville, TN 37219.
All rights reserved. Used by permission.

'I'm Going in a Field':
Words and music by Ivor Cutler.
© 1967. All rights reserved. Used by permission of the Estate of Ivor Cutler.

'Live and Let Die':
© 1973 MPL Communications Inc and Danjaq S.A., U.A Music Ltd.
All rights on behalf of Danjaq S.A. and U.A. Music Ltd administered by Sony Music Publish-

ing LLC, 424 Church Street, Suite 1200, Nashville, TN 37219.
All rights reserved. Used by permission.

'Letting Go':
Written and composed by Paul McCartney and Linda McCartney.
© 1975 MPL Communications Inc
All rights reserved. Used by permission.

'Love in Vain Blues':
Words and music by Robert Johnson.
© 1937 Standing Ovation and Encore Music.
Copyright renewed.
All rights administered by Concord Music Publishing.
All rights reserved. Used by permission.
Reprinted by permission of Hal Leonard LLC.

'Love Me Do':
© 1962 MPL Communications Ltd and Lenono Music.
Administered in the U.S. by MPL Communications Inc and Lenono Music.
Administered in the U.K. by MPL Communications Inc.
Administered for the World excluding the U.S. and U.K. by Sony Music Publishing LLC, 424 Church Street, Suite 1200, Nashville, TN 37219.
All rights reserved. Used by permission.

'Medicine Jar':
Written and composed by Jimmy McCulloch and Colin Allen.
© 1975 MPL Communications Ltd, administered by MPL Communications Inc.
All rights reserved. Used by permission.

'On My Way to Work':
© 2013 MPL Communications Inc and MPL Communications Ltd, administered by MPL Communications Inc.
All rights reserved. Used by permission.

'Please':
By Leon Robin and Ralph Rainger.
© 1932 Sony Music Publishing LLC.
All rights administered by Sony Music Publishing LLC, 424 Church Street, Suite 1200, Nashville, TN 37219.
All rights reserved. Used by permission.

'Please Please Me':
© 1963 MPL Communications Inc, Lenono Music, and Universal / Dick James Music Ltd.
Administered in the U.S. by MPL Communications Inc and Lenono Music.
Administered for the World excluding the U.S. by Universal / Dick James Music Ltd.
All rights reserved. Used by permission.

'Say Say Say':
© 1983 MPL Communications Inc and Mijac Music.
All rights on behalf of Mijac Music administered by Sony Music Publishing LLC, 424 Church Street, Suite 1200, Nashville, TN 37219.
All rights reserved. Used by permission.

'Strawberry Fields Forever':
Written and composed by John Lennon and Paul McCartney.
© 1967 Sony Music Publishing LLC.
All rights administered by Sony Music Publishing LLC, 424 Church Street, Suite 1200, Nashville, TN 37219.
All rights reserved. Used by permission.

'Tell Me Who He Is':
© MPL Communications Inc.
All rights reserved. Used by permission.

Index

Main song entries are not repeated in this index.
Page numbers in *italics* refer to illustrations.